Fishermen Against the Kaiser

By the same author

The Saltdean Story
The Church in a Garden
Foul Deeds and Suspicious Deaths around Brighton
Crime and Vice in Brighton, 1800-2000

Fishermen Against the Kaiser

Volume 1
Shockwaves of War

Douglas d'Enno

Pen & Sword
MARITIME

First published in Great Britain in 2010 by
Pen & Sword Maritime
an imprint of
Pen & Sword Books Ltd
47 Church Street
Barnsley
South Yorkshire
S70 2AS

ISBN 978 18441 59 796

A CIP catalogue record for this book is available from the British Library

Typeset in Sabon 10.5 by Lamorna Publishing Services

Printed and bound in UK by the MPG Books Group

Pen & Sword Books Ltd incorporates the Imprints of Pen & Sword Aviation, Pen & Sword Maritime, Pen & Sword Military, Wharncliffe Local History, Pen and Sword Select, Pen and Sword Military Classics, Leo Cooper, Remember When, Seaforth Publishing and Frontline Publishing.

For a complete list of Pen & Sword titles please contact
PEN & SWORD BOOKS LIMITED
47 Church Street, Barnsley, South Yorkshire, S70 2AS, England
E-mail: enquiries@pen-and-sword.co.uk
Website: www.pen-and-sword.co.uk

Contents

List of Plates

Dedicated to the fishermen of these islands who made the ultimate sacrifice in the Great War and all those who were prepared to.

That day is gone for ever, with the odds against them of five or six to one, more than four hundred years ago, men warped their strange craft out of Plymouth Harbour to encounter and drive away the Spanish Armada. For days and days, worn with fatigue, scant of food, they hung grimly on to the invader until that great Armada was scattered to the four winds of heaven and the fear of invasion was gone for centuries. These men were the ancestors of the fisherfolk who man our fishing fleet today. Forged on the anvil of duty and true to the simple traditions of their craft, they obey with the loyalty and silence of their breed. I am sure of this, that when the war is over, or if their rest comes during the war, we shall find that the work has been done as speedily, as effectively, and as untiringly as was the work their forefathers did in the days of old in driving the invader from these shores and these seas.

RE Prothero, President of the Board of Agriculture 1916–1919,
spoken on 15 June 1917

What would King Garge 'ave done without these 'ere trawlers?

A West Country skipper in the Aegean, 1915

Preface

This book is the first of a two-volume history. So great was the impact of hostilities on the nation's fishermen and fishing vessels that a full account of its many initial ramifications warranted this introductory volume. Taking the story to the end of 1915, it describes how grievously our fishing ports suffered yet how quickly they became nurseries for the Navy; how the Admiralty remorselessly requisitioned the best vessels and recruited the ablest men for war service; and how the fishing industry almost collapsed under the strain – the last straw being the closure of, or restricted access to, vast areas of the most important and prolific grounds. No fishing vessel at sea was safe, whether from surface craft, mine, U-boat or even the air. Innocent crews were captured and many saw out the war in the inhuman confines of POW camps. A goodly number of fishermen exchanged their trawls and drift nets on the North Sea or other home waters for sweep wires and depth charges on the freezing seas off Northern Russia or on the often placid, but mined and submarine-infested, waters of the Adriatic or Aegean. Quite simply, the war could not have been won without their efforts. Had they not kept the English Channel carefully swept and patrolled, British and Empire troops could never have reached France safely in the numbers they did.

The idea for this book first came to me as long ago as 1986 – and the project has been worked on, intermittently, ever since. I had been engaged in researching a volume dealing with food and farming in the First World War and became increasingly interested in the fisheries aspect. At all events, I was working in the right place: the headquarters of the Ministry of Agriculture, Fisheries and Food in London, where I had access to all kinds of material not readily available to an outside researcher. When the Ministry of Defence's Naval Historical Branch Library moved into the Great Scotland Yard building opposite my office window, my task was facilitated even further!

By the time I retired from the Ministry in 1995, I had more than enough material to complete this book – on the basis of paper sources at least. I had by then made a tour of much of Britain's coastline, from Lowestoft, via Aberdeen, to Fleetwood, but was disappointed to witness an industry seemingly in its death throes. And now a friend in the Granite City reports that there are only one or two fishing boats left in that once-thriving port and there is talk of demolishing the fishmarket.

Other projects intervened – and mercifully so, since it has become abundantly clear that without the resources of the Internet and electronic communication, the quality and accuracy of the text could not have held a light to what it has been possible to produce over the last decade.

Books covering a variety of aspects of the fortunes of fishermen and fishing vessels during the First World War have been produced in some number since 1918 (a start was even made during the war itself with, for example, Walter Wood's *Fishermen in War Time* of that year). Some are remarkably detailed. I would, however, venture to claim that this volume is the first attempt to portray this vast canvas in the form of a single history. There was not space to include everything I would have wished but the volumes are as comprehensive as they could be at their present length.

It is hoped that the extensive bibliography will encourage readers to pursue their own lines of interest independently and/or will provide sources of which they may not previously have been aware. Endnotes have been added in support of particular passages or statements in the main text.

Despite the immense pains taken to ensure factual accuracy, it would be futile to imagine that a work of this enormous scope could be free from error or omission. I accept responsibility for any that may be encountered. Corrections will be incorporated in any future edition.

Douglas d'Enno
Saltdean, April 2009

Acknowledgements

Profound thanks are due to Roderick Suddaby, the Keeper of Documents at the Imperial War Museum, London, who gave his full support, moral and documentary, to the project at the outset and maintained interest in its progress over many years. Donald MacLeod of Aberdeen also deserves special mention for providing much valuable and varied family and naval documentation relating to Scotland and the Islands. My commissioning editor at Pen & Sword, Rupert Harding, kept my nose to the grindstone and drove the project forward with his advice and enthusiasm.

I am also grateful to the following persons who helped in many and various ways with the text over the years. Without their assistance this book could not have been written: Bailey, Peter (Curator, Newhaven Local and Maritime Museum); Banton, Ms M (TNA, Kew); Barker, Lesley (The Fishermen's Mission [formerly the RNMDSF], Whiteley, Hants.); Bate, Derek (Ex-Librarian of former MAFF Fish Laboratory, Lowestoft); Bell, George (Hoylake, Wirral); Blow, William (Cleethorpes); Boardman, Michael (former Director of Leisure Services, Grimsby); Bourke, Edward (Dublin); Bowden, the late Leslie (Grimsby); Brady, Ms Anita (Librarian at the former Royal Naval College Library, Greenwich, London); Britton, Gus, the late (Naval Affairs Consultant, RN Submarine Museum, Gosport); Buckie & District Fishing Heritage Centre Ltd, Banffshire; Butcher, David (Lowestoft fishing industry historian); Clampton, Bernard (former Secretary, RNMDSF, London); Clarke, Alex (Ilford); Clarke, Betty (Ilford); Clarke, Delia (Cheltenham); Cook, Russell (Editor, *Lowestoft Journal*); Cooke, Ian (British Library, London); Crask, Chris (Grimsby); Cullen, Tim (formerly Acting Chief Librarian, MAFF, London); d'Enno, Caroline, Corin, Juliet and Neal (input services); Fyfe, Ms Morag (the National Archives of Scotland, Edinburgh); Gill, Alec (Hull fishing industry historian); Greiling, Meredith (Aberdeen Maritime Museum); Hallifax, Trevor (Grimsby trawler historian); Halpern, Prof. Paul (naval historian); Harris, Colin, MA (MOD Naval Historical Library, London); Hansombe, Mrs Cheryl (input services); Hines, Peter (High Salvington, Worthing, technical advice and computer services); HM Treasury Library, Treasury Chambers, London; Johnson, Barry (Milford trawler website); Jones, Stuart (Port of Lowestoft Research Society); Kennedy, Ms Brenda (Hull); Liddle, Peter H (The Liddle Collection, Brotherton Library, University of Leeds); Lörscher, Oliver (Trier, Germany); Mckay, Ms Glynis (Great Yarmouth Central Library); Macauley, John (Librarian, RUSI, London); McWilliam, Jane (Marine Laboratory Library, Aberdeen); Malcolmson, George (Archivist/Historian, RN Submarine

Museum, Gosport); MOD Naval Historical Library, Fulham; MOD Wrecks
Section, Hydrographic Department, Taunton; Moore, John (Sea Fish Industry
Authority, Edinburgh); National Maritime Museum, Greenwich; O'Carroll,
Ms Linda (Leeds); Read, Philip (formerly Deputy Archivist, Department of
Documents, Imperial War Museum, London); Royal Institution, London;
Sieche, Erwin (Austria); the late Smith, Capt. Sydney T (Scarborough);
Stephenson, J (with Messrs ETW Dennis & Sons Ltd, Scarborough, in the
1980s for the loan of various issues of *Olsen's Nautical Almanack*); Ms
Stephenson-Knight, Marilyn (Dover War Memorial Project website); Suffolk
Record Office, Lowestoft Branch; *Yachting Monthly* office, London.

I should like to thank the following for their valuable assistance with images:
Blow, William (Cleethorpes); Chapelhow, John (MAFF, Lowestoft); Fantoff, P
(Central Library and Arts Centre, Rotherham); Griffin, David (MAFF
Reprographic Section, London); Lindsay, Mrs D (Picture Research
Department, National Maritime Museum, London); Tallett, Kyle ('Man of
Kent' website); Roberson, Reginald (MAFF Reprographic Section, London);
Sieche, Erwin, Austria; and Weaver, Brian (MAFF Reprographic Section,
London).

I should add, as a keen collector, that partworks devoted to the war and both
British and German picture postcards have yielded a number of striking images
for this volume which would not normally be seen elsewhere.

Abbreviations Used

ABS	Armed boarding steamer
A/P or AP	Auxiliary Patrol
APV	Auxiliary patrol vessel
BAF	Board of Agriculture and Fisheries (England)
BDV	Boom defence vessel
BoT	Board of Trade
BVLAS	*British Vessels Lost at Sea, 1914-18*
CMB	Coastal motor boat
DORA	Defence of the Realm Act
FBS	Fisheries Board for Scotland
FN	*Fishing News*
FT	Fishery Trawler
FTG	*Fish Trades Gazette & Poultry, Game & Rabbit Trades Chronicle*
GRT	Gross Registered Tonnage
GY	Grimsby
HMD	His Majesty's Drifter
HMT	His Majesty's Trawler/Transport
HMY	His Majesty's Yacht
ICW	In Company With
JRUSI	Journal of the Royal United Services Institution
LT	Lowestoft
LV	Light Vessel
MAFF	Ministry of Agriculture, Fisheries and Food (now DEFRA)
MB	Motor boat
ML	Motor launch
NMM	National Maritime Museum, Greenwich, London
pdr(s)	pounder(s) (re: guns)
RNMSDF	Royal National Mission to Deep Sea Fishermen
RNRT	Royal Naval Reserve Trawler Section
RUSI	Royal United Services Institution, London
SF	Steam Fishing
SFC	Sea Fisheries Committee
SFCo	Steam Fishing Company
SNO	Senior Naval Officer
SS	Special Service/Steam Ship
TB	Torpedo boat
TBD	Torpedo boat destroyer
TD	*Toilers of the Deep* (monthly publication)
TN	*The Navy* (monthly publication)
USN	United States Navy

Chapter 1

The Bolt from the Blue

In peaceful days, a kid of three
I plunged into Geography;
Said Mother, 'Say this after me,
North Sea, or German Ocean.'...

...In nineteen fourteen, August four,
The Hun came banging at our door.
I grasped the point I'd missed before
'North Sea OR German Ocean'!

From *North Sea or German Ocean* by Alice Brooks[1]

4 August 1914. At 8 p.m., a messenger hurried across Whitehall from the Admiralty to the offices of the Board of Agriculture and Fisheries. War had come. It was time to clear the North Sea for the great naval battle that had been expected for so long. The instructions he carried ordered all fishing vessels to return to port by daylight on the following day and prohibited any vessel being allowed to sail for the North Sea fishing grounds. The orders were immediately telegraphed to the harbourmasters at all East Coast ports. As there was no other means of contacting the Lowestoft smacks (sailing trawlers), a steam trawler was dispatched to warn them and order their return, although reaching them all would be a major undertaking.

There were then hundreds of single or grouped British steam trawlers on both the North Sea, where a fleet of over 200 smacks from Lowestoft was busy, and further afield. The summer herring fishery was in full swing off England's north east coast and steam drifters in their hundreds were following the herring southward, having begun the season off the Shetlands. Single boaters (vessels worked individually, going to sea and fishing until enough fish had been caught to make it worthwhile to return to port), beam trawlers and liners (line-fishing vessels) were all enjoying profitable voyages.

On the 'German Ocean', four fleets of steam trawlers – the Red Cross, the Great Northern, the Gamecock and Hellyers' – were hard at work; they were descended directly from the old fleets of sailing smacks which fished the Dogger and other banks and had their catches conveyed to Billingsgate by steam carrier. Remaining at sea for two months or longer at a time, they returned to port for only a few days to refit and obtain fresh water and stores. The steam trawlers making up the modern fleets of 40 or 50 vessels stayed in unbroken succession on the fishing banks, with a vessel leaving for port to re-coal and get fresh water and stores after being at sea for four or five weeks. The old system of fleeting, under which fast cutters ran the fleet's catch ashore on a daily basis, was in operation, each fleet being under the control of an 'admiral', an experienced and specially selected fisherman. His duty was to select the best fishing grounds and thus secure the most satisfactory results. Under him was a vice admiral who, in his chief's absence or as necessary, could take over the direction of the fleet.

Grimsby, the world's greatest fishing port, was the headquarters of an enormous fleet of steam trawlers, mostly engaged in single-boating. Many of these sturdy vessels made the Iceland trip, lasting about three weeks, and voyages were undertaken also to the White Sea and elsewhere. The fleeters belonged mostly to Hull. Extensive operations were conducted from other bases, such as Aberdeen, and great numbers of vessels worked from lesser ports like Scarborough. Yarmouth and Lowestoft maintained their position as the chief ports for the steam drifters and smacks. Before the war, therefore, there was a substantial aggregation of first-rate steam fishing vessels, many members of whose crews spent almost their entire lives on the North Sea, since a fleeter would enjoy only about three weeks ashore per year.

This industry, employing in England and Wales alone some 44,000 men and vessels whose aggregate tonnage exceeded 216,000 tons (not to mention many thousands of persons whose livelihood was bound up by the distribution and curing of fish) was now in danger of being brought suddenly to a standstill. The country stood to lose fish supplies equivalent to nearly a half of the total quantity of meat consumed in the British Isles. The bulk of that supply was normally landed at ports on the east coast – the coast most exposed to enemy attack – with more than three-fifths being obtained from the North Sea. Here the greatest sea battle in human history would, it was generally believed, be fought to a decisive conclusion.

The Unexpectedness – and Reality – of War

Yet the fishing trade journals had made barely no reference to the looming conflict, while the industry for its part seemed to be taken almost completely by surprise. Everybody knew that the European situation was threatening, but few believed that a war involving Great Britain was really imminent. The first symptom of anxiety in the trade was an enquiry, on 30 July, by the Hull Fishing Vessel Owners' Association as to what measures were being taken for the protection of fishing vessels in the event of hostilities. It was informed that no special measures could be taken as only coastal fishing boats could be regarded as immune from capture.

One oblivious skipper among many was Walter Samuel Wharton from Lowestoft, who was later to write in his unpublished reminiscences[2] that he was:

> ...trawling peacefully in the North Sea, 60 miles E.S.E. of Lowestoft on the morning of the 5th of August, 1914, not thinking or knowing anything about war being declared between Great Britain and Germany (although there had been some rumours that England would help France before we sailed from Lowestoft on the 30th of July).

The Board of Agriculture's research vessel had only recently left for a special cruise to carry out the Department's share in the programme arranged by the International Council for the Exploration of the Sea, which was at the time under the Presidency of a German delegate.

In Germany, Britain's declaration of war similarly appeared, in some circles at least, totally unexpected. JD Smith, the English agent of one of the chief herring importers in Stettin[3] and a well-known figure in the trade, was quickly arrested and, together with the British Consul and other refugees, had to make his way back home – in his case, Fraserburgh – as best he could. In the event, they travelled via Denmark. When on board the Copenhagen steamer *Express* he wrote, in a long letter:

> To begin with, the declaration of war by Britain came as a very great surprise to the Germans, as well as to the British subjects staying in Stettin. We all thought that by remaining neutral we had everything to gain and nothing to lose, and that the quarrel was certainly outside any necessity for direct interference on our part. Up to the very last moment we were treated and entertained more hospitably than I have ever before experienced in the 'Vaterland'. Our healths were drunk in every restaurant we went to, and free drinks to the Britishers were the order of the day.
>
> The first intimation of war we had, appeared in the papers on Monday morning 3rd inst., advising the departure of the British Ambassador from Berlin. So many incorrect reports had been appearing, however, that I did not place any reliance on this one.
>
> …Our reception after the news [was confirmed] was, to put it mildly, considerably cooler, and it was scarcely safe for a foreigner to walk the streets. The better class of people would not have molested one, but everyone seemed to be on the outlook for spies, and anybody looking in the least foreign-like ran grave risk of being very severely assaulted.

Another aspect of this strange time was recorded by Frederick Palmer, the accredited American correspondent at the British Front, in *My Year of the War*, published in 1915:

> Crossing the Atlantic on the *Lusitania* we had a German reserve officer who was already on board when the evening editions arrived at the pier with news that England had declared war on Germany. Naturally he must become a prisoner upon his arrival at Liverpool. He was a steadfast German. When a wireless report of the German repulse at Liège came, he would not believe it. Germany had the system and Germany would win.
>
> …His English fellow-passengers on that splendid liner which a German submarine was to send to the bottom showed him no discourtesy. They passed the time of day with him and seemed to want to make his awkward situation easy. Yet it was apparent that he regarded their kindliness as racial weakness. *Krieg ist Krieg.*[4]

One JF Hooper, an entrepreneur writing on 20 October 1917 in the *Fish Trades Gazette*, recalled:

> We believed war between two nations such as Germany and Great Britain an impossibility. When certain retired Naval men ventured to express their opinions and thoughts, they were termed 'scare-mongers,' and statesmen told the nation to

take no notice, and 'sleep peacefully in your beds'. Even so late as the last Goodwood Race Meeting in 1914, the majority regarded war as such an impossibility that they treated the whole thing as stupid rumours, and newspaper boys 'inventing the awful possibilities of war' were laughed at by the holiday crowd, who gave them 6d. for their paper and their humour. But before the conclusion of the 'Glorious Goodwood' a dark cloud fell, anxiety prevailed, Cowes with all its society and gaiety was cancelled, and Britain was at war.

The reality of the conflict was brought home sharply to the men of the Grimsby trawler *Zenobia*. On reaching her home port on the evening war was declared, she reported that while fishing off Heligoland, a German gunboat peremptorily ordered her to sail westward. The skipper at once steamed south, whereupon the gunboat chased her, ordered her to stop and placed her under arrest. She was made to return to Heligoland and was detained there for five hours. Her papers were examined and the skipper was closely interrogated before being released, and told to get out of German waters without delay. Three weeks later, this unlucky vessel was captured by torpedo boat and her crew taken prisoners; her fate is officially listed as 'not known'.

In Aberdeen, the boot was on the other foot. Here, Britain's first prizes of war were seized. For years, German trawlers and other vessels had landed their catches at the port. In the month war was declared, two were detained there. The first, boldly flying her national flag, was the trawler *Else Kunkel*, which was boarded by the authorities and arrested. A crowd quickly gathered and over a dozen policemen were drafted to the scene. The onlookers jeered the captive crew, one of whom reluctantly hauled down the national flag, much to the crowd's jubilation. However, no violent hatred was shown to the enemy by the townspeople – indeed, the hungry crew members were even supplied with provisions (a bizarre incident in connection with this vessel is recounted in a later chapter). A sister vessel, *Dr Robitzsch*, was likewise placed under arrest. Both vessels, as *Chirsin* and *Clonsin* respectively, were taken into British service, as were 27 other German fishing vessels captured at sea, largely during destroyer and cruiser sweeps in the North Sea.

Restrictions and Paralysis
The recall of fishing vessels from the North Sea and the detention in port of those that had not sailed was a preliminary measure of precaution. Then the whole of the North Sea was closed to British fishermen, with the exception of an area between Cromer on the Norfolk coast and Kinnaird Head, Aberdeenshire. The entire west coast of Scotland similarly became a forbidden region for fishing by any other than local boats, as did the north-east coast of Ireland. The Channel was also barred as far as Portland.

A flurry of official notices was issued by the Board of Agriculture and Fisheries on information received from the Admiralty.[5] The following, dated 11 August, is typical:

> Fishing craft in the North Sea may continue their operations with the following restrictions: Steam trawlers may go out at their own risk, but they must remain in sight of land, and they must return to port before nightfall. Drifters may go out to sea at their own risk, but they must not attempt to enter ports at night. Fishing craft

may carry out their operations without any restrictions, but at their own risk, to the westward of the fourth meridian of longitude (west).

On 25 August 1914, restrictions were ordered forbidding fishing in the North Sea to the east of a line drawn from the Hook of Holland to Sumburgh Head (at the southern tip of the Shetland mainland) and to the south of the latitude of Lowestoft; these were intended to keep British fishing vessels clear of the Southwold minefield (dealt with in Chapter 6) and the German coast. Despite the presence of fields off the Tyne and Humber, the Admiralty imposed restrictions with some moderation – a policy due to the director of its Trade Division, Captain Richard Webb, who considered a prohibition of fishing to be undesirable on both economic and military grounds. Unemployment in the fishing industry and ancillary activities would be aggravated, fish supplies diminished and an invaluable channel of information blocked. In naval terms, fishing craft could be indicators of minefields (albeit through their destruction) on those very Tyne and Humber fields.

Webb's views prevailed for a time but developments towards the end of the year forced a rethink and a new stringency. In early November, the North Sea was declared a military area, with the Admiralty making the following announcement through the Press Bureau at 10.45 on the evening of Tuesday, 3 November:

During the last week the Germans have scattered mines indiscriminately on the open sea on the main trade routes from America to Liverpool via the north of Ireland. Peaceful merchant ships have already been blown up with loss of life by this agency. The White Star liner *Olympic* escaped disaster by pure good luck. But for the warnings given by British cruisers, other British and neutral merchant and passenger vessels would have been destroyed.

These mines cannot have been laid by any German ship of war. They have been laid by some merchant vessel flying a neutral flag which has come along the trade route as if for the purposes of peaceful commerce, and while profiting to the full by the immunity enjoyed by neutral merchant ships, has wantonly and recklessly endangered the lives of all who travel on the sea, regardless of whether they are friend or foe, civilian or military in character.

Mine-laying under a neutral flag, and reconnaissance conducted by trawlers, hospital ships and neutral vessels, are the ordinary features of German naval warfare. In these circumstances, having regard to the great interests entrusted to the British Navy, to the safety of peaceful commerce on the high seas, and to the maintenance within the limits of international law of trade between neutral countries, the Admiralty feel it necessary to adopt exceptional measures to the novel conditions under which this war is being waged.

They therefore give notice that the whole of the North Sea must be considered a military area.

Within this area, merchant shipping of all kinds, traders of all countries, fishing craft and all other vessels, will be exposed to the gravest dangers from mines which it has been necessary to lay, and from warships searching vigilantly by night and day for suspicious craft.

All merchant and fishing vessels of every description are hereby warned of the danger they encounter by entering this area, except in strict accordance with Admiralty directions.

Every effort will be made to convey this warning to neutral countries and to vessels on the sea, but from November 5 onwards the Admiralty announce that all ships passing a line drawn from the northern point of the Hebrides through the Faroe Islands to Iceland do so at their own peril.

Navigational directions to and from Norway, the Baltic, Denmark and Holland were then given to ships of all countries wishing to trade, although

...any straying, even for a few miles from the course thus indicated, may be followed by fatal consequences.[6]

At the instance of the Board of Agriculture's Fisheries Department, the total ban on the presence of deep-sea fishing vessels in the North Sea was modified to the closure of specified areas in which the success of naval operations might be jeopardized or where vessels and their crews faced serious risks of destruction or capture through fishing vessels being present.

What was the thinking behind the Admiralty's restrictions? For the answers, the naval authorities' view of fishermen and their place on the sea need to be considered. The Navy had a job to do, and fishermen might get in the way. They were a nuisance. The Navy was in a hurry, while fishermen's methods were leisurely. Admittedly, some account was also being taken of the fishermen's safety, but to be realistic this was not a paramount consideration on the part of Their Lordships. The presence of fishing vessels with their nets down might obstruct the operations of naval vessels. Destroyers encountering a fleet of drifters at work might get their propellers fouled, while a cruiser squadron might have to turn aside from its direct course to avoid a scattered fleet of trawlers unable to give way because their trawls were down. Fishing vessels were so ubiquitous that the task of inspecting them individually would make heavy demands on the patrol and examination vessels. Minefields laid by the British might be fouled by the trawl or other fishing gear, and their position thus indicated. The Navy was responsible for protecting fishing vessels and British shipping generally, and such protection would be difficult to give to so many independent and vagrant groups and individuals. Finally, the presence of trawlers on the sea afforded an opportunity to the enemy for disguise – possibly using captured British trawlers (a number had been seized within a few days of the outbreak of hostilities); under cover of such disguises, mines might be laid, intelligence collected and submarines provisioned. That they were put to use with unaltered identities was the conviction of Skipper Wharton – and his could not have been the only sighting:

After this [the loss of the *Aboukir, Hogue* and *Cressy* on 22 September 1914], the Admiralty gave the Fishermen a certain area to fish in. We were not allowed to trawl to the south of Cromer. One trip I was bound for Botney Gut, about 80 miles off the Humber River. Two days after we left Port we sighted a Steam Trawler, the first vessel we had seen since we left the Smith Knoll Spar Buoy. Thinking it was a Grimsby Trawler we altered our course towards him [*sic*], when we got close we found she had no number on her bows, nor name on her stern. We spoke to her, but got no answer, and whilst I was looking about her Bridge and Life Buoys which were hanging up, for a name or number, my mate took the glasses and made out a number on her Funnel, which was 'B.N.90'. I had been supplied with a book from the Custom House telling us to look out for Trawlers with certain numbers, that had been captured by the German Submarines whilst peacefully fishing. I soon found that the B.N.90 was one of the vessels that had been taken. We had orders before we sailed to return to Port if ever we came across one of these vessels, which we did, as fast as the light weather would let us. ...I arrived home safe and made a report to the Naval Authorities about the Steam Trawler and Submarine [sighted on the return trip], for which they gave me a good reward.

The Boston trawler Wharton saw was in fact the *Indian*, which had been captured with a crew of nine together with seven of her sisters on 22 August 1914.

In early June 1915, the crew of the steam trawler *Noogana* of Milford Haven were awarded £10 by the Admiralty for giving valuable information as to the whereabouts of a submarine.

Ground rules for the granting of rewards were laid down in an Admiralty notice of 22 October, conspicuously displayed at every port, with the eye-catching heading:

£1,000 REWARD

NOTICE

To Owners, Masters and Crews of Fishing and other Vessels.

News of the Enemy

In order, it read, to encourage fishermen and others to bring in immediate reports of the movements of the enemy, the Admiralty had decided to pay a sum not exceeding £1,000 for information leading directly to the actual capture or destruction of an enemy vessel down to and including a minelayer or submarine; a sum not exceeding £200 for information leading to the enemy vessel, minelayer or submarine being sighted and chased, the information being proved to be accurate although the vessel was not destroyed; and a sum not exceeding £1 (per mile travelled off the direct course in order to report quickly) for information which proved to be accurate and valuable and was delivered at the earliest possible moment. Vessels observing enemy warships or ships engaged in minelaying or other hostile or suspicious action were to proceed AT ONCE towards the nearest British warship or port and make their reports immediately to naval officers, coastguards, customs officers or fishery officers. Fishermen could therefore, even inadvertently, play a useful scouting and reconnoitring role simply by being allowed to follow their calling.

Cooperation and Compromise in London and Edinburgh
The spirit of compromise between the Board of Agriculture's Fisheries Department and the Admiralty marked a new relationship of understanding

and sympathy, a development remarked upon in the Board's detailed report published in 1919 and entitled *Fisheries in the Great War*. Admiralty Orders were framed in consultation with, and as a rule issued by, the English or Scottish Board of Fisheries as appropriate. The central and local naval authorities availed themselves freely of the assistance of the Board; local inspectors were appointed and accredited to the various naval commands and there was established, between the naval authorities on the one hand and the fishery departments on the other, a system of cooperation and mutual understanding which was – to the great advantage of the industry and of the nation – to continue. All possible steps compatible with the requirements of the naval situation were taken by the Boards and the Admiralty to enable fishing to proceed.

So that both the Board and the Admiralty might be in the closest touch with the daily situation, careful records were obtained day by day of all fishing vessels leaving port, based on returns supplied by the Board's Collectors of Fishery Statistics. Some 270 War Notices and Circulars, telegraphic or otherwise, were issued by the Fisheries Divisions during the first 18 months of the conflict. The 40 notices entitled *Operations of Fishing Vessels* which were issued during the first year of the war included: *Regulations as to Prohibited and Restricted Areas, Mines, Drift Net Fishing in the North Sea* and *Herring Fishery of the East Coast*, while notices on miscellaneous subjects covered matters such as *Identification Marks on Sails, Warning as to Torpedoes, Mines, Shells etc. found in Fishing Nets*, and *Lights on Fishing Vessels*.

Frequently, information and instructions needed to be conveyed with the utmost secrecy. In such cases, communications were made to skippers by word of mouth through Inspectors, Collectors of Fishery Statistics, or other representatives of the Board, to whom necessary instructions were issued with a covering note.

In Scotland, close liaison was established between the fishing industry and the Admiralty through the former's Secretary also receiving a commission as a Staff-Paymaster in the Royal Naval Reserve (RNR); throughout the war, he was in constant touch with the Admiral Commanding Coast of Scotland and the Senior Naval Officers at the various Scottish bases. Numerous conferences were also held at the Admiralty which, as a result of the Board's efforts, led, after a thorough appraisal of the situation, to valuable concessions being won for the fishermen both as regards the areas in which vessels might fish and the extent to which the naval authorities might fairly draw upon the industry for the men. The concessions obtained for the different localities varied according to the circumstances, which included proximity to a naval base (where freedom of action was essential for naval vessels moving at high speed), the degree of danger to which vessels operating in the area were exposed and the extent to which protection could be afforded by the Navy at the time.

The system of prohibited areas led to the system of fishing by permit; enforcement proved difficult, however, in the face of the fisherman's well-known contempt for danger – and orders. Control was therefore best exercised in harbours, where warnings could be given of the possible cancellation or suspension of permits where the rules were found to be disregarded. The permit system was brought into use gradually. Most of the work fell on the Fishery Departments; once they were satisfied as to the eligibility of applicants, they prepared the permits and forwarded them to the naval authorities for countersignature. When countersigned, they were returned to the Fishery Departments, which then issued them to the fishermen.

Nearly 200 orders affecting fishing in Scottish waters were promulgated during the period of the war. The permissive orders provided that every skipper of a fishing vessel operating in regulated areas should receive permits signed on the Fishery Board's behalf and countersigned by the competent naval authorities. The total number of permits issued exceeded 18,000.

Dr Willway's Memorable Record

Few indeed are the surviving accounts of conditions in the North Sea in the early months of the war as witnessed from a vessel attached to the newly-reinstated fleet of fishing vessels operating in those dangerous waters. Fortunately, Dr Frederick W Willway of the RNMDSF submitted a report of his visit to the fishermen in October 1914, which was published in the following month's issue of the Mission's journal, *Toilers of the Deep*:

We are rolling on the October swell. It is a moonless night, our trawl dragging heavily behind us, and around are the lights of the fishing vessels engaged in the routine duty of supplying the London market with the fish for which it ever clamours, though it seems to pay but little for it when the demand is met. We are a week out, and already the world at large has grown remote and the echoes of its doings dim.

...We are at war, and the air is full of rumours, as is ever the case where news is difficult to obtain and belated when it comes. We are at war, but who would know it out here? And yet, as we know to our cost, the sea is full of deadly perils for those who voyage to and fro upon its waters. We watch the arrival of vessels fresh from port, and wonder how near destruction some of them unknowingly may have been. We shriek farewells upon our syren [sic] to vessels leaving for home, and we wonder if they will reach the haven of their desire in safety. Nothing out here is certain, and nothing would surprise us, though we should be immensely disgusted, to put it mildly, if our fishing operations were summarily put an end to by the appearance of a hostile submarine or other kind of warship. It is a possibility that is in all our minds, though, after the fashion of our nature, we make light of it and bandy jokes to another across the sea as we pass and re-pass one another.

The story of our being out here is not without interest, so I will try to set it out in a few words. All our readers will know that when the war broke out the fishing fleets were recalled, and for a time the fishing grounds were deserted. It is the opinion of not a few that it might have been wiser to abandon fishing altogether in these waters for a time; be that however as it may, fishing was gradually resumed under the plea of 'business as usual,' and for a time all went well; then came the staggering blows Grimsby and Hull and Boston have reeled under, in the losses that have befallen them, whilst across the sea are men who are doubtless wishing they had stopped at home, and beneath the sea are lying those who so long sailed fearlessly upon its bosom, matching danger with dauntless skill and coming triumphant through many a peril with that dogged courage and pluck that have done so much to make us what we are as a nation and people.

After a time the Fishing Companies formed themselves into a combined fleet to fish in that portion of the North Sea that lies to the westward of a line drawn from Sumburgh Head in Shetland to the Hook of Holland.

Naturally, the men at once began to ask 'Where is the Mission Ship?,' and equally naturally the Mission began at once to arrange to send a Mission Hospital Steamer to attend to the needs of the men at sea, only waiting to make sure, as far as one can make sure of anything just now, that the enterprise was being carried out in earnest.

Thus we are here following the fleet as it fishes up and down the line mentioned above, and, in a whisper, let me add sometimes so near the line that we are not sure whether it is east or west of it we are to keep.

...Today rumour, ever busy in our midst, is saying that high officials ashore are very angry because the fishermen will go where they are told not to and unless we all promise to behave ourselves we shall be sent home like naughty children. I fear some of us wouldn't find it very heavy punishment to exchange the life out here for our more accustomed life ashore. It is only fair to add that rumour doesn't accuse the fleet of doing more than look over the wall; it is those incorrigible single boaters that can't see the wall at all.

We sailed from Great Yarmouth on Wednesday, October 7th, for North Shields, where we were to coal before proceeding to join the fleet. As we left the harbour the Destroyer Flotilla was coming in from sea, reminding us of the untiring watch kept by the Navy night and day, whilst out upon the horizon were the mine sweepers carrying on their hazardous occupation.

Our skipper was armed with a sheaf of papers and primed with instructions from the Custom House. We were obligingly supplied with a fearsome illustration of what a mine looked like supposing it to be upon the surface, and were advised not to be too curious in our examination of any we came across. I am prepared to state that none of us intended to be, though it was difficult to see how we were to carry out our observation without going near the object of suspicion. Happily, so far, we have not been called upon to decide whose special duty it shall be to count the knobs and decide upon the character of any strange objects, for the simple reason we have seen nothing more alarming than a fish trunk floating in the sea.

...It was instructive to notice that, with the single exception of a Norwegian timber vessel, every ship we sighted was flying the Red Ensign. We had no need to ask ourselves where is the Navy or what is it doing, the answer was around us on every hand. Our passage across the Wash brought us by an unnamed lightship, whose captain shouted through his megaphone our course to the Spurn. Night overtook us before we reached the Humber, and it was eerie work feeling our way along the unlighted coast, though we were glad to be clear of the shoals that infest the passage further south. All through the night our skipper kept his watch upon the bridge, and those of us who turned in felt that all that was possible was being done for the welfare and safety of all on board. The morning broke fine but foggy, and nothing was visible but the sea around us. Judging by our log that we were nearing the Tyne, we turned shoreward under reduced speed, and presently heard the firing of troops at practice, that turned all our thoughts to the other side of the sea, where similar sounds might be heard under conditions of horror and sadness too deep for words.

Arrived off the Tyne, we found a crowd of vessels brought up waiting the inevitable examination, and the special signal, which we found was changed every two hours, before receiving permission to enter the port. Soon the examining steamer came alongside 'Where are you from? Have you got a set of code signals?' came through the megaphone. 'Very well, hoist N.P. and take a pilot.' So, although our skipper was as familiar with the Tyne as the Yare, we had to take a pilot, and were glad to get in with so little difficulty.

Soon after berthing our ship we heard of the sad loss of the drifter 'Lily' whilst sweeping for mines a few miles off the port. It was very distressing news, and we could only hope it wouldn't unnecessarily alarm those we had left behind, who always have the hardest part to bear – the suspense and wonderment as to what is happening to dear ones far away.

...Friday, October 9th, at noon, we left Shields for the North Sea. We were ordered to steam south as far as Seaham before heading for the fishing grounds where we expected to find the fleet, so as to avoid what was known as the Tyne mine area. We also had marked down on our chart a danger spot that lay right in our track that we were strongly advised to avoid. We acted on that advice!

Without mishap or adventure, though not without some delay owing to the fleet shifting their ground, we found ourselves next evening in the midst of the vessels forming the combined fleet, and now our task is simply to follow the Admiral as he leads us to and fro and up and down the invisible line that marks off the lawful from the unlawful waters in which we may fish. Everybody was glad to see us, and, to my astonishment, I found I was not unknown, though it is now eight years since I was out here with the men of the Red Cross Fleet.[7]

The *Lily* had in fact been a North Shields trawler and seven of her crew of 10 were lost. Three were saved through the efforts of the Yarmouth fishing boat *Oakland* and one dead body was picked up by her sister-vessel *Floandi* (concerning which much more later). The survivors and body were later landed from the Tyne.

Chapter 2

Turmoil Round the Coast

The North Sea Ground

Soles in the Silver Pit – an' there we'll let 'em lie;
Cod on the Dogger – oh, we'll fetch them by-an'-by;
War on the water – an' it's time to serve an' die,
For there's wild work doin' on the North Sea ground.

Good luck to all our fightin' ships that rule the English sea;
Good luck to our brave merchantmen wherever they may be;
The sea it is their highway, an' we've got to sweep it free
For the ships passin' over on the North Sea ground. ...

From *Punch*, 24 March 1915

On 15 August 1914 the *Fishing News* remarked:

> Never in the history of fishing have the East Coast ports been so congested as they are at present. Lowestoft, Yarmouth, Peterhead and Fraserburgh are simply blocked with drifters that drift not and the larger ports are not a whit better. At Grimsby on Tuesday [the 11th], 430 trawlers were berthed, and by the end of the week the remainder of the fleet will be in port. Hull is the home of the fleeters, and the 'Dogger' being closed, the units of the various fleets have come in for safety.

'King Herring' Dethroned

Herring fishermen, herring curers and the army of other workers whose liveli-hood depended on the 'Silver King' suffered severely from the opening of hostilities. The prosperity of the industry depended on the export of pickled herring. Of a total catch of some 500,000 to 600,000 tons landed in the United Kingdom, it had been the practice to export at least some 85 per cent. The two principal markets for pickled herrings were Germany and Russia, which in 1913 had taken over 2.4 million barrels between them. The Russian market was reached mainly through Germany or through the Baltic ports, markets which were now firmly closed – as were those in other countries adjacent to enemy countries. The loss of these markets was crippling.

Yarmouth herring fishermen were very hard hit; once the fishing closed, they took engagements with the Shipping Federation as firemen and able seamen. Over 100 were sent to London and Liverpool to join large trading steamers or Government transports. They were excellent material for the purpose. It was feared that, with regular berths found for them, they might be lost to the fishing industry in the future, as that only afforded them part-time employment, usually from May to November.

The port suffered not only the usual deprivations of war but, like Scarborough, was to be attacked directly from the sea more than once. Indeed, it was the first town in the UK to be assailed by the Germans, being bombarded by a flotilla of seven German cruisers and attendant warships.

The condition of the herring fishery in Lowestoft was vividly described in the unpublished *Trawler Boy to Trawler Man* by Skipper Victor Ernest Crisp (1900-1975). Extracts from it were published in 1976 and 1977 in the *Lowestoft Journal*. In the first instalment we are given a vivid picture of the preparation and packing of herring:

> During this Home Fishing[8] a large influx of Scots girls came into the town, most of these women being married and middle-aged. With them came their large clothes chests and barrels of oatmeal for their consumption. They lodged with different local people who were glad of the extra money. At the same time, a large fleet of Scots drifters manned by many husbands, brothers or other relations of the 'Lassies' arrived to join the large fleets of Lowestoft and Yarmouth herring fishing boats, steam and sail.
>
> Millions of fish were landed every day. These were cured for export to Russia, Germany and other European countries after the home market had been supplied, the Scots folk gutting and curing these fish in yards which were scattered about the central part of the town, also the village beach area. Where I lived was almost in the centre of this area.
>
> ...Saturday was bath night with us. During the fishing season we were allowed to sit at mother's bedroom window and watch this work going on for ten minutes before getting into bed.
>
> The flare of the naphtha lamps lit up the area of the yard which was directly opposite to where we lived. Today this is a thing of the past; many houses are now built where those yards used to be.[9]

In 1913, no fewer than 12,000 Scottish women gutters had followed the migrant herring, 3,500 of them setting out from the Western Isles in June and 5,000 coming south for the autumn season in East Anglia.

In the latter half of September 1914 there came to England an influx of another kind: Belgians. They arrived both in the shape of trawlers and the families of fishermen, together with owners and managers. The situation in Ostend had made it essential for the extensive fishing fleet either to lay up or seek a hospitable port in England. On 12 October, the Royal Naval Division re-embarked at Ostend and two days later, the Germans entered the port. Its fleet of 30 steam trawlers, mostly built in this country along the lines of our own vessels and a well-known feature of that harbour, accordingly steamed over to England. About one-third of them were later taken up for minesweeping, sunk or sold to British owners, while the remainder used to be seen fishing out of Milford, Swansea and Fleetwood, albeit with a British pilot on board.

Writing for *Toilers of the Deep* in a piece entitled 'With the North Sea Smacksmen' on 15 October 1914, the Revd CH Hicks reported that at Lowestoft, Ostend smacks had arrived that afternoon with many hundreds of Belgian refugees. He thought that he would doubtless have come across some of these same vessels in the days of peace, as he used to board them on the North Sea and in that port.

The inland arrival of these refugees was vividly described by the war correspondent, Frederick Palmer:

In Ostend I had seen the Belgian refugees in flight, and I had seen them pouring into London stations, bedraggled outcasts of every class, with the staring uncertainty of the helpless human flock flying from the storm. England, who considered that they had suffered for her sake, opened her purse and her heart to them; she opened her homes, both modest suburban homes and big country houses which are particular about their guests in time of peace. No British family without a Belgian was doing its duty. Bishop's wife and publican's wife took whatever Belgian was sent to her. The refugee packet arrived without the nature of the contents on the address tag. All Belgians had become heroic and noble by grace of the defenders of Liège.[10]

Returning to the herring fishery, this branch of activity in England came to a complete standstill up the coast in North Shields. Some boats were almost depleted of crews as RNR men were hurriedly called up, and all were forbidden for a few days to fish. From all along the north coast drifters hurried home, as did buyers, curers and Scottish girls. After a while, a few herring boats took up fishing again and the kipperers were busy; but curers were forced out of work. Only after nearly six weeks' inactivity did many of the trawlers prepare to fish again. But Scottish ports were the worst-hit of all.

During the last two weeks of July, herrings of splendid quality were landed in the Fraserburgh Fisheries District and there was every prospect of a good fishing. It seemed there were large shoals of fish on the ordinary fishing grounds and the trade was looking forward hopefully to the future. Then war was declared and the industry was practically brought to a standstill. The Naval Reserve was called up and about 500 men, mostly hired hands, left early in August. With the exception of a shot of 190 crans (a cran typically being about 1,200 fish but variable from 700 to 2,500[11]) landed by a Wick crew, no herrings were landed during the first two weeks of August. From 17 August until 25 September a few steam and motor boats were employed at herring fishing on the inshore grounds, and landed a light general fishing, which sold at moderate prices. Four cargoes of the 56,000 barrels or so of cured herrings were sent to Archangel, and 11 cargoes to Norwegian ports.

Only one steam drifter ventured to the English herring fishing, and grossed less than £100, which would have done little more than cover expenses. Five crews of fishermen went south to work English steam drifters but they had only been at sea a few times when the attempted raid by a German fleet, and the sowing of floating mines off Yarmouth, practically put an end to that fishing. When war was declared it was expected that the community would be plunged into a state of poverty, but, on the contrary, there was very little distress, although business generally was curtailed.

An interesting point was raised in Parliament on 25 November 1914 when William Cowan, MP for Aberdeenshire Eastern, asked the Secretary to the Admiralty whether his attention had been called to the fact that the Admiralty, while employing a considerable number of Peterhead steam drifters for patrol purposes in the North Sea, was not similarly employing any Fraserburgh steam drifters, notwithstanding the fact that the whole of the Fraserburgh fishing fleet was then laid up on account of the war; and whether he would now take steps to provide for the employment by the Admiralty of a proportion of Fraserburgh steam drifters in order to more equitably distribute, as between different ports, moneys expended by the Admiralty for such service. Dr Macnamara replied that his suggestion would be 'borne in mind'.

In and around Peterhead, the year 1914 would long be remembered for the disastrous effects which the outbreak of war had upon the fishing industry. Much capital had been invested in the herring trade and stood to be lost. If the paralysed state into which the herring fishing industry was plunged in early August had only ended with the home fishing, matters would not have been so bad, but the English fishing, on which so much depended, was also interfered with, and with dire results. Only 32 local vessels ventured south to Lowestoft and Yarmouth, compared with four times that number in 1913, but owing to the risk to life and property from mines in the North Sea, they only remained for a brief period. For the short time they were engaged in fishing they did well, their earnings amounting to £420 per vessel. This, however, was but a pittance compared with the earnings of previous years.

With so many men lost to the services, thousands of fishermen were thrown out of employment. Even those vessels which could muster their full complement of men experienced difficulties almost as great as had to be faced by those compelled to be ashore from sheer necessity, due to the great personal risk facing crews attempting to fish any distance from the land.

In Lossiemouth, fishing of all kinds, except for a few small boats, came to a halt by Government decree. The harbour was filled to bursting point with drifters tied up, but very soon the Government found uses for the fleet and in a few months practically all the drifters were either on patrol or minesweeping duties. Many of the older men were not taken into service by the Admiralty, so they formed themselves into crews and resurrected what was left of the sailing 'Zulus' (very fast two-masted boats which carried three sails and were very popular along the entire east coast) and went fishing again. There was still a fair fleet of small boats going line fishing, manned as usual by the older men and boys.

Wick continued to maintain its position amongst the leading fishing centres of Scotland, chiefly through the importance of its herring fisheries, although operations in August were greatly disorganized and conducted by a comparatively small fleet of boats on account of the outbreak of the war. Earlier in the year, shoals had been met with in such abundance from Whiten Head to Strathy Point as to cause considerable losses of netting.

The first blow struck at the industry by the war was the mobilizing of the Royal Naval Reserve on 3 August. At that time there were well-nigh 400 boats in Wick harbour, few of which did not have members of that force as part of their crew. Then came the difficulty of effecting insurance against war risks. Nonetheless, for two or three weeks in August, a very successful fishing was prosecuted by a small fleet on grounds at a convenient distance from the harbour.

Curers had 50,680 barrels of cured herrings on hand since the German and Russian markets were cut off. Nor could payment be obtained by curers or herring merchants who had herrings in those countries. Shipments subsequently made to Archangel, Malmö, Bergen and New York reduced the stock to about 14,000 barrels.

The interruption of the fishing caused severe employment problems, with fishermen, coopers, gutters, packers, labourers and carters all being seriously affected. Most males, however, secured temporary employment. A fair number of the fishermen were mobilized in the RNR, while others were employed on steam drifters serving as tenders at the naval base of Scapa and on board motor boats used for patrol work. Others found employment in coaling war ships.

Only one of the steam drifters from the district went to Yarmouth, realizing £363 from its catch during its five-week absence. When on its way south, the crew rescued the crew of a naval biplane in the vicinity of the Bell Rock and afterwards towed the machine to Inchkeith, in the Firth of Forth.

The Islands, too, had their problems. In Shetland and district, the estimated numbers of fishermen and others on naval and military duty was about 1,000 yet this did much to compensate a class of men who were irregularly employed during the greater part of the year. In other respects, the fisheries suffered severely through the outbreak of war. The herring fishing, which had until then been very good, was brought to a premature close and the line fishing was subsequently neglected at most of the outstations due to most of the younger men serving in Royal Naval Reserve. Fishermen from outside at once left for their own homes, and local men commenced to dismantle their boats. None of the Shetland boats, steam or sail, went to the English fishing but a Lerwick crew did go to Lowestoft and manned and worked an English drifter, making a fair enough season.

In terms of volume, 1914 was a good year for the herring fishery but not in terms of price. The total quantity landed in Shetland was 273,493 crans, the average price of which was 21s 9d. per cran, compared with 202,657 crans and 32s 9d. per cran in 1913. Curers had great difficulty in finding a market for their herrings but managed to sell some to America.

In and around Stornoway, Isle of Lewis, the number of naval reserve men serving the fleet was 1,903, while the number of men who joined the land forces, from nearly every trade and occupation in the district, was 1,100 – 1,200. In addition, about 100 men left the district for Glasgow and Liverpool to fill vacancies on merchant ships created by reservists having been called up for naval duty. All expenses were paid and high wages were given. Generally speaking, the inhabitants of the district were seldom better off, as it was estimated that about £4,000 from the men on service was coming to the island each week.

Fishing had to be completely suspended in the Orkneys from the commencement of the war owing largely to the strategic situation of such operations in certain parts of the fisheries district. All the different parts of the industry were more or less affected, either directly or indirectly, but the people hardest hit were those whose livelihood depended on the herring fishery and the curing industry. The calling up of the RN Reserve on 4 August disorganized the fleet of fishing craft to a great extent – unfortunately at a time when the fleet was at its full strength and the best results were being obtained. Had the fishing been continued throughout August the catch might very easily have been a record one, or one at least equal to the 1912 figure of 154,600 crans. Fully 90 per cent of the season's catch was landed at Stronsay. With the calling out of the Reserve the fishing practically closed. Fishermen returned to their home ports and curers closed down their stations as quickly as possible.

Despite the crisis, the total catch for the year exceeded the 1913 figure by 2,987 crans although, as in Shetland, the value (£61,963) was less, largely on account of the outbreak of the war. Dense shoals of herrings of excellent quality were just then on the fishing grounds so the fishermen would very likely have had a more prosperous year than in 1913.

Fortunately most of the district's herring fishermen had crofts and did not depend entirely on the fishing for their livelihood. Many of those thrown temporarily idle when the crisis came soon found employment on farms and also with the Admiralty, while 45 fishermen were RNR men and were called up. Others prosecuted the lobster fishing.

Luckily the stocks of cured herrings on hand in August 1914 were relatively low – 47,760 barrels, the bulk of which was of a good quality. Much of this stock went to Norway, and roughly half was consigned jointly to America and Archangel. Owing to an order issued by the Admiralty forbidding foreign vessels from landing in the Orkneys, Faeroe smacks were prevented from landing their fish, and local curers and fish workers suffered in consequence. Line fishing by local fishermen was practically suspended during the last five months of the year owing to the movements of our warships, and there was a great decrease in the quantity of cod landed.

Difficult Times in White Fishery Ports
Early in August 1914, England's Board of Agriculture and Fisheries initiated inquiries to ascertain conditions due to the war which had led, or tended, to distress among fishermen and their dependants and to devise some remedial measures aimed at the temporary or (preferably) permanent development of fishing resources.

In a surprisingly sanguine report on 29 August, the investigating officers found they were able to state that the position was generally satisfactory:

> The only cases calling for immediate attention are those of the small fishermen affected by the local military and naval restrictions on grounds near the dockyards, &c. Next in urgency will be the case of herring fishermen, whose main markets are closed, and who will have difficulty in substituting new markets at home or abroad.

Local and necessary naval restrictions on fishing operations pressed heavily on some of the minor ports. Dredging and dumping on a large scale for the improvement of harbourage were causing damage to fisheries here and there, while wrecks were already beginning to cause loss of gear, especially those which occurred in the neighbourhood of much frequented fishing grounds. On the whole, however, there was 'little grave distress'.

Yet from the beginning there was the danger from mines – floating mines deliberately cast adrift by the enemy and anchored, or moored, mines as yet undiscovered. The danger from submarines grew from comparatively small beginnings to an all-pervading menace. Thirdly, there was the danger from enemy surface craft – a danger which diminished with the growing reluctance of the German naval authorities to risk their surface craft at sea.

In September, Miss Grace, the RNMDSF Superintendent at North Shields, reported to the Mission's journal, *Toilers of the Deep*:

> In the past fortnight we seem to have lived through many weeks, and though there will have been the same happenings in other fishing ports on the eastern coast, those living inland will have difficulty in realising what it has meant and is meaning to us. Besides all the regular RNR and Army Reserve men – of whom there were very many here – being called up and going away, for eight days continuously our fishermen were signing on and our trawlers making ready to go mine sweeping. In other places they would have to wait for the men and the boats coming in from the sea; here, owing to the strike, they were all at hand. My time was spent almost continuously about the Quay seeing the men ere they left, and I never felt prouder of our men! Neither excited nor downcast, calmly and resolutely they went about their hurried preparations; only the extra light handclasp on saying farewell showing their realisation of what might be before them.
>
> Of all our trawlers 18 have gone off thus – 180 men – and now I am spending every available minute in visiting the wives and families left behind. ...

Some idea of the uncertainty prevailing at the port may be gained from a letter to the journal written some months later:[12]

> When war was declared, I was at Shields, and we had the order to bring the boat home; and when we were going to start we had the order to stop; and that is how it went on for a week. But at last we came home and were at home for three weeks. We had to be down the market every day to see if we could go away again, and at the end of three weeks we went to Scarborough. We were there four days and had to come home again, and were at home three weeks, and then we wanted to start the home fishing, and then the trouble and worry began again. I was a fortnight getting a crew, as so many of our people belong to the Naval Reserve, and they were called up, and a lot had joined the Army. So you see we had a job to get a crew, but 70 of our boats had to lay up as they were unable to get crews at all. Then we were on the fishing voyage a month and then we had to stop again.

Only three days after hostilities began (7 August 1914), Grimsby was to suffer the loss of the 227-ton steam trawler *Tubal Cain,* sunk by the German warship *Kaiser Wilhelm der Grösse* 50 miles WNW off Iceland. A month after the war broke out, Miss Newnham, local superintendent of the RNMDSF, reported:

> The horrors of war are upon us as a nation, and everywhere amongst all classes will its dreadful effects be felt; here in our own town of Grimsby we already feel some of the consequences.
>
> The whole of our steam trawlers have to lie idle in the dock, save for those vessels used for mine-sweeping, and thus in one short week thousands of Grimsby workers are out of employment. Our vessels number some 600-700 and, with the exception of those already mentioned and a few at the distant Icelandic fishing grounds, are

ordered by the Government NOT to fish in the North Sea. This means that some 6,000 fishermen, besides the vast army of pontoon workers, are absolutely stopped – a fact which is impressed upon one day by day as one sees the hundreds of men in Riby Square and in the docks.

...More than 1,000 men have gone off to their different Reserves, and day by day others are joining, yet still many are left, and there are the wives and children!

...Ever the first to help in times of need in our town are the trawler owners themselves, but it will be seen at once that this war affects them in a very terrible way as well as those who man the vessels.

I am well aware that all the east coast fishing ports and the great herring industry will suffer very acutely, but perhaps in no one place will the suffering be felt more than in Grimsby, the capital of the Fisheries, on account of the vast number of persons involved.

Grimsby's vessels lay idle for nearly three weeks; then they were gradually got to sea under agreement to abide by the Admiralty restrictions as to fishing. Almost immediately the danger of floating mines appeared and soon over 20 Grimsby vessels were destroyed.

In the first year of the war, the port lost no fewer than 73 steam trawlers, not including any on minesweeping duties. Of these, as many as 27 were lost with their entire crews and 17 were sunk with their entire crews interned. By October, nearly 200 of the town's fishermen were thought to be in Wilhelmshaven as prisoners of war (see Chapter 8). At first there seemed no hope of any Government help for the wives of men who were POWs, nor any compensation for those lost at sea, although proper arrangements were reported to have been made by Miss Newnham a year later. The area to be covered by her visitation was very large – there were over 180 widows, many with large families. The Relief Committee cared in a very kindly way and much valuable work was also performed by the Mayor's Fund for the Relief of Distress.

Any aliens in the port (and, of course, Germans in particular) were dealt with harshly. On 20 November 1914, one George Bruhm, a German fisherman, was sentenced to two months' hard labour for failing to register. Although he had registered at Hull on the outbreak of the war, he later went to Grimsby but did not report and had been sailing on a Grimsby trawler. The Court recommended that Bruhm should be detained in a concentration camp on completion of his sentence.

Large numbers of Grimsby's fishermen were called up for service with the Royal Naval Reserve, while others served with the complementary Trawler Reserve, of which more later. Not until 6 June 1926, however, was a memorial lamp dedicated to their memory in St Andrew's Church.

Afternoon tide sailings had proceeded from Hull as usual until the end of July, with instructions to skippers as to procedures in the case of eventualities, but as the outlook grew more serious, sailings were suspended with effect from 1 August. The large 'boxing' fleets which worked in the North Sea were recalled and on the morning of the 5th about 100 sail boats were anchored in the river, with others constantly arriving as they passed up from Spurn.

The docks quickly became congested with trawlers, while the number of men thrown out of employment grew daily; naturally, a considerable number volunteered for service in the Trawler Reserve.

In August 1914, there were 375 Hull-owned trawlers and cutters, a figure which by mid-January 1916 had been reduced to 93, of which 32 were supplying the London market direct, leaving 61 to supply Hull. Over 260 were, or had been, on Admiralty work. The loss of the *Imperialist* (see Chapter 6) combined with the removal of aids to navigation on the east coast was responsible for the transfer of a further number of Hull vessels, notably to Fleetwood. The sinking of the trawler, one of the finest vessels extant, and the death of her popular skipper, Joe Wood, created a deep impression on the community.

In early September 1914, arrangements were made to dispatch the Gamecock Fleet to sea and a number of vessels left dock on Thursday the 10th, but recall orders were later issued and the fleet remained laid up. Nevertheless, there was some easing of the situation with the carriers from the fleet working the west coast grounds beginning to arrive regularly. With a fair number of the fleeters being altered and adapted for independent voyaging, landings from the nearer grounds improved.

At the RNMDSF Institute, Skipper Arthur Windass and Albert Burke were the local workers, but both very soon joined the minesweeping service; the former was promoted to Chief Skipper and the latter did long service in the Mediterranean.

Scarborough's fishing trade was completely disorganized as a result of the war. Several of the local trawler crews refused to put to sea, with the result that their vessels lay idle and supplies were greatly affected. Buyers were also operating under difficulties owing to the unsteadiness of the inland markets.

On the night of Saturday, 8 August, the harbourmaster received instructions from the Admiralty to stop all fishing vessels operating, although on the following Monday it issued further instructions permitting the boats to fish during the day only and to 'lie to' during dark hours. Reports of floating mines in the fishing areas, however, were to keep many of the fishermen from venturing out to the grounds. On Friday, 4 September, only one trawler landed, with a cargo made up mainly of cod and sprag (juvenile cod intermediate in size between cod and codling); values ruled high, with demand far outweighing supply. On Monday the 7th, there was again only one arrival, the Hartlepool trawler *Loch Garry*, while the next two days were blank, with no fish at all being landed. Trawlers did gradually resume fishing operations, however, thereby alleviating the situation.

Towards the end of August, 1914, disaster befell the Boston trawling fleet and a part of the Grimsby fleet. The incident was reported in the following terms by the Admiralty:

A squadron consisting of 2 cruisers and 4 destroyers have succeeded in sinking 15 British fishing boats in the North Sea, and the crew of fishermen have been taken to Wilhelmshaven as prisoners of war.

The effect of this encounter was to cripple Boston as a deep-sea fishing port for the remainder of the war. It was not only the decimation of the harbour's fleet which led to this standstill but the potential threat posed by the reports of numerous vessels striking mines near the Outer Dowsing. The suspension of operations by the Boston Deep-Sea Fishing and Ice Company resulted in virtual paralysis for the port as early as mid-August, with 24 of the company's trawlers lying idle in the dock and the remaining three due back to port imminently for confinement. Nevertheless, work soon began on fitting out a number of the vessels for war work and before long seven were on patrol and minesweeping service.[13]

Private companies continued to operate a handful of vessels, two being sent out, for example, in the week beginning 10 August, while on the night of 7 September, a lone vessel, owned by the Witham Steam Company, sailed from the harbour. The *Fishing News* of 24 October reported that the only vessel to have landed during the week had been the local *Arctic* (whose fate is described in Chapter 7). Her 10-day trip had fetched very low prices yet had been satisfactory financially.

Anti-German feeling in Boston ran high. In the third week of August, a mob attacked the premises of Messrs Frank & Co, pork butchers, in the High Street. The business was carried on by two Germans, Leonard and George Cantenwine. A crowd of around 1,000 people gathered round the shop and a missile thrown through one of the plate-glass windows was the signal for an attack. The shop windows were riddled and some of the upper windows of the residence were smashed. The premises were hastily closed and the Cantenwines made their escape, being sheltered by friends. The disorder continued until an early hour on the morning of Sunday 23rd. The police formed a cordon and, using their batons, cleared the thoroughfares. A young boy was injured and taken to hospital and one man was arrested.

In mid-December, 1914, a meeting of the Kent and Essex Sea Fisheries Committee was held at Fishmongers' Hall at which it was reported that the fisheries had been very much affected by the war, especially at Brightlingsea and Harwich. The Thames had suffered less repercussions. So far, however, there were plenty of winkles and cockles and an abundance of whitebait. There had been a great fall of oyster spat, so that a good yield of oysters in 1915 could be looked forward to.

Yet on the North Sea, as one speaker pointed out, the position was serious on account of the mines. None of the smacks could get out. The younger men had therefore enlisted, preferring to 'have a go' at the Germans rather than being blown to pieces. Many of the men had gone to London and joined the Fire Brigade and the supply of fish had therefore suffered.

The Secretary had supplied the Board of Agriculture with information, for the Admiralty, as to the fishermen's distress. The fisheries for the whole Thames estuary were in a difficult situation.

As far as Billingsgate market was concerned, supplies had been fairly normal except for the preceding three weeks, when the shortage had been due to the gales. The sprat fishing had just commenced. In the previous three years, the bulk of the supply had been exported, but this would no longer be possible. However, this would make sprats cheap for home supply if the public supported the fishermen through their demand and made it worth their while to bring their catches home.

What of the south and west? The severe restrictions imposed on fishing in the North Sea meant that many east coast operators had to look elsewhere to continue their work. Commenting on the situation on 21 November 1914, the *Fishing News* confirmed that the North Sea was 'practically totally closed to fishing boats' and considered the two alternative areas available – the south coast and the west coast. Yet for some reason:

> ...the south coast has not had the same appeal as the other, and the reason is all the more difficult to find when we consider that actual results obtained seem to stamp it as a more lucrative area than the west coast. Of the three, east, south and west, the latter occupies the lowest place in a comparison of the total landings of fish, having about one-fifth of the amount to its credit that the east coast can boast of and about a third of the landings on the south coast. Yet this may easily be explained by the probability that the resources of the west coast fishing grounds are not fully utilised.

In Devon, particulars of the effect of the war on the Plymouth fishing industry and suggestions for coping with the situation were, at the end of August 1914, laid before Stephen Reynolds,[14] Assistant Fisheries Inspector, author and champion of the inshore fishermen, who held an enquiry on the subject at the Seaman's Bethel, Barbican, on behalf of the Board of Agriculture and Fisheries. The Devon Sea Fisheries Committee and the National Relief Fund for Plymouth were represented and the fishermen themselves attended in good numbers.

Reynolds sought information on four points: how the war had affected fishing at Plymouth, how best the industry could be kept going, the extent of distress among the fishermen and the best means of meeting that distress. From the evidence supplied, it emerged that before the war some 450 fishermen were following their calling from the port. Of these about 80 had been called up as naval reservists, and 20 or 30 had gone to work at Devonport dockyard. Some 150 men working on the quay as carters and in other capacities were dependent on the fishing industry. On account of the lack of crews, four trawlers and 20 small boats were laid up. So far no specific application for assistance had been made to the Relief Fund by any of the fishing class.

The distress among fishermen was not acute, but many were earning very little and just struggling along. Although mackerel had been plentiful it had been sold very cheaply. The better class of fish were in short supply, since the men could not go out far enough or at the best time. In addition, the port was closed at night.

One member of the audience pointed out that a contributory factor to distress was the recent suspension of payment by the Naval Bank; a large number of fishermen had their life savings in the bank and were very hard hit by the collapse. There was hope at least on the employment front, since official information had been received that all the men at the dockyard were likely to be fully employed for some time.

Regarding restrictions on vessel movements, those present thought it would hardly be practicable for boats to be convoyed in and out as a fleet. As an alternative port to work from, Looe met with little favour; Brixham was thought preferable as it offered better facilities for handling fish. The re-opening of Start Bay (long closed to British trawlers) was urged as a means of assisting the industry.

Reynolds also met representatives of the trade from Porthleven at around the same time to ascertain what steps could be taken to assist those who might suffer on account of the war. It was stated that the pilchard fishery had so far probably been the worst season within memory and there would without doubt be much distress. Many crews were seriously hampered by the absence of reserve men.

Concerning Brixham, the *Fishing News* reported on 8 August 1914, that over 200 men had been called up to serve in the Royal Naval Reserve and that stirring scenes had marked their send-off on the Sunday. The Brixham Torbay Royal Regatta was postponed indefinitely.

A number of Belgian refugees took up quarters in the town and many of them settled. In May 1916, a Brixham fisherman by the name of Coleman reported at the 35th RNMDSF Annual Meeting:

> We have 300 Belgians working out of Brixham, some in their own vessels and some in ours. They have adopted our methods. When they first came they did not do much, but they are getting along better now.[15]

The West Country fisherman has been known down the centuries for his chivalry and heroism – in 1346, the town of Fowey supplied 47 ships and 770 men for the investment of Calais. In 1914, Cornwall soon felt the effects of the depletion of manpower, the response by the county's fishermen to the call of King and Country being as prompt and enthusiastic as ever.

In Newlyn, 150 seamen belonging to the town were sent away and, with the Royal Naval Reserve men also going, they were left practically without men. Then the Admiralty sent the ML boats and Newlyn became a naval base. Later the airmen came and found a refuge with the RNMDSF, so there was not a day when the Mission's house was not packed with all kinds of servicemen.

A correspondent wrote to *The Times* in 1916:

> When the Navy first made ready for the War, nearly 600 men left the county on one Sunday evening, and it is said that as many as 300 followed them the next day. Three hundred went from the St Ives district alone. These were the naval reservists, and they are now at sea or waiting somewhere in their ships for the German fleet to come out from the Kiel Canal. Since those first days the men who were left have gone in twos and threes, and sometimes in greater numbers, to take up those other activities at sea which have their dangers and hardships, although the crews engaged upon them are classed as non-combatants. The draining of men has gone steadily on until in many places only one-third of the original male fishing popula-tion is left to man the boats.[16]

Writing of his childhood in Cornwall in *Harbour Village – Yesterday in Cornwall*, Leo Tregenza who, with his brothers, grew up in the fishing village of Mousehole, remembered one neighbour, a:

> ...fisherman, [who] like many others in Mousehole, belonged to the Royal Naval Reserve, and I well remember that Sunday morning in August 1914 when someone must have come into the chapel and told them that war had been declared for they all walked out one after the other in the middle of the service.

For his part, Alfred J Pengelly, BEM, recollected in his autobiography *Oh, For a Fisherman's Life:*[17]

> At the outbreak of the First World War, my father who was attached to the Royal Naval Reserve, was called up for service. It was on a Sunday morning that the call went through the town for all reserve men to assemble at the Coastguard Station, Church End, East Looe. I remember sitting on my father's kit bag waiting for the men to be off. In the afternoon with a band leading the procession, more than a hundred fishermen from Looe and Polperro marched to the station to entrain for the Naval Barracks, Devonport. It was an impressive sight even for us youngsters.

Pengelly's family moved to Devonport, which made it much more convenient for his father to come home on night leave from the Royal Naval Barracks.

The Harbour Trust of Swansea stated in its 1915 report that the industry at the port was reviving, the landings for 1914 having shown an increase of 1,000 tons, largely thanks to the Belgians. It was also noted that seven additional trawlers were being built for local owners.

'Good-bye till we come to stay' had been the curious words used a little over two years before the war in Milford Haven by a German naval officer bidding farewell to a lady from that port. This story was recounted by the vicar of Swindon in the course of a discourse on duty and the war, which he preached to the congregation of men at his own church. The vicar was referring to the elaborate system of spying which Germany had instituted. While he was staying at the Welsh port, a German warship had appeared and dropped anchor and the crew came on shore. They were given a very warm welcome and everything possible was done to make them happy. All the time, however, they must have been engaged in spying out the land around the Haven. The *Fishing News* correspondent reporting this item referred to a case as far back as nine or ten years earlier where the doings of a suspected German spy on the occasion of naval manoeuvres at Milford substantially boosted sales of local papers; the admiral in charge of operations not only knew about the spy but gave his consent to pressmen investigating the circumstances and turning it into 'copy'.[18]

In the event, the only 'invasion' to be suffered by the port in wartime was from fellow fishermen ousted from the east coast and the refugees from Belgium. No fewer than 25 Belgian trawlers elected to transfer to Milford early on, with several moving to Swansea. A Belgian trawler was nothing new at Milford, but this was indeed an invasion – albeit a most welcome one, since the vessels just about made up for the home trawlers then minesweeping. They were planning to work the herrings first and exploit the hake grounds later.

Among the fleet were three old Milford boats, formerly the *St. Clair, St. Brides* and *Athalia*. No fewer than five Ostend firms were represented, and the owner of one, J Bauwens, himself arrived with his family and servants to take up residence. All the guests greatly appreciated the kindness shown them on their arrival at the Welsh port.

Soon five Grimsby trawlers were working out of Milford and these would later be joined by others which could no longer operate in safety off their home coast. By September 1914, quite a few boats belonging to GF Sleight of Grimsby were already using the port, as were vessels owned by a number of other Grimsby and Hull firms. Fleetwood, on the north-west English coast, was also to be largely frequented by British steam trawlers driven off the North Sea, and a number of fishermen took their wives and families from the east to the west coast to live.

The wrench away from familiar surroundings was softened by the comfort and guidance given by the RNMDSF at its institutes. This body was itself affected by the crisis in unforeseen ways: with the withdrawal of the fleets and the recall of the single-boaters from the North Sea, its three Steam Hospital Mission Ships (and four Sailing Bethel Ships[19]) were, for the first time in the Mission's history, 'comrades at the quay with nothing to do', according to Dr Willway. The sailing vessels were quickly fitted out with the necessary stores and sent round to Milford to work in what were then untroubled waters. The steamers were offered in turn to the Admiralty and the War Office but were not accepted, so the *J & S Miles* and the *Alpha* were fitted out as single-boaters and sailed round to join their brethren working out of Wales. (The *Queen Alexandra* was fitted out for duty in the North Sea, subsequently working in the combined fleet later established there).

Turning to Scotland, port congestion in Aberdeen was still unusually marked in mid-August 1914, although the new Torry dock, being thrown open for the accommodation of drifters, provided some relief. The Fish Market, extended for the fourth time in February 1914 and opened by Messrs WH Dodds & Co. as agents for the German trawler *Brake*, had lost its bustle and the arrival of a trawler became an event of some importance. Dismay prevailed as a result of a notice displayed at the market stating 'Please circulate widely that the Admiralty order no fishing vessels to go out until further notice.' On Thursday 13 August, 220 trawlers and 50 drifters found berthing room, while nearly 100 of Aberdeen's fleet were at sea engaged in sweeping operations. With the exception of two – the *Jack George* (Yarmouth) and the *Levita* (North Shields) – all the English boats had left for home. The fleet of 50 drifters confined to the harbour was composed of locally-owned craft.

Chapter 3

Fisher Jacks

Lads, you're wanted. Come and learn
To live and die with honest men.

You shall learn what men can do
If you will but pay the price,
Learn the gaiety and strength
In the gallant sacrifice.

Take your risk of life and death
Underneath the open sky.
Live clean or go out quick -
Lads, you're wanted. Come and die.

From *Recruiting* by EA Mackintosh[20]

Various classes of reservists were liable for war service and these were promptly called upon under proclamations of 3 August 1914.

The most important of these at that time – numerically as well as from the point of view of efficiency – was the Royal Fleet Reserve, established in 1900 and consisting entirely of seamen, naval police, stoker ratings and Royal Marines, together with a few ships' police, who had completed their term of enlistment in the Navy. Yet its authorized strength of 31,137 petty officers and men was rapidly outstripped in numbers by the Royal Naval Reserve, a force raised by an 1859 Act of Parliament which was recruited entirely from the merchant service and fishing fleets. Officers and men were required to put in a certain amount of periodical training with the fleet in return for a retainer and, of course, for placing their services at the disposal of the naval authorities in the event of war. The main body of the RNR consisted of 1,790 officers and 17,299 men plus 600 and 400 men in sections in Newfoundland and Malta respectively. In 1911 a new branch had been created for the specific purpose of minesweeping in war – the Trawler Section. In 1914 its authorized strength was 142 skippers (warrant officers) and 1,136 men.

The third and youngest of the Navy's reserve forces was the Royal Naval Volunteer Reserve, established in 1903 and consisting for the most part of shore-keeping men with the necessary enthusiasm and spare time to equip themselves to stand their footing with regular seamen in the event of war. Its various divisions were known as London, Clyde, Bristol, Mersey, Sussex, Tyneside, and South African, and its strength at the outbreak of war was 4,700 officers and men – a small force, but one whose efficiency was quickly established and acknowledged. Part of it, plus a Royal Marine Brigade, formed the nucleus of the Royal Naval Division, which would see splendid but ultimately ineffectual service at Antwerp in October 1914, and later on in Gallipoli and on the Western Front. It was a purely land force, formed at the outbreak of the war at the specific request of Winston Churchill. Due to the insufficiency of ships for the men available to crew them, the First Lord of the Admiralty wished to prepare for active service a new unit which would be trained as infantry but retain naval elements in rank, uniform and procedure.

When war broke out, then, the total active list of the Royal Navy stood at 151,000, of whom 129,425 were navy personnel, 3,130 coastguards and 18,445 Royal Marines. This manpower was supplemented by over a third in the form of the reservists, who totalled 57,204. Of these, 37.3 per cent were represented by the pure Naval Reserve (20,089) and the RNR(T) force (1,278) combined. By the spring of 1917, some 76,000 men belonged to the Naval Reserve and 33,000 to the Volunteer Reserve. Many thousands would have to be deducted from the aggregate on account of the Royal Naval Division and the RN Air Service, of which a certain proportion was employed with the land forces.

Of course, a number of fishermen joined the army, exchanging mine-strewn and submarine-infested waters for fields of mud and barbed wire. James Spring, the chairman of Hull City Football Club, received an interesting letter from the trenches in the summer of 1915 from one George Wood:

I am a Hull lad, and my occupation is that of a fisherman, my last ship being the Flicker[21] of the Gamecock Fleet. I came home when all the fleets were brought in from the fishing grounds, and I have been out here since November. ...Out here the trenches we are occupying are only 23 yards apart, and between us and the Germans is a poor Belgian woman and her child, shot down in cold blood by the Germans. Perhaps her husband is fighting. You can believe me, sir, that there is practically not a house or building left standing. Now, to crown their efforts to get to Calais – which they will never do – they find themselves beaten in modern warfare, and are trying to poison us. To tell the truth, I do not know what implement of torture they will adopt next; but whatever they adopt, you can rest assured that French's 'contemptible little army' will be always ready for Kaiser Bill and all his colleagues. The weather conditions are now fine and we are all quite happy amid our dangerous surroundings. I hope you will convey my greetings to Mr Stringer and all the members of the team. Thank you for sending the football.

Spring told the *Fishing News*, which published the letter,[22] that footballs were still wanted by the men at the front in their intervals of rest.

Flocking to the Colours

Throughout these islands, enrolment by fishermen to the various services was nothing short of overwhelming. A journalist, HM Tomlinson,[23] described such a scene in England to the *Fishing News*:

When war was declared I was in one of these East Coast towns, and stayed on, expecting to get there the first news of any naval action. Its fleet of trawlers came in gradually, and stayed in till the harbour was full. There was little chance to fish, and the men idled about till one night Whitehall sent word that those who thought they would like it could go fishing for mines and submarines, under the White Ensign. They were to present themselves next morning. I was there at the time, and saw that morning in a queue all the fishermen of the town, those with white whiskers and those with none, eager for the chance of this new fishing. It was their job, they thought. That harbour began at once to change, not in the nature of its work, but in the kind of prey its ships went out to get. Its fleet began to fish once more, its crews applying the ancient lore of their kind merely to a new kind of sea-work.[24]

Portsmouth comes readily to mind as one of the country's great naval bases yet perhaps only a flying visit might be paid to it by reservists called to action, as in the case of Donald Macleay RNR of Shader, Barvas, on the Isle of Lewis. He had for years pursued his fisherman's calling around the Hebrides, off Fraserburgh and, once a year, as far south as Lowestoft and Yarmouth. It was on a Sabbath that the summons to the Reserve came and it was peremptory. He and his fellow reservists were in Fraserburgh waters but there was no question of them even having dinner before leaving. They immediately boarded southbound trains, spending just two days in the historic naval barracks, then a week on Whale Island for gunnery training. Some hundreds of them then took trains to Liverpool, where they joined the converted transatlantic liner *Carmania*, which had been taken over by the navy as an armed merchant cruiser at the beginning of the war. Over 30 of the crew were ex-fishermen from the Western Isles.

The vessel was to see spectacular action, sinking the German armed liner *Kap Trafalgar* off the east coast of South America on 14 September 1914 after an engagement lasting one hour and forty minutes. So fierce was the duel that the *Carmania* was hit by no fewer than 79 projectiles. On fire and severely mauled, she was unable to render assistance to the five lifeboats crowded with survivors from her enemy. Only 279 of the *Kap Trafalgar*'s original 423-man crew reached Buenos Aires, where they were interned. The battered *Carmania* was escorted to Gibraltar by the cruiser HMS *Cornwall*. For her action against the *Kap Trafalgar*, the *Carmania* was commemorated by the British Navy League, who presented her with a silver plate from the dinner service of Viscount Nelson. Her casualties were nine killed and 26 wounded, among whom was Donald Macleay, who lost his right arm and right leg:

> I was carrying a shell in my two arms to number 2 gun on the port side when one of the German shells came and struck it on the point, and the shell burst and scattered about me. I don't know how I was not in bits.[25]

Had it not been for his brother preventing it, Macleay would have been thrown overboard with the other fatalities from the battle.

On the HMS *Orama*, an armed merchant cruiser which took part in the Battle of Coronel off the Falkland Islands in November 1914 and which was torpedoed by a U-boat in the Atlantic on 19 October 1917, all 70 reservists were ex-fishermen from the Islands – 25 of them Macleods from Stornoway.[26]

The RND and HMS *Never Float*

Within the RND, two naval brigades and one marine brigade were constituted, of which Admirals of the fleet, Lord Fisher and Sir Arthur Wilson, and Admiral Lord Charles Beresford, were appointed honorary colonels. The strength of the naval brigades was to be made up to 15,000 by the addition of 5,000 men so that the Division might be raised to the strength of an infantry division, complete with field hospitals, transport, ammunition column, signal companies, cyclists, motor cars and machine guns. An aeroplane squadron from the Royal Naval Air Service was also to be available when required.

Before the Division had even been in existence for a fortnight and before it had any equipment or its new recruits had had even rudimentary training, a contingent of 2,200 of all ranks had to be rushed into the fighting line to assist in the defence of Antwerp, as mentioned. In this action, many prisoners were taken, including numbers of fishermen (see Chapter 8).

For training purposes in connection with recruits for the Division, the Admiralty took over the Crystal Palace in south-east London. Headquarters for the staff were established near the Admiralty at 41, Charing Cross, London SW. The Palace, originally a giant glass and iron exhibition hall in Hyde Park that housed the Great Exhibition of 1851, was taken down in 1852-54 and rebuilt at Sydenham Hill, at which site it stood until 1936, when it was virtually destroyed in a spectacular fire. The towers which survived were finally demolished in 1941 since they were thought to be a dangerous landmark for incoming German bombers.

By April 1915 no fewer than 17,000 men had passed through this centre since its takeover as an RND depot. Brigadier BB Rackham (RND *Hawke*) remembered the discomforts of the cold, draughty stone-floored buildings, while one HC Kerr recalled it as the 'Glass Frigate' or 'HMS *Never Float*' and recollected in particular the tremendous efforts to create a naval atmosphere there. In October 1914, the daily schedule comprised a run before breakfast, parade, rifle drill, signalling, a route march and skirmishing.[27] Phillip Boydell (of whom more later) remembered:

> The track around the Football ground was the place where the brutes of P.T. instructors almost literally ran us to death.

The men received two months' training, after which they were sent to other camps for another period of training before being drafted as needed for active service. A great many fishermen had joined the Division and the various battalions had been able to supply large numbers to undertake the perilous task of minesweeping.

A vivid record of life at the Palace is afforded by another ex-trainee. In his self-published reminiscences entitled *SURRENDERED – Some Naval War Secrets* written under the pen name 'Griff (ASG)',[28] the author recalled the change of use of the premises from an exhibition centre to a training establishment for the RNVR:[29]

> In 1914 the Admiralty took over the Crystal Palace and made it the head-quarters of the Royal Naval Volunteer Reserve. The great glass-house was in a terribly dilap-

idated state at the time, but the extensive grounds offered excellent training quarters for a large body of men. Before long recruits poured in from every part of England. R.N. and R.N.V.R. Commanders from their various divisions, which had been established throughout Great Britain, transferred their work to the Crystal Palace depot under the leadership of Commodore Sir Richard Williams-Bulkeley. The R.N.V.R. depots in London, Bristol, Tyneside, Clyde and Mersey, which were for many years their training quarters, were utilised now as recruiting centres, to provide men for the Royal Naval Division at the Palace Head-Quarters.

Speedily the great building was transformed into a naval base... The ever-increasing number of recruits who found their way into the building daily became so numerous that the Exhibition houses in the Palace grounds had to be used for sleeping accommodation. Around all the galleries rows and rows of hammocks were slung, and on the ground floor spacious mess decks were arranged.... The number of recruits became so large that in its earliest days the crowds of men wandered about the building in amazement, not knowing one iota where to go, or what to do. Bugle calls rang out which conveyed little meaning to anyone, for they were not understood.

A large number of re-mobilised marines were drafted into the depot to cope with the crowd, who were running wild in the grounds, and who seemed to be enjoying sightseeing amongst the various exhibits.

Before long, however, steps were taken to stow all the exhibition relics away, as there was serious work to be done. The internal appearance of the whole building rapidly changed, but the enormous glass roof leaked like a sieve and even proved a health hazard. At last a new glass roof was provided throughout the length of the building:

Steps were at once taken to prohibit the public from entering the depot, but before this sensible measure was adopted all manner of curious people wended their way to the Palace, to see what was going on. Girls by the hundred joined in the dancing each evening round the bandstands, where the sailors whirled them round till closing time.

Little by little law and order was established, and the recruits soon fell into the ways of the Navy. Instead of a general stampede to the mess decks, the men marched, and when the bugles sounded the recruits fell in to their proper divisions and marched off to the parade grounds. The difficulties experienced in coping with such a vast number of undisciplined men were increased by an inadequate staff. The war was young, and all those who joined up were so full of enthusiasm that they meddled with each others' affairs in the organisation of the training. It is strange how this mass of humanity, herded together in a building, found their way eventually into some sort of order, and knuckled under to discipline.

...The reason why these soldiers, destined to Gallipoli and France to fight in the field, were dressed up in sailor rig I could never understand, for not one of these men had ever paraded on the decks of a warship. The same applied to their commanding officers. Everything was carried out in a similar way as at Naval Barracks, which gave the recruits the impression that they would be required for sea service; their disappointment was very marked when they discovered that this was a ruse to obtain volunteers for the Army.

The collection of recruits that entered the depot consisted of men in every station of life-from the lowest type to the man of gentle birth, lawyers, barristers, clerks, professional men of all kinds, road sweepers, musicians, actors, and burglars who had escaped from the arm of the law.

...We were getting on famously with the HMS *Crystal Palace*, when suddenly orders were received from the Admiralty to cancel the unauthorised name of our ship. ...In spite of the unkind remarks which the Admiralty chose to thrust at us, hundreds of men left the depot for ships, possessed of an accurate knowledge of their work, often superior to the men who were already at sea. Dummy guns, without a bark, peeped through the balustrades of the terraces; these were loaded by the men with imitation projectiles and cartridges for instructional purposes. Each gun crew closed up to their gun daily, until they became acquainted with the breech block mechanism of different sized weapons.

Recalling the departures for the training camp at Blandford, Griff wrote:

Each week when the drafts of men were ready to entrain for Blandford Camp, the Naval band formed up at the main entrance, and preceded the fully equipped Naval ratings on the march to the Crystal Palace Station, with their respective officers. A great send off was always awaiting them; also en route they received marked attention from the various houses as they passed by. Little flags were waved from the windows, and good wishes were shouted from the numerous onlookers, which the men acknowledged with cheery smiles, although lumbered up by their bulky kit bags and fighting equipment.

On 17 April, press representatives were permitted to visit the Palace to see what was being achieved; the six battalions then under training were paraded for inspection, with the divisional march past being recorded as a 'fine spectacle' in the *Fishing News* one week later.

Evidently on the basis of this visit, a correspondent for *The Navy* reported in the May 1915 issue that:

7,000 men, who have only worn the naval uniform for a few weeks, impress the spectators with astonishment at the accuracy and swing with which they perform their movements. Many of the men have volunteered for the perilous work of mine-sweeping. Nearly a thousand signallers have also been supplied to the War stations. But there is a pressing need for men, more men.

In the July issue of the same periodical, further impressions were recorded and revealed the diversity of the trainees and their lives within its precincts:

Miners, University men, artisans, artists, men who have tilled the soil, have all donned the blue jacket... Not all go to sea, but after an initial training in military drill the aptitude of each for individual service is taken into account. Mine-sweepers, signallers and the ordinary rank and file of infantry are recruited from the ranks of the Royal Naval Division. Some are sent to coast stations, others join the land forces in Egypt or the Dardanelles, others are detailed to the Expeditionary Forces nearer home. Strenuous physical drill and recreation occupy the leisure hours of the men. Boxing rings and concerts make up the light side of life. A savings-bank has been established, reading-rooms and writing-rooms are provided, and many features of club life break the monotony of ordinary routine. Study is not neglected, and French, among other subjects, is well taught.

A 'graduate' of the Palace was Phillip Boydell, quoted from earlier who, in 1977, wrote a memoir of his life in two volumes. The first volume covers in some detail his service in the First World War as a wireless telegraphist in the

Royal Navy and on board the hired patrol tug *Blackcock* on salvage work and towing off the African coast, in the Persian Gulf and in the Channel until the boat was finally lost following an accident in the White Sea in January 1918, after which he briefly served in a trawler fitted with a hydrophone for anti-submarine work.[30]

He recalled the Palace as 'an extraordinary place' and remembered being housed in the Canada building. After successfully taking his passing-out examination, he was assigned to his first posting to a minesweeping trawler.[31] Some two years later, when serving on the *Blackcock*, he learned from a fellow trainee that passing the examinations was no guarantee of acceptance on board a service vessel. The fishermen in this case clearly closed their ranks against the outsider:

> It was late one evening when we slowly entered Lock [*sic*] Ewe. It was like steering into a tunnel getting darker and grimmer the further we crept in and it was within dim sight of a single white cottage ashore, the only sign of human habitation we could see, that we dropped anchor.
>
> There were a few trawlers lying at anchor near us and [Signalman] Bunts was just able to read their names in the dusk before we went below. One of the trawlers' names seemed to ring a bell in my mind and looking through an address book I discovered that 'Chubby', an old Crystal Palace team mate, was on board her. Back on the bridge Bunts and I made morse lamp signals directed at the trawler time after time without response and eventually gave up believing them dead aboard as well they might be in this ghostly God-forsaken place.

An hour or so later, 'Chubby' Charlton appeared on board. Recognizing his old friend, he fell with his arms around his neck and wept unashamedly, despite not being 'that kind of chap'. All night they exchanged news. After the usual experience at sea as a second operator, Charlton had been posted some two years earlier to this 'dead alive place Lock Ewe'. Like Boydell on joining the *Blackcock*, he had been violently repulsed by the ship and everyone aboard it. He hated deeply what he regarded as the disgusting foulness of mind in which he saw no redeeming feature, from the skipper to every single member of the crew. And not one of them would have anything whatever to do with him. He was, as it were, sent to Coventry of his own making and for two years, except for leave, he had suffered complete isolation. He was now in a shocking state of mind and nerves. The tug crew did their best to cheer him up with sympathy and suggestions for a rethink about his attitude toward his shipmates and a move towards some kind of reconciliation. At any rate by the time he reluctantly left them in the morning he was beginning to look more like his old cheerful self. As the *Blackcock* moved off and made the open sea, it broke regulations by exchanging goodbye, good luck messages over the W/T.[32]

At the Crystal Palace depot, a large section of the building was handed over for the training of airmen. At the close of the war, it was utilized for demobilizing soldiers. When the last batch left, the Palace became an exhibition once more, with a very fine display of both Allied and enemy war trophies. Every department of the war was represented from the battleship to the small trawler in the Naval Section, and Army equipment was exhibited in the Northern Section. 'Griff' recollected:

> All these remnants of the war are now installed in the South Kensington Museum, and the old depot, where so many happy days were spent by the R.N.V.R., has returned to variety shows and musical festivals. Firework displays take place on the terraces, which was the scene of many thousands of trained sailors and soldiers, who paraded before their departure to the war areas. There remains very little in the building and grounds that reminds one of the splendid purpose which the Crystal Palace was used for during the period of the Great War.

The locations of RND training camps included Chatham, Portsmouth, Plymouth, Portland, Gravesend, Browndown, Tavistock and Alnwick. Writing in the November 1914 issue of *The Church and the Sailor*, the Chaplain at Deal, the Revd PL Neagus, reported that two Royal Naval brigades had been encamped for some weeks in the neighbourhood of the town. The first was at Walmer and the second at Betteshanger Park, some six miles away. The brigades were made up of Royal Fleet Reserves, RNR, RNVR and a few Army recruits. In the camps were men drawn from every grade of society – several doctors, lawyers, public school men, an ordination candidate and Yorkshire miners from Pontefract. Every British accent, from John O'Groats to Land's End, was to be heard. There were Scottish Naval Volunteers from the Clyde and others from the Mersey, Tyne, London and Sussex. A few of the men hailed from Stornoway and when speaking in broad Gaelic were unintelligible to onlookers.

Chatham Barracks

The Naval Barracks at Chatham need no introduction. The report of a visit later in the war to this establishment was printed in the partwork *The War Illustrated*. It was penned by regular contributor Sydney A Mosely and refers to a German air raid which took place on 3 September 1917:

> To the new-comer nothing inspires so deep a consciousness of the greatness and conservatism of the Navy as a visit to a Royal Naval Barracks. A sense of grandeur, a spirit of intense dignity is ever present.
>
> It was an excellent idea to send us newly-gazetted officers to take our training at Chatham. From the moment we entered the town till the moment we left it to take up duties elsewhere we were never allowed, by the bearing of officers and men alike, to forget our status as officers of the King's Navy. The streets were packed with seamen and soldiers, but not one failed to recognise our rank, comparatively humble as it was. ...
>
> ...By a coincidence I was afforded an example of Jack's imperturbability in an unexpected crisis. I had come up from the Grand Fleet base to report at the barracks. I found I would have to stay the night ...and the Huns chose that evening to pay us a visit from the air. I heard the noise of gun fire and bomb-dropping, but we had grown accustomed to such music, and I did not trouble to stir. In a few minutes, however, a steward came in to inform me that 'they were over the building and had dropped a bomb.' Officers, he said, were ordered below.
>
> That bomb, you remember, was one of the few Hun bull's eyes. It fell on the top of the men's quarters and killed a large number of the fellows I had seen drilling a few hours previously. The Huns were still above the building when I went across to

the drill-hall. In the semi-darkness, the scenes were weird and soul-piercing. But what was so stirring to watch was the whole-hearted contempt the surviving sailors had for the presence of danger. I believe I was the first officer present, but there was no need to give orders to such men. They worked expeditiously and carefully, removing from the debris of broken glass and timber the dead and dying bodies of their comrades.

I shall never forget this example of the British sailor's thoroughness. Before the raid was over all the victims had been removed for treatment or burial, and the drill-hall was once more – apart from the damage – cleaned up and made ship-shape.

Among the casualties were two ex-fishermen naval reservists from Lewis, Neil MacKay and Alex Kennedy.

On his return to Rosyth, Moseley, having successfully completed his course of instruction in coding, was able to 'take over' at once and it was regarded as being 'one more feather in Chatham's cap'.

Although Scotland did have camps and centres of its own, many men were sent south to the Palace, as when, following a recruiting meeting on 30 September 1914 for the Naval Brigade in Fraserburgh, 55 names were handed in from that port and its district. A special train conveyed the recruits to the Palace one week later.[33] So great was the response to the call to arms north of the border that new companies of the Royal Naval Brigade were formed, two from the Moray Firth district and the others from Aberdeen, Dundee, Edinburgh and the Clyde. The reservists were housed in the Crystal Palace. Although the headquarters of the Scottish Brigade were at Govan, recruiting offices had also been opened at Leith, Dundee, Aberdeen, Cullen and Banff. Special trains conveyed the recruits to London each Wednesday.

Granton
The extensive harbour of Granton on the Firth of Forth, a few miles west of Edinburgh, had been in operation for over 70 years before the outbreak of the war, work on it having begun in 1837, with a broad approach road from the centre of the capital. It was financed by the Duke of Buccleuch and was intended to be the grandest port on the Forth and the main ferry terminus for Fife and the north. It was opened on 28 June 1838, the day of Queen Victoria's coronation. The harbour quickly became an important fishing port and provided a home for a fair number of vessels until well into the twentieth century. By 1911 it had 59 registered there, all but one of them steam trawlers. It is indicative of the prosperity that could arise during the years of conflict that one operator, Thomas L Devlin, had 20 boats at the port in 1911 and 25 in 1915 (the enrichment of fishing companies and trawlowners – as trawler owners were referred to in the trade – would be a contentious issue during the war).

It was, however, as a base for the Armed Trawler Fleet that Granton was to become prominent in 1914-18.

When war broke out there were at Granton six officers and 30 men in trawlers under the command of a Commander Pocock RN. The work of what was to become the naval base was carried on in the Custom House under

Captain Hope Robertson, assisted by Lieutenant Sheather RN, who combined the duties of Executive Officer, Victualling Paymaster and Chief Master-at-Arms. Before long, larger premises were needed, so the shed at the end of the pier and two adjoining offices were commandeered on 11 August. Here Captain Cecil Fox succeeded Robertson. Three yachts were added to the command. The personnel comprised the two officers and 250 men, registered on the books of HMS *Columbine*.

Expansion proceeded apace and new premises were built. Then one snowy, stormy night in March 1915, Commodore Sir James Startin, holding the rank of captain, came to take command. He was appointed to the only Admiralty trawler at Granton, HMS *Gunner*, and she became the parent ship.

In *The Crisis of the Naval War* Startin was later to be glowingly described by Sir John Jellicoe, the Commander of the Grand Fleet and subsequently First Sea Lord, as 'the life and soul of the patrols and minesweepers working from Granton'. His success was doubtless due to the enthusiasm and imaginativeness he brought to his work. For instance, he effectively exploited the fishermen's interest in financial gain and the rivalry between trawler crews by arranging for prizes to be awarded to those gun crews which attained the best results in target practice, while competitions were held to identify those vessels which could lay out their modified sweeps in the fastest time. Since most of the men at Granton had never laid eyes on a submarine, he doubted they would be able to identify a U-boat. He accordingly arranged for exercises to be carried out by a British submarine in their presence. The forms of disguise he continuously evolved for the trawlers became ever more ingenious, so much so that on 20 July 1915, a large German submarine was damaged by the Granton armed trawler *Quickly* posing as a small Norwegian cargo vessel, in company with the trawler *Gunner* similarly disguised. Startin was himself aboard one of the vessels and his achievement earned him a tribute from Admiral Sir Robert Lowry, commanding the Coast of Scotland station:

> He has inspired with his own energy and spirit of keenness the officers and men under his command at Granton, drunkenness and insubordination have almost ceased there, and all hands are only eager to get their opportunity for serving their country.

The Naval Base rapidly grew under Startin's able command until by the end of the war the personnel numbered 400 officers, about 8,000 men and 100 Wren officers and ratings. A mass of buildings, some stone, some wooden, crowded the pier over which fluttered the broad pennant of the commanding SNO. As far as vessels were concerned, there were attached to the base in 1917 and 1918, 55 minesweeping trawlers, 57 escort trawlers, eight drifters, 25 motor launches, six yachts, 29 special service vessels, six paddle sweepers and one whaler, all of which were armed. Target practice was carried out by the trawlers, drifters and motor launches monthly, and by the special service vessels every time they returned to port.

Operations and life in general (gunnery training in particular), were sharply portrayed in the *Log of HMS 'Gunner', 1914-1919* by W Atkinson et al:

There was very little gunnery and no gunnery staff at Granton when I arrived in November 1914.

The Base consisted of about four yachts and several trawlers, which were employed in patrol work and mine-sweeping. Each yacht had a unit of six trawlers, their duties being to patrol the coast from Aberdeen to Berwick-on-Tweed, and to seaward for about 150 miles.

The heaviest armament at the time was 3 or 6-pounders in yachts and in a few trawlers, but the majority of trawlers had 3-pounders. Personally, I was very proud of my two little 3-pounders on the 'Quickly', they being the largest guns I had ever been in contact with.

We went out on patrol for seven days and in harbour for two. At sea – weather, etc., permitting – we had gun drill in the forenoons and signal exercises in the after-noons.

It was astonishing what an enormous lot of supposed enemy submarines were reported; but when investigated they invariably turned out to be floating spars, or stumps of trees. They proved useful in that they gave the trawler crews a little gun practice.

...In May 1915 a sort of gunnery training establishment was formed, in order to train the men in shooting, gun drill, etc., and I was taken from 'Quickly' for this purpose, and at the same time becoming available for proceeding to sea at a moment's notice with the S.N.O., when submarine hunts were taking place.

...The system of training the men in gunnery in 1915 was to get the men from the ships when they were doing their 'stand off' and drill them at their respective guns. After they had learnt this drill they were taken to sea and exercised at firing practice, commencing at first with the small aiming rifle, and eventually getting to the full calibre firing, when the best shots were picked out and put in the special service vessels, where they got more pay, and much easier times.

In 1916 a drill battery was constructed and fitted up with all types of guns used at Granton, when more efficient training was organised. Batches of twenty men at a time were taken out of their ships and put under regular daily gunnery training in the battery until they thoroughly understood all the mechanisms of the guns, and all relating to the ammunition for these guns and the gun drill. As soon as the C.G.I. [Chief Gunnery Instructor] in the battery reported that the men were ready for examination, they were examined by the gunnery officer as to their knowledge in taking guns to pieces, putting them together, in ammunition and the precautions to take when handling explosives, and what to do in the case of an accident. The men who obtained over 60 per cent. of points were passed out, and after they had passed their full calibre firing test, were allowed to take charge of a gun on a trawler; and later, when volunteering for a special service ship, they were again put in the battery for extra training and a much more severe test in full calibre firing, the men then being required to find the range and hit the target in five rounds, the target not being nearer than 3,000 yards.

With the Sweepers at Invergordon

Many miles north of Granton, also on the shores of a firth and 11 miles north-east of Dingwall, stood Invergordon minesweeping base. Due east, on the northern tip of Black Isle, lay the great naval base of Cromarty, guarding the entrance to the bay and firth of that name.

To Invergordon came, in the autumn of 1914, Commander AB Campbell[34] to work with the men of the flotilla, many of whom were fishermen. At the time the place was still little more than a village, and only occasionally did a big ship call in to give leave or pick up mails. Of the ships of the Grand Fleet little was seen.

Campbell had held a commission with the Naval Reserve for many years and in June 1914 had been doing his annual training with the Navy (in HMS *Valiant* off the Island of Arran) when orders were received that no reserve officers were to be allowed to leave. Only the fact that he was a sea-serving officer enabled him to get away. Even so, he had to report daily to Whitehall.

When war was declared, he was scheduled to join the Cunarder *Mauretania*, but was disappointed to learn that, in the drive to reach England quickly on the threat of war, trouble had started in her engine room and she had had to return to New York for repairs. Instead he joined her sister-ship, the *Aquitania*, although that same night she collided with a freighter when patrolling the Irish Channel. Although no lives were lost, her bows were seriously damaged and she had to return to dock.

Campbell then joined the *Lakonia* at Devonport, a 5,000-ton vessel of the Donaldson line scheduled to convey a cargo of British mines to a naval ship. A week or so afterwards came his posting to Invergordon:

> I was sent by the Admiralty to a delightful spot on the Scottish coast. I was attached to the mine-sweeping trawlers, manned by as fine a lot of shipmates as I've ever had the luck to be with. They knew little about service routine, but mine-sweeping came naturally to them. The 'gallows' on their little vessels, normally in use with the trawls, were easily adaptable for the 'sweep' wire, and the otter-boards that kept the net mouth open in fishing served admirably for controlling the depth at which the sweep wire worked.
>
> Senior naval officers were in charge of these units, and in those early days there were times when the merchant seamen found themselves somewhat irked by the stern discipline of naval routine that was so foreign to their free-and-easy ways. This condition sometimes caused trouble not unmixed with comedy.[35]
>
> …Some naval officers, especially those who had so gallantly responded to their country's call and joined up after retirement, failed to realize that they now had to deal with men who had not been taught by years of service and discipline to do things in just-so style and at a nod. They failed to appreciate, I think, the splendid qualities of the trawler men, whose blind devotion to duty sent them out to sea in all weathers, handling their little craft with matchless skill in the teeth of dangers, and who, I know quite well, were indifferent to the terrible risks they ran. It was grand sea-going material, and it grieved me very much to see that at times it was so woefully misused.
>
> …it took many months for some [of these naval officers] to recognize that in the great brotherhood of the sea the men of the merchant service stood shoulder to shoulder with their brothers of the Senior Service.[36]

Campbell remembered how the British public took the minesweepers to their hearts, particularly in the early days of the war; in fact, they were so inundated with gifts that the Naval Store Officer 'got fed up with handling the stuff'. As Christmas drew near, the spate of gifts increased:

> Balaclava helmets, socks, cardigans, pullovers, scarves, and a myriad variety of woollen goods poured in on us. It was something of a welcome change when we heard from the station-master that a large barrel of walnuts, addressed to 'the

officer i/c mine-sweepers' was lying in the goods yard. It was not too securely packed, he said, and it ought to be removed at once, for he could not be responsible for the contents.

Campbell, with two hands accompanying him, found an alternative store for the nuts in a small outbuilding of the Town Hall, since the sweepers had as yet no store of their own. When they came to collect the barrel some days later, however, it was covered with a dirty roll of canvas; on being removed, the contents fell onto the cement floor. It was a dead Chinaman. Evidently, the body had been brought ashore off an oil-tanker the day before: the outbuilding served as the town mortuary. Despite fears that the nuts might be affected by the beri-beri from which the Chinaman had died, an old skipper pointed out:

> Wha wad want tae eat the shells? As long's we dinna crack them wi' oor teeth we shouldna catch aught.

Campbell was relieved to report that nobody did 'catch aught'.

After they had been sweeping for three months, he was sent a letter from the Admiralty expressing great appreciation of the work the men were doing. A visit from Admiral Doveton Sturdee[37] was therefore being arranged so that their lordships' thanks could be conveyed by word of mouth. Campbell arranged for some of the skippers to be ashore to meet him. Only three were available and there was no chance of collecting others. The trio made every effort to dress for the part: each wore a brightly coloured tie (there was a red one which 'positively sang'), two wore buttonholes of flowers, and the third flourished a sprig of heather in his cap:

> They were marvellous. I loved them. I hadn't the heart to admonish them for their variations from uniform attire, and criticism would have made them very ill at ease. The Admiral, I decided, would have to take them as they were. I ushered them in.
>
> At the sight of my three gallants Admiral Sturdee had to shake himself out of what the Scots call a 'dwam'. But he was too great a man to allow himself to be more than momentarily incredulous, and he was grasping the hands of the men before they could gather anything of his first reaction. Then he cleared his throat and told them the object of the meeting. And Sturdee could express himself well. He told them of the Admiralty's appreciation of their splendid work. The skippers listened in silence, quite without embarrassment. Probably most of what the Admiral said went over their heads, but they grasped the meaning all right. The skipper with the sprig of heather had primed himself for the occasion. His smile grew wider and wider as the speech developed, and one could see that he was gathering himself to herald the climax. The Admiral reached the end of his peroration (I think he had expected a larger audience): 'On behalf of their lordships, on behalf of your country, on behalf of your King, I thank you!' It unleashed 'Heather Jock'. Up he sprang to his feet, waved his sprigged cap wildly, and bellowed 'Hooray! Hooray!' with all the force of his magnificent lungs. The other two added their stentorian efforts to his. Then Admiral Sir Frederick C. Doveton Sturdee, K.C.B., C.V.O., C.M.G., straight-faced, gravely shook hands all round again, and I ushered them from the room.[38]

For many, the first Christmas of the war was unforgettable, and the Invergordon minesweepers had every reason to remember it. Orders had been passed along that every possible vessel was to be out and on duty, since the idea was going around that the enemy meant to launch a great attack on that day, hoping to find them off guard. The people had not forgotten the trawlers, and as Christmas approached the flood of gifts swelled daily. A prominent peer sent word that he was dispatching a turkey to each sweep in the minesweeping flotilla, and a London paper followed this up with gifts of plum-puddings.

The men nevertheless suffered real hardships during that first winter of the war with their long spells of duty and until proper supplies and accommodation were arranged; being Scotland, it was impossible to get a drink when on shore leave on a Sunday, so that 'mouchers' carrying bottles of fake whisky hung round the ports. They tempted sweepers into their houses for a drink and sold them bottles of poisonous filth at exorbitant prices. In one week alone, two men were found dead of alcoholic poisoning.

To remedy this situation, Campbell proposed a scheme for a canteen which would be open to the men for drinks even on a Sunday. He obtained sanction for it and it was officially opened by Admiral Sturdee and Colonel Grant of the Camerons. After the speeches, the flags behind the two speakers were rolled back to reveal barrels and barrels of beer:

> At this enthralling spectacle the men were for a minute held mute. Then, loud as the sound of a thousand guns (more or less), broke their answer to that delectable revelation. They cheered as though they wanted the biggest thirst procurable for slaking. The Admiral (a strict teetotaller) took a cup of tea and Colonel Grant and I drank a pint of ale apiece to the success of the new institution.[39]

When the time came for Campbell to take up a new post as paymaster of the armed merchant cruiser HMS *Otranto*, on its return to England for refitting after taking part in the Coronel and Falkland engagements, he was sorry to leave the men:

> I say it with sentiment, but I hope without sentimentality, that those men of the drifters and trawlers had established themselves in my heart.
> ...they escorted me in a body to the station. When the train steamed out they put up a rousing cheer. It was through misty eyes and with a tightness in my throat that I saw the last of them.[40]

A Glimpse of Scapa Flow and Cromarty

GHP Mulhauser, in his absorbing volume *Small Craft*, gave an interesting account of a visit to various naval bases in the earlier part of the war. He was serving as 2nd officer at the time aboard the *Sagitta*, a 750-ton armed yacht which had belonged to a French duke. His work, continuing that begun aboard his previous yacht, the *Zarefah*, was used to form a connecting link between the patrols and the various groups of minesweepers from the North Foreland and the Outer Dowsing Light Ship, and the base at Lowestoft. That was nominally the brief, but in practice Mulhauser and his crew were mostly employed on other jobs, looking for reported floating mines and so on:

On the 6th January, 1915 'Sagitta' had done her trials and was ready to sail.

...On leaving Portsmouth we made for the East Coast, and were in the Tyne on the 16th January when orders came late at night for us to be at a certain time at Peterhead to meet the A.M.S. [Admiral of Mine-Sweeping], and take him to visit the chief Naval Bases on the East Coast.

The night was pitch black, and there was a N.N.W. gale blowing with frequent snow squalls. It was not a pleasant night to put to sea, however, 'growl you may, but go you must,' and we cast off at 11 p.m., and groped our way down the river, and out to sea. It was very rough outside, and before long one wave carried away the starboard breakwater on the foc's'le, while another one leaped inboard amidships, and smashed one of the engine-room scuttles, sousing the heated and lightly clad engineers with ice-cold water. They thought a shell had struck the ship. ...By degrees the rough night dragged slowly through, but it was not until noon next day that we got some shelter from the snow-clad Scotch hills. Just before dark we entered Peterhead, and anchored. The A.M.S. came on board during the evening.

At intervals next day, as we passed up the coast to Scapa Flow, War Signal Stations on shore challenged us, and patrols came up and chatted. Our replies being satisfactory we were allowed through, and made for the Examination Boat off Hoxa boom. She told us how to enter, and told off a drifter to lead us in. All the entrances to Scapa Flow were blocked by booms, sunken ships, or other obstructions, but some of the booms had 'gates' which could be opened.

The Grand Fleet seemed to have chosen a very desolate and depressing place for a home. The Flow is a deep water anchorage at the southern end of the Orkneys, measuring roughly seven miles east and west, and four miles north and south. On the north side lies the mainland of the Orkneys, and on the south, east and west sides lie islands, all hilly, bleak and inhospitable. It is a dreary and depressing spot in winter. No one, however, paid any attention to the scenery. The Grand Fleet was the thing, as it lay in ordered lines of big battleships. Here at last was the 'sure shield,' and it looked the part. A comforting and inspiring sight. It was impossible to help reflecting that on these ships and their leader hung the fate of the civilized world.

We steamed quietly and as unobtrusively as possible past them to our anchorage in Weddel Sound.

The next day, as the AMS had finished his business, they left for Cromarty,

...where the battle-cruisers were lying in a beautiful Firth surrounded by high hills. Here also a boom stretched across the entrance, while batteries crowned the two hills between which the Firth lies. By this time all the harbours were protected by booms, but at the start of the war there was not a single anchorage where the Fleet could go for coal, water, provisions, and ammunition and lie in safety.

...On leaving Cromarty, we worked down the coast and arrived at Lowestoft two or three days later.

Chapter 4

An Armada is Born

So many a ship of peaceful purpose was called to the tasks of war,
Was manned and armed and made anew for work unguessed before,
Came quietly into the dockyard and, converted, slipped away;:
Yacht, trawler, ferry, liner, tramp. So came the 'Jervis Bay'.

From *The Jervis Bay* by Michael Thwaites[41]

During the war, no fewer than 1,455 trawlers, 1,372 steam drifters and 118 motor drifters were pressed into naval service.[42] Nor should the humble smack be forgotten, for a number were assigned to special duties – often with dramatic effect – as will be described later.

The early emphasis, however, was on the trawler, a vessel which, in tandem with a sister, lent itself admirably to the sweeping of mines. It was mines which were viewed early on as the greatest threat to Britain's navy in any future conflict.

Charlie B's Idea

Admiral Lord Charles Beresford (1846-1919) laid the foundations of the minesweeping service when he visited Grimsby in July 1907 and recognized the potential of trawling gear for mine clearance work.

Writing of this visit in *The Sea Fisheries of Great Britain and Ireland – Notes from the Author's Diary, 1854-1928*, George L Alward recalled:

I had the honour of explaining to his Lordship the working of the Otter Trawl, in which he was deeply interested. It was at his suggestion that the Admiralty chartered from the Author two steam trawlers with their fishing crews, by which experiments in sweeping up mines were carried out.

In another recollection following Beresford's death in September 1919, Alward described the meeting thus:

When Admiral Beresford, in command of the Channel Fleet, visited Grimsby ...we had a long chat about fishing methods, and I explained the working of the otter trawl to him. He was keenly interested, asking many questions and finally explained: 'I believe I've found what for a long time I've been looking for. In the next naval war, sea mines will be a great feature and', he added, 'I may be called upon any day to meet an enemy in the North Sea, and what I need is something that can go before the fleet to destroy mines before big ships come in contact with them.'[43]

In his previous position as Commander-in-Chief of the Mediterranean Fleet, Beresford had tried sweeping experiments with tugs and destroyers, but neither class of vessel was found to be suitable.

One of his questions to Alward was whether trawlers could operate in all kinds of weather. He was assured that the weather would have to be severe indeed for trawlers to be unable to work, whether by day or by night. Upon enquiry, he and his lieutenant were informed that the otter could be kept in a vertical position during the roughest weather. In later correspondence with Beresford, Alward pointed out that the build of the modern steam trawler was such that:

> ...it was, without doubt, the safest vessel afloat, and in defending our islands, these vessels, fitted with wireless and various other necessary equipment, would act as watch dogs all round the coast, day and night.

Beresford made a passing reference to his early thoughts on the trawlers' potential as sweepers in his own memoirs:

> There being no provision against mines dropped in time of war, it was suggested by me that the North Sea trawlers should be enlisted to sweep for mines, because they were accustomed to the difficult work of towing and handling a trawl. The proposal was afterwards adopted.[44]

Beresford's 1907 visit led to him suggesting to the Admiralty that a trial should be made with these craft and that if they were successful, a number of them should be requisitioned for the different ports so as to be ready for service in the event of a crisis situation arising with a foreign power.

Early Experiments and the First Acquisitions
In response to Beresford's suggestion, the Admiralty approved of him conducting a practical test. At the beginning of the following year, Commander EL Booty of the *King Edward VII* was sent to Grimsby, where he selected two typical steam trawlers, the *Andes* and *Algoma*,[45] placed at his disposal by Alward with Skipper Hoole in charge. (The vessels had identical careers. Both had been built in North Shields and launched in 1899, were taken up for the experiments in 1908, transferred to the Fishery Reserve in 1917, returned to the mercantile in 1919 and purchased by The Spurn SFC of Grimsby with registrations GY 5 and GY 6 respectively.)

Reaching Portland on 5 February, with their skippers and crews of eight apiece, they proceeded to sweep up dummy mines for the next eight days. The trials were supervised by a Channel Fleet Mining Committee, of which Sturdee, then commanding officer of the *New Zealand*, was president. Beresford himself had been unable to be present at this experiment. Associated with him were Captain RF Phillimore and two torpedo lieutenants, together with a mining expert from HMS *Vernon*, the base in Porchester Creek, Hampshire, where work focused on torpedo trials, on the research and development of anti-submarine devices and training and on mines. The committee reported that the experiments had proved sufficiently satisfactory to justify the taking up of trawlers for service in war, to assist in keeping clear the approaches to harbours liable to be mined. In his own report, Lord Charles stated that the trawlers would prove invaluable for sweeping duties, as the skippers and crews (who had entered into the trials with enthusiasm and delight) had been accustomed to earning their living with precisely this class of work. The trawlers for their part were of such a shape and build as to render sweeping easy and practically no additional gear was required.

In sweeping for mines, the towing-warp did the work of the sweeping-wire. There was a 'kite' and a 'shoot' as well as hundreds of fathoms of heavy wire warp. Using all these called for great skill and extreme care. Even so, danger was ever present and there were accidents. On one occasion, a man on a sweeper was working between the 'kite' and the 'shoot' when the vessel rolled and the 'kite' swung over and killed him. When sweeping, a pair of trawlers steaming abreast would drag a weighted steel hawser which, when it struck the mooring of a mine, brought the mine to the surface. There it was promptly exploded, either by gunfire from an accompanying destroyer or armed trawler, or by rifle fire.

The Portland experiments convinced the Admiralty that trawlers could be depended on to clear a channel with practically only their own resources. One distinguished officer, Captain Bernard Currey (afterwards Director of Naval Ordnance), pointed out that they would be indispensable in wartime as an Auxiliary Sweeping Service, and suggested the desirability of preparing a contract with the trawler-owners so as to enable a number of these craft to be taken up on the approach of war. With this suggestion Captain EJW Slade (later Admiral Sir Edmond JW Slade), then Director of Naval Intelligence, concurred, and he further emphasized the fact that trawls were obviously more efficiently worked by men accustomed to their use than by untrained crews. The solution of the manning problem, therefore, appeared to lie in employing Royal Naval Reserve men, of whom a large number were fishermen. The proposal was approved by the Admiralty's First Sea Lord, Sir John Fisher.

The *Andes* and *Algoma*, with the same crews (this time under Skipper Thomas Roberts), were engaged by the northern section of the North Fleet to carry out another trial in St Andrew's Bay. Here, the weather was more favourable than it had been at Portland and the experiment was again a success. Fourteen dummy mines were laid down, and the two trawlers, at full speed (9 knots), ran parallel, 80 fathoms apart, for about a mile and cleared the channel. Two or three methods of minesweeping were carried out. Admiral Calligan on the flagship *Shannon* became deeply interested and several of the captains from other warships were on board the trawler with Skipper Roberts.

In *The Auxiliary Patrol*, E Keble Chatterton recalled how:

Lord Fisher in 1909 had caused five trawlers to be bought at Grimsby, Fleetwood and North Shields for experimental work, and a good deal of unostentatious practice went on after the Japanese War in learning all that could be discovered about minefield clearance. And I remember being at sea in 1909 quite close to the sweepers and watching them keenly at work between Weymouth Bay and St Alban's Head.

Taking the work further, the Admiralty purchased, between April 1909 and October 1914 inclusive, the first trawlers of its own. First came the *Seaflower* (ex-*Osprey II*), *Seamew* (ex-*Nunthorpe Hall*), *Sparrow* (ex-*Josephine I*) and *Spider* (ex-*Assyrian*). In December it was decided to allocate the *Sparrow* and *Spider* to the *Vernon* at Portsmouth and the *Seamew* and *Seaflower* to the *Actaeon* at the Nore.

Appendix 1 provides a list of acquisitions and also shows the survey trawlers *Daisy* and *Esther*, which were purchased on the stocks on 14 February 1911 and would, like the other boats, become minesweepers and be incorporated into the Auxiliary Patrol organization.

On 28 March of that year, the Hon. Waldorf Astor asked in the Commons whether trawlers and fishermen were to be enrolled at Grimsby for the purpose of trawling for mines; whether a subsidy or annual retainer was to be paid to the owners of the trawlers and to the fishermen, and whether it was proposed to give trawler-owners and fishermen of ports other than Grimsby an opportunity of earning the subsidy or retainer. Dr TJ Macnamara, the Parliamentary Secretary to the Admiralty, answered the first and last parts of the question affirmatively, while as regards the second part, annual retainers would be paid to the skippers and the men of the trawlers but no subsidy would be paid to the owners.

The *Fishing News* dated 30 May 1914 reported that many of Milford Haven's men were 'out on the deep trawling for mines' and that they 'always look forward with interest to their half-yearly training'. The first detachment had made a start with its training a week earlier on board the *Spider* and *Sparrow*. Recruits were rapidly coming forward and the vessels were expected to operate from Milford until the end of June.

Sadly, the *Spider* would soon be lost, being wrecked on 21 November 1914 off Lowestoft. Later casualties to the small force were the *Jasper* (ex-*Rayvernol*), sunk by a mine in Moray Forth on 26 August 1915 and the *Javelin* (ex-*Braconlea*), also mined that year, on 17 October, off the Longsands.

The Formation of the RNR Trawler Section

Now the Admiralty had obtained these trawlers, its next step was to secure the personnel.

Naval officers needed to be detailed to take charge of the trawler units when sweeping but there were very few officers with sweeping experience. Thus early in 1910 it was decided to detail and train certain officers on the emergency and retired lists for this special purpose. The initial requirement was for 22 lieutenants or commanders, each of whom would, in time of war, command a unit consisting of six trawlers. Among those invited, 20 or so commanders and lieutenants agreed to serve and underwent a 14-day course in the *Vernon*. Another course for an additional intake followed.

The vessels would be manned by members of the Trawler Section, the regulations for which were drawn up in October 1910. Existing titles of ranks and ratings – 'Skipper,' 'Second-hand', and so on – would be retained. Pay was based on the wages current in the trawling industry less about 20 per cent. The skipper, who must have commanded a trawler for at least two years, held a

Board of Trade certificate and had undergone eight days' training in one of HM's steam trawlers before receiving the Admiralty warrant, was to be given the rank of warrant officer.

Since the slack season in the trawling business occurred immediately after Lent and especially between June and September, it was decided to make the training season coincide with it as far as possible.

The first enrolment of fishermen for the Royal Naval Reserve (T) was postponed until the beginning of 1911, when the Admiralty set out to recruit 50 skippers and 50 second-hands for training on board the six trawlers now attached to the Torpedo Schools, the names of the recently-added pair being the *Rose* and *Driver*, attached to Devonport. Aberdeen was selected for the commencement of this training and there the six Admiralty trawlers were to assemble, together with HMS *Jason* and *Circe*; these two gunboats had been selected on account of their commanding officers' training and experience in minesweeping. The first course at Aberdeen began on 20 January 1911 and ended by mid-April, during which period 28 skippers, 27 second-hands, 20 deck-hands, 21 engineers and 20 trimmers had been recruited and trained. This was the first batch of the Trawler Reserve. Commander Holland of the *Circe* afterwards reported that the class of men enrolled was very good, much better than expected. They had all taken a very keen interest in their work and were amenable to discipline.

When the war was not much more than a year away, the *Fishing News* reported on the continued success of recruitment at the Scottish port:

The annual training of the Naval Reserve (Trawler Section) is now in full swing at Aberdeen, and there are at present two Admiralty mine-sweeping trawlers in the harbour. Since last year the conditions of service of all ratings on board these trawlers have been greatly improved, and the training is looked upon by the fishermen as something of a holiday – a well-paid holiday at that. The mine-sweepers proceed to sea daily, going out each morning, and returning about 4 o'clock in the afternoon. Mine-sweeping operations are carried out in the bay, and each skipper in turn takes complete charge of an operation. A class on board consists of anything from 10 to 40 members.

The different grades which are enrolled are skippers, second-hands, enginemen, deck-hands and trimmers. The list of skippers in Aberdeen is now quite full, as also is the list of second-hands, and no more in these grades can be taken on, with the exception of a few on the short service system (five years). We understand, however, that there are still vacancies for enginemen, deckhands and trimmers, and a few volunteers in these grades can yet be enrolled.

The age limits for enginemen and second-hands has now been raised to 40 years, so that there is now an opportunity for some of the older men – who were debarred on account of age last year – becoming members. The conditions of entry of the deck-hands has also been considerably improved during the last twelve months. They now receive a uniform similar to that worn by bluejackets in the service. Pay is increased from 3s to 3s 6d per day, with a gratuity of from 10s to 12 6d at the end of four days' training. The yearly retainer is also increased, and now amounts to £5.

The Admiralty have been very generous in their treatment of the trawler section of the Naval Reserve. As evidence of this, the following rates of pay applicable to the various ratings are interesting:

> Skippers receive £3 6s for their four days' training; and a retaining fee of £10 per annum.
>
> Second-hands and enginemen receive £2 4s for four days' training, and a yearly retaining fee of £8.
>
> Deck hands receive £1 6s and a retainer of £5.
>
> Trimmers get £1 6s and a retainer of £4.

In addition to these payments, a generous uniform allowance is given to all ratings, and at the end of 20 years' service a gratuity of £50 is given.

It is hardly necessary to say that in Aberdeen this section of the Royal Naval Reserve is proving extremely popular, and all ratings express themselves as vastly pleased with their training.

In Grimsby, however, it was a different story. When recruiting began there in early April 1911, the results were disappointing. Not more than a dozen men volunteered, and not one of them was a skipper. There were a number of reasons for the lack of enthusiasm. The Admiralty had made the age limit for skippers 25 to 35, which the Grimsby men objected to as being too young. They felt the best skippers in the port were much older than 35. Nor was the pay attractive. In June, prominent trawlowners met the gunboat commanders in conference at the port. The Admiralty not only raised the age limit for skippers but withdrew the right to draft them into other branches of the Navy in the event of their service being required (skippers had refused to join unless they had some guarantee of continuity of employment following the training period). The trawlowners were happy and several days later, the first two trawl masters to enrol went for their training on the Government trawlers. A third of the men required had, reportedly, signed on for the new service and the remainder was optimistically awaited in the wake of the skippers' cooperation. Recruiting and training went on through to the autumn of 1911 and the ports of Hull, Fleetwood and Milford were visited. These yielded a total of 526 men: 52 skippers, 94 second-hands, 198 deck-hands, 88 enginemen, and 94 trimmers.

To meet the need for a mobilizing officer at each trawler port, a number of retired naval officers were selected in March 1912 to take charge of minesweeping trawlers at Sheerness, the Firth of Forth, Dover, Portsmouth, Portland, Devonport, and Milford. Directly these officers received a telegram ordering them to mobilize, they were to go to their respective ports in charge of the respective groups of sweepers. Officers for Aberdeen, Hull, Grimsby, Milford Haven, North Shields, Granton and Fleetwood were appointed in July. Each year, all the officers were to visit the Admiralty for one day to confer with the Inspecting Captain of Minesweeping and were subsequently required to attend a 3-day course at their appointed ports to establish contact with the RNR Registrars, the local harbour authorities and trawler owners and familiarize themselves with the docks and locality. In September 1912, an allocation of minesweeping trawlers was made right the way down the coast from Scotland along the North Sea, down the Channel, up the Irish Sea to Milford Haven, and even as far west as Queenstown.

By November, there were 64 trawlers on the Admiralty list, each allocated to their port and each with their skipper and crew trained for sweeping.

When war came, the owners of suitable craft were to remove from them any fish, ice and fishing-gear (save for the warps) and prepare them for sea, with enough coal water, oil, and provisions to last seven days. The skippers would be given their charts and sailing orders by the mobilizing officers and would steam off at full speed to their allocated ports. There they would draw their special sweeping stores and be assigned to a group of sweepers, each of which was under a parent ship. The vessel would have its fishing letters and number painted out and be given an official number, to be painted in white two feet long on each bow. She would be painted navy grey overall and fly the White Ensign. A naval petty officer, who would be third in command, would also join the trawler to advise the skipper (especially on purely naval matters) and assist in signalling and keeping accounts. In addition to the officer, the crew was to consist of the skipper, second-hand, four deck-hands, two enginemen, and one trimmer.

By August 1914, a total of 82 trawlers – plus, of course, the trawlers already purchased by the Admiralty – had become available nationally under the various arrangements implemented. They were based on Cromarty, the Firth of Forth, North Shields, the Humber, Harwich, the Nore, Dover, Portsmouth, Portland and Devonport and could thus be dispatched within a few hours to sweep up the first minefield laid by the enemy off our coast. Thus in a period of just seven years, a minesweeping fleet ready for service as a reserve force had been created – and at a minimal cost to the nation. Had it not been for this trawler organization, shipping could not have gone up and down the North Sea as it did during the first few months of the war.

By 8 August, at least 114 trawlers were in service or fitting-out. A further 100 were requisitioned within the next two weeks and sent to Lowestoft for fitting-out. There very large quantities of sweep gear and assorted stores were maintained and the port became the chief depot for minesweepers on the east coast. The other principal fishing ports also became fitting-out bases but on less of a scale than Lowestoft.

To the Admiralty's thinking, the usefulness of these vessels lay not in acting as fleet sweepers (i.e. sweeping ahead of the Grand Fleet) for they were too slow and a number of old gunboats were in any case already earmarked for that duty, but in clearing the entrances to harbours and fairways. Here the fishermen were in their element, being highly proficient in the use of the otter gear, whose net averaged 100 feet or so in length, with a spread of 80-90 feet.

Regarding the hire rates for the vessels used, an arrangement had been made before the war between the Admiralty and certain trawler owners. As soon as possible after receipt of notice of charter, the latter would hire their vessels to the Navy against payment of 12 per cent per year on the then value of the trawler. The first cost was to be ascertained by valuing the hull and outfit at £18 per ton of the gross tonnage on the BoT certificate and the machinery and boilers at £40 per nominal horse-power. This estimated initial cost was to be depreciated at the rate of 4 per cent for every year of the trawler's age; the class of vessel targeted comprised craft no more than 10 years old and able to carry enough coal to steam at least 1,000 miles at 8 knots.

Recollections of Lowestoft and Portsmouth

In mid-September, Rear-Admiral Edward B Charlton took up the post of Admiral East Coast Minesweeping (AMS) at Lowestoft. Leaving the inspecting captain to attend to the business of supply, he took charge of minesweeping operations and technical arrangements. The service he headed comprised the gunboats, trawlers, drifters and other vessels engaged in minesweeping and in watching the channels in the area from the Goodwins to St Abb's Head. The organization of the yachts and armed trawlers, drifters and motor craft engaged in patrol work, however, remained unaffected. Two minesweeping gunboats, *Halcyon* and *Spanker*, were based at the port but otherwise all operations were carried out by trawlers and drifters.

Under the title *The Work of a Trawler in the Aegean Sea*, an anonymous contributor to the *Naval Review* described the early days of training at Lowestoft prior to departure for the Dardanelles in the spring of 1915:

AUGUST, 1914.   Got drafted to a new base opened at Lowestoft, with 19 petty officers who had been out of the service for years. Most of them were to fit the trawlers out with sweeping gear and rig new stays, etc. Most of the trawlers all wanted stays, etc., and general refit.

I was running a motor boat for about one month. We were all living on the pier; band playing daily; not a bad change.

After that I was to do duty as gunnery instructor. Two 12-pounders arrived. Several R.N.V.R.'s were doing writers' duties. Two more field guns were coming, to make four. Captain Higginson (retired), Commander Bruce, R.N.R., the former in charge of fitting groups of sweepers and patrol, the latter of charts and locating the groups which the Admiralty required. There were five retired lieutenants, R.N. Lieutenant Seymour was middy on the *Cordelia* with me, my part of the ship; first time I met him since. In addition to drilling the base I had to fit guns and rifles and drill the trawler ratings. Quite a busy time, working under heavy pressure the first five months, day and night. Got many trawlers fitted out and drilled up. I got fed up with trawlers. Thirty were going to the Dardanelles, and I left on March 17th, 1915.[46]

WJ Collyer from Suffolk told the author George Ewart Evans[47] about his early years spent with the Lowestoft fishing fleet and later in the Navy's Trawler Section:

...I became a member of that, and I carried on fishing till I was required. And it was nine months after I'd enrolled in that before I got called up. Then I got called up in April 1918. And we was up in Oban in Scotland then. They sent the papers down there; and I came by train from Oban; left the boat to come by train to go and join up.

...When we got on the train at Halesworth, 'course when we got there – me and another one – we soon found out plenty more chaps that come from Lowestoft. Yes, fishing-chaps that got called up the same as us; because they called them up in batches. But then we got to Portsmouth, where we were sent to, there was about thirty of us in a gang. A petty officer met us on the station there at Portsmouth. He picked us up and he say:

'Come on, you boys,' he say; 'I know where there's a nice little pub. We can go and have a drink!'

So he cart us round to two or three different pubs; and of course we kept treating this owd petty officer; and at 2 o'clock-time, then we had to go to the Barracks in Portsmouth. We went strolling in there, hands in our pockets. But there as soon as we just got inside the gate there was some shouting:

'Take your hands out of your pockets! Take your hands out of your pockets!'

We strolled in there like we do on the old fishing-boat; and of course, we'd had a drink. He took us to the officer who took our names and particulars; and they sent us up to our Mess: they told us where we had to go to to get a number and one thing and another. Two or three big long tables. They got great thick rounds of bread and jam laid on plates; rounds about two inches thick, you know. There was plenty of jam on. But we thought we'd have a good feed; but it was one bit each. I scoffed one bit and got hold of another:

'You mun have any more,' he say; 'that's somebody else's.'

We had only one round! It was three days before they gave us our uniform, we was really in then; and they let us out of the gate, now and then.

After a month's training at Portsmouth, Collyer and his fellows were drafted up to London to join an unusual type of minesweeping vessel in the London docks, a tunnel-sweeper of the Dance Class[48] named *Cotillion*. The vessel was sent across to be based at Dunkirk and would sweep daily from that port down as far as Calais and back again. The port was a dangerous place to be on account of bombardment from the air or from long-range guns, with a shell being sent in every half-hour or so. The vessels remained outside, however:

There weren't no ships damaged because they had to bring up outside at nights – in the roads; and they wouldn't let us in the harbour. We done about three months there.

Then they sent a few of each ship that had experience to go with some more men. I got on a trawler after that – from the Dance Class to a trawler. And we were sent round to Ireland; and on our way there we stopped at Falmouth. That's where we was when the Armistice was signed. They let us go ashore that night because we were all making merry. But you couldn't get no drink. The pubs were open, but there weren't no beer. So we had to do the best we could up and down the streets – shouting.

Neglected Sisters

Much attention was devoted at the time of the crisis – and before – to trawlers. Drifters were relatively neglected.

The pre-war agreements between the fishing industry and the Admiralty did not contemplate the mobilization of steam drifters. These craft were not fitted with appliances for towing, nor had they the same engine-power as steam trawlers. The part they would play by using their nets against submarines was not foreseen, although they were deployed in minesweeping – on occasion with tragic consequences.

The two great classes of fishing vessel – trawler and drifter – were in contrasting positions in terms of fishing, especially during the first few months of the war. While trawlers, despite the necessary restrictions on their movements, had the prospect of profitable voyages, especially in the case of those which worked western and Icelandic waters, drifters, with their chief fishing grounds off the east coast of Scotland and England, found themselves largely excluded from their most productive fishing areas. Their owners were, not surprisingly, anxious to have their vessels taken off their hands by the Admiralty – without raising any questions as to the rate of hire. The large firm of Bloomfields Ltd, fish merchants of Yarmouth, for example, possessed a fine fleet of 20 steam drifters, all new and up-to-date. In August 1914 they immediately placed these at the disposal of the Admiralty, which naturally accepted the offer. The boats were taken over and on a Sunday afternoon Mr Bloomfield had to give orders to the men to be ready to go to sea on the following Tuesday. He scoured the county using motor cars to get his crews, together and by Monday these assembled at Yarmouth Custom House to sign on for the Admiralty.

The better vessels, then, were readily taken up. The *Fish Trades Gazette* reported on 25 September 1914 that most of the first-class drifters had already been commandeered by the Government, although a large sailing fleet remained.

Generally the outlook for drifters in those early months of hostilities was so serious that, early in 1915, the Board of Admiralty approached the Port of London Authority and the Mersey Dock and Harbour Board with the suggestion that some of the vessels might be used as carriers or tugs to relieve the serious congestion prevailing at the docks of London and Liverpool. For various reasons, neither of these authorities could see their way to taking up this offer but before long the case was met by the increasing demands for small craft for patrol and other naval work and the drifter, like the trawler, took its place as an essential auxiliary arm of the Navy in the Mediterranean, in the Straits of Dover and elsewhere. At home, of course, many vessels continued to perform the vital job of feeding the nation.

At a conference held in London in May 1915 between representatives of the fishing industry, at which the position of the trade as affected by the war was discussed, a committee was formed to draw up and submit to the Government and to the Admiralty suggestions for the relief of the trade and the better supply of fish to the public. A deputation from this committee subsequently met Commodore Lambert, the Fourth Sea Lord, and put before him the case for the trade, urging the Admiralty, for the sake of the national fish supply, not to interfere with it further than was absolutely necessary and unavoidable.

It was pointed out that if the seizure of vessels continued at the present rate, the trade might be killed off at some ports. The deputation requested that a nucleus of the fleet at least should be left at every port, so that the industry, and trade connections which had taken years to build up, would not be wiped out.

As it was, a number of drifters had been requisitioned – which was a fortunate thing for the fishermen, seeing that they would otherwise have been idle – and the deputation's suggestion was that in future drifters only should be drawn upon by the Admiralty and trawlers left alone. The reply by the Fourth Sea Lord was that it was not possible to employ drifters in place of trawlers to any great extent and that it would be necessary to take more of the larger class of trawlers. He gave an assurance, however, that the authorities would endeavour to leave some vessels at each port, if possible.

In a feature in the *Fishing News* of 13 May 1916 (*OUR STEAM DRIFTER FLEET – Its Value to the Nation*), the contributor remarked that the harbours at weekends '…instead of showing a forest of sails as in the days of old, are full of smoking funnels of steam drifters'.

It was, the feature continued, a good thing for the country that when the war broke out there was a fleet of steam drifters in being, largely created as it was by the enterprise of the fishermen themselves. It was also a good thing that the vessels were owned or commanded by men who were expert in the handling of them, or else they would have been of little use in patrolling or sweeping the seas for deadly mines.

In due course, then, the naval value of the drifter was amply recognized – so much so that the Admiralty would add to the fleet by having its own built. This, as in the case of trawlers, was the ultimate accolade to these craft.

Chapter 5

The Auxiliary Patrol

On Patrol
A Lay on the Patrol Service

Up and down. Up and down.
Not for us is any glory or renown!
We're useful, we suppose,
But the Lord Almighty knows
That it's weary, weary, cruising
Up and down. ...

Up and down. Up and down.
We shall either get a medal, or we'll drown.
Perhaps a little bump,
An explosion, and a jump,
And we'll know if we are going
Up and down.

From *The Log of HMS Gunner, 1914-1919*

Duty, courage and perseverance were the bedrock of Britain's auxiliary navy. Had this secondary force, composed largely of fishermen and their vessels, not developed to the extent it did, the war would have taken a very different course.

The expedient of lesser craft supporting the nation's capital vessels went back centuries but it was only in the 1914-18 conflict that their role would become so vital. Warfare had changed. The twin menace of mine and submarine demanded the employment of enormous numbers of boats of every description. These, luckily, were available. The Admiralty was nonetheless faced with the daunting task, when it came to trawlers and drifters (and, to a lesser extent, smacks) of balancing the imperative defence of these islands with the essential role of the fishing industry in supplying an important element of the population's diet.

It was not really until the end of 1915 that the Auxiliary Patrol was honed into the formidable force that would be remembered with gratitude by later generations. During the autumn of that year the multitude of vessels engaged in patrol work and numerous other duties were officially joined by their minesweeping sisters. On the personnel side, the initial difficulties in relations between fishermen and their naval co-sailors had, by and large, been overcome to the extent that they could work together reasonably harmoniously.

The growth of the patrol as far as trawlers and drifters were concerned can best be illustrated by the fact that on 1 January 1915, the force comprised 549 of the former and 88 of the latter while by 1 January 1918 these totals would stand at 1,000 and 984 respectively. Personnel in 1918 numbered no fewer than 18,000.

Inception and Non-Fishing Vessel Components

It is to the Assistant Director of the Admiralty's Operations Division, Captain, later Admiral, Sir Herbert William Richmond,[49] that we owe the idea of an extensive flotilla of armed yachts and trawlers to combat submarines and minelayers and protect the fleet. He had been agitating since the eve of the war for measures to counter enemy minelaying but his memoranda were not acted upon for several weeks. Active resistance against the twin threats was wanted as opposed to the purely defensive role of minesweepers and unarmed watching drifters; of the latter he opined: 'I doubt if any more childish scheme could be imagined.' His proposal for units of armed yachts, trawlers and motorboats to be allocated to the Grand Fleet bases was expounded in a memorandum dated 22 August 1914.

The idea of motorboats (MBs) used in this capacity had, in fact, already come up before and been implemented. The Motor Boat Reserve had been formed in late 1912 with naval patrol service in mind and became directly associated with the Royal Naval Volunteer Reserve (RNVR) in January 1914. These craft, with their shallow draught, could relieve warships of many important tasks in harbours, estuaries and other sheltered waters. The training and organization of the Motor Boat Reserve was, in fact, still under discussion at the outbreak of the war, when the owners immediately placed their craft at the Admiralty's disposal. Originally intended to examine inlets and harbours for the submarines then believed to be lurking along the indented Scottish coast, the boats lacked the speed to take any offensive action against a U-boat, despite their crews being armed with rifles and revolvers (the boats were not strong enough to mount a gun). The Motor Boat Reserve was incorporated into the yacht patrol organization on 1 October 1915 and diverted to the traffic control or harbour police work for which it was better equipped.

Motor launches (MLs) were built as replacements for motorboats. Several hundred were constructed in Canada. By early November 1916, 550 had been shipped over, supplemented in February 1918 by a further 30. They carried a 3-pdr gun and were manned by RNVR personnel, many of whom had formerly been in MBs. At least 82 ML patrol units were formed (Units 500-581) consisting of six vessels each. They sometimes served at considerable distances from their bases and were employed in the Patrol as scouts, anti-submarine craft, smokescreen generators, inshore minesweepers and hydrophone vessels. Although more seaworthy than MBs, they still had limitations. The fire hazard from their petrol engines and overheating resulted in a decision being taken in mid-1916 to use a fuel mixture of one part petrol to two parts paraffin.

It was, however, yachts which formed the nucleus of the early Patrol. Directly approval was given, in September 1914, to the formation of the AP, Richmond wrote to several prominent yacht owners offering them commands if they, or their nominees, would serve in their craft. By the end of September, some 25 steam yachts had been taken up and this number would rise steadily. No fewer than 152 hired yachts are listed in *British Warships, 1914-19* by FJ Dittmar and JJ Colledge, who comment that most of them served as AP group leaders and carried wireless equipment while others were formed into special yacht squadrons and served in home waters and in the Mediterranean.

These craft, too, had their limitations, however, the chief of which was their lack of real seaworthiness. Older and smaller yachts in particular were especially unsuitable for patrol work and these vessels as a class could never be satisfactorily disguised.

Yet there was the occasional success. In 1916, the large yacht *Narcissus* – whose name was changed to *Narcissus II* in September 1915 and which would serve again under the name *Grive* in the Second World War – repelled a U-boat. She so damaged *UB.49* on 8 September 1917 that she fled into Cadiz, whence she limped back to Germany. The incident was recounted in *Mystery Ships (Trapping the "U" Boat)* by Alfred Noyes, who additionally observed:

> Today, the best of these yachts act as flagships to the vast fleet of trawlers, drifters, and whalers. These last three were taken in the order given. …These fishing auxiliaries may almost be described as the people's fleet and their names are like stray bars of folk-song.

Reference was made by Captain Halton Stirling Lecky, CB, AM, RN (of whom more later), in a lecture on the Auxiliary Patrol given in 1933, to 20 cases of serious yacht actions with enemy submarines in which damage in varying degrees was inflicted on the enemy. After an action in Lyme Bay on 26 May 1918, for example, the yacht *Lorna* (ex-*Beryl* and also a future Second World War craft) sank *UB.74* by depth charges. The submarine's entire crew of 35 was lost.

A squadron of eight biggish yachts, all commanded by retired admirals, was based on Gibraltar for work in the Straits and on the Spanish and African coasts. Their services at these locations were highly valued.

Exceptional among yacht owners was one Harold Swithinbank. On the outbreak of the war, he offered his yacht *Venetia* (which was renamed *Venetia II* in February 1917 and also saw service in Hitler's war) to the Admiralty free of charge. A member of the Royal Yacht Squadron and of the Admiralty's committee under Sir Arthur Farquhar investigating the feasibility of the patrol around northern Scotland, Swithinbank ordered his yacht to work with the armed trawlers at Scapa Flow.

Among the other craft constituting the patrol were paddle steamers, whalers, tugs and sloops.

In response to a request for some very light-draught vessels of good size and speed for patrol work, the Mediterranean command was given paddlers. Lecky recorded being assigned a brace of such steamers formerly on pleasure service off the Isle of Wight. Dittmar and Colledge list 73 paddlers as having served, not including the Ascot class and Sea Bird class.

Distinct reservations were expressed about the whalers whose use was urged by Lord Fisher. Fifteen of these craft were ordered and launched in 1915, all built by Smiths Dock Company of Middlesbrough using designs prepared for whalers to be built for the Russian government. They were originally numbered Z.1-15 and were later named. Although suitable as anti-submarine escorts in coastal waters, they were not good seaboats and their usefulness as patrol vessels was also circumscribed by their small coal endurance. From 1915-18 they formed three squadrons, respectively based at Stornoway, Shetlands and Peterhead or the Humber – patrol areas where their limited radius of action would cause the least inconvenience. The commanding officer of the eight whalers at Peterhead recorded that, in a wind of Force 6 or above, they became 'very lively and wet'. Their speed, at least, made them more suitable than armed trawlers for escort duty.

A makeshift unarmed patrol of 12 tugs was hired in the Liverpool area by Captain HH Stileman, the SNO at that port, while the trawlers for his area were being commissioned and armed. They served for a very short time during late 1914 and were soon used for other purposes. A few were purchased by the Admiralty and one later served as a rescue tug. Other categories of tugs employed included boarding tugs, rescue tugs and a substantial fleet of hired screw tugs.

Sloops, diverted to patrol duties in the Western Approaches during the latter half of 1915, could withstand the heavy seas off the west coast better than a trawler and possessed twice the speed and armament. In October 1915, the Director of Naval Ordnance stated that 72 sloops had been ordered and were built or building. Of these, one-third would be armed with two 12-pounders and the remainder with two 4.7-inch guns and two 2-pounder pompoms.

Trawlers and drifters

In Volume I of *The Merchant Navy*, Archibald Hurd states that of the craft requisitioned for service in the Auxiliary Patrol, it was the trawlers which came closest to attaining the goal of replacing the warships. While their speed was substantially inferior to that of a destroyer – it averaged 8 or 9 knots but corresponded to the submerged speed of the best of the German submarines – they possessed far superior sea-keeping ability. While patrol destroyers, which were nominally capable of up to 30 knots, were frequently obliged to seek shelter during the winter months, trawlers were seldom driven back to port by weather conditions, except in the open waters to the westward which experienced the full force of Atlantic gales. Varying in tonnage from about 100 to 300 tons and in length from 90 feet to 140 feet, with a powerful single-screw engine, they had a coal capacity which enabled them to remain at sea for three or four weeks at a time. Their big fish hold allowed them to store extra coal, ammunition and anything else that might be required. With their sturdy upstanding bows for ramming, and their solid sterns, they were strongly constructed in every way. Perhaps their only drawback was their draught, which might be as much as 14 feet aft. Although it gave them a good grip, it was a great disadvantage in minesweeping and led to many being lost.

Lecky recalled in his lecture:

As time went on we took up trawlers by the dozen at a time at the various fishing centres and fitted them out locally. ... We started with the idea that a yacht, six trawlers and four motor boats should form a unit, but this idea was soon dropped and the numbers of each type were adapted to the Areas in which they served. In any case the motor boats were not capable of keeping the sea with the other craft.

By 17 November 1914, 30 yachts and 166 trawlers had arrived at their bases and a further 30 trawlers were being taken up each week. So great became the demand from the Admiralty for these vessels that it embarked on a construction programme of its own from 1916. Details are provided in Volume 2.

The range of duties they performed was wide, even extending to minelaying. Sixteen of them were fitted out for that purpose: six in May 1915, two in May 1916 and the rest between March and August inclusive in 1918.

Concerning drifters, Lecky's concise description is a good summary of the features of these craft and their usefulness in war:

The drifter is a much smaller type of vessel than the trawler. They range in size from about 40 to 80 tons, and in length from 70 to 90 ft., with a beam of 15 ft. and a draught of 7 to 8 ft. As their name implies, they are not intended to drag a heavy trawl, but to lay out light surface nets and, lying to their tow, just drift while the fish run into the net. They are, for their size, strong, buoyant, handy and seaworthy craft. They have single screws, and do not need such powerful engines as the trawlers. We took them up at the various herring drifter bases by the hundred. Their cost being much less than trawlers, they were often owned by single men, or by a family or by two families jointly, who would put their life savings into their purchase. The very personal nature of their ownership was indicated by such names as *Children's Provider, Family Trust, Three Friends, Husband's Thrift* and *Grandfather's Pride*.

Although not originally intended to do so, a good many eventually carried guns when they became available. These vessels laid and watched specially made wire nets across the known routes of enemy submarines.

Few were requisitioned in 1914 due to limited coal capacity restricting their value as patrol vessels but, as mentioned, hundreds were taken up in 1915 as the indicator net came into widespread use. During January, the Admiralty ordered 150 of them to Poole and 50 each to Falmouth, Milford and Larne. Preparations were also made for the establishment of net bases elsewhere. Each vessel could stream 500 yards of buoyed wire netting which extended down about 16 fathoms. Working together in large groups, they were able to create a net barrier many miles in length. The Dover and Otranto Straits were the best-known areas where these barriers were employed, against German and Austrian U-boats respectively. The obstacles hampered rather than prevented U-boat traffic and the exposed drifter lines suffered fearful casualties when attacked by enemy surface vessels. In the closing months of the war, when the net barrages were replaced by far more effective barriers composed of deeply moored mines, many drifters became minesweepers.

The drifters, some of which were fitted with wireless, also carried depth charges, lance bombs and, later on, hydrophones. They performed any and every duty of which they were capable, including the towing of targets, carrying of stores and ferrying of men as well as lighter assignments, such as examination service throughout the conflict and the delivery of mails. So valuable did they become that, as in the case of trawlers, the Admiralty augmented the stock via a construction programme of its own. This was embarked upon in 1917 and produced some 226 vessels of both wood and steel. On completion, the vessels were incorporated into the Auxiliary Patrol and many became minesweepers and fleet tenders. On the suggestion of Admiral Sir G Lionel Preston, Director of Minesweeping, they were named after various aspects of the elements, such as *Milky Way, Starlight, Sunlight, New Moon, Iceblink, Hoarfrost*, etc. Further details are provided in Volume 2.

Motor drifters became part of the Trawler Section on 22 September 1916. These craft, which were smaller than their steam-driven sisters, were hired for use in more confined waters as harbour tenders and coastal service craft. Practically all 118 of them came from Scottish ports.

Mention must be made, in connection with fishing vessels, of the sometimes dramatic part played by humble sailing trawlers/smacks as auxiliaries to the Navy as 'special service' or decoy (Q) vessels. Normally fishing singly and unarmed, they were easy targets for German submarines and many of their number were lost. Yet when they were armed they fought back stoutly – with the occasionally remarkable results we shall see.

Areas and Organization

The post of Admiral of Patrols, held by Rear-Admiral George A Ballard, had been created in the month before war broke out. It was at a conference with the Fourth Sea Lord on 7 October that Jellicoe recommended the introduction of a system of trawler patrol areas off all the bases used by the Grand Fleet. The Admiralty immediately accepted the Commander-in-Chief's request. It promptly ordered the requisitioning of another 60 trawlers and substantially increased the number of armed auxiliary vessels allocated to the Grand Fleet bases.

Following the initial concentration in the Scapa Flow area, vessels were allocated around the rest of the British Isles. From 20 December 1914, the 22 areas of the home Auxiliary Patrol, each based at a naval centre, were designated numerically.

Auxiliary vessels were also sent as far afield as the Mediterranean, where the patrol zones were divided according to the responsibility of the British, French and Italian navies, and to the White Sea, the Suez Canal, Trinidad, Canadian and African waters.

Responsibility for the running of each British area lay with the specially appointed area commanders, many of them retired naval officers. The three patrol areas off England's east coast as far south as the Naze, however, remained temporarily under the command of Ballard, whose responsibility for the Dover Straits had ended in October 1914. In February 1915, all the AP vessels in Area X (those based at Lowestoft and Harwich) were also removed from his control.

Since the command of several areas was sometimes under the same admiral, there were fewer parent ships than patrol areas. When in pursuit of an enemy vessel, no vessel had any hesitation in leaving its area.

After January 1917, Areas II and III (the Shetland and Orkney Islands) were combined, as were Areas VI and VII (both Granton), while a new Area XIIIa (Devonport) was created from within Areas XIII and XIV (Portland and Devonport) from 1 April 1917. In the following month, changes were made in Ireland, with original Area XIX (Killybegs) becoming new Area XIXa with altered boundaries and Area XX (Galway Bay) being downsized and re-numbered to become the new Area XIX. The remaining southernmost portion constituted the new Area XX (Berehaven).

Until he was appointed to command the 10th Cruiser Squadron, Admiral Sir Reginald Tupper headed stormy tide-ridden Area No I. He recalled later:

> I went to Area No. I on the 1st January, 1915, at twenty-four hours' notice. I was taken to Stornoway in a yacht called the *Vanessa*, which became my headquarters. I had no staff whatever, but I picked up my coxswain at Portsmouth Barracks before I started North, and happened to meet Mr. Norman Craig, K.C., who was serving as a Lieutenant in the yacht *Lorna*; and, as I was made Competent Authority of the Hebrides, said to him 'You know something about the law, if you don't about anything else, so come along and be my Flag Lieutenant and legal adviser and helper'. I had an eighteen year old youth as a Secretary to start with, and it took me something like five weeks before things were working efficiently. At the end of six months I had 6 yachts, 36 trawlers, 40 drifters, 8 M.L.s and 6 of those extraordinary things called whalers to carry out the duties of the Area.
>
> I spent at least four days a week at sea, visiting my patrols and searching all the fiords and so on. It was well that I did so, for the first time I went afloat I found nearly all my patrol craft in harbour; they said they went in every night because they thought that was the right thing to do! I soon disabused them of that idea, and the result was that they did very good work.
>
> I claim that my little patrol destroyed three submarines and picked up ninety-five mines; only one merchant ship was torpedoed during my fifteen months in command. Ships of the Grand Fleet used to go down to dock through the Area and nothing happened to any of them.

Personnel and Duties

Lecky became connected with the new service in October 1914. Since 5 August, he had been in charge of a group of six minesweeping trawlers at Harwich. They had been sent out immediately, unarmed and without wireless, to sweep for the *Königin Luise* minefield, concerning which more later, and subsequently used to leave harbour at 2 a.m. to sweep the channels which might be used by Commodore Tyrwhitt's light cruisers and destroyers later on in the day.

Hailed from a light vessel one morning, he was informed that he was to return to Harwich immediately. The scheme so far on trial was outlined to him and he was told to develop it, probably because he had served on the staffs as Gunnery Lieutenant of both the Admiral Commanding Reserves and the first Admiral of Patrols.

In reply to his question as to what kind of ships he was to take up and from where, he was told to 'take up anything seaworthy that has not got a hole in its bottom'. Enquiries as to naval personnel for guns and RNR ratings to complete their crews were met with point blank refusals from both the

Director of Mobilization and the Admiral Commanding the Reserves, who held themselves responsible only for manning the main fleet and certain subsidiaries. On asking about RNVR ratings, whose role was to support the Navy in its operations, he was informed that the First Lord had turned them into soldiers to serve on shore in Flanders, that a large number were already interned in Holland, and that the rest were being recruited for military service elsewhere.

He reported to his superiors that neither RN, RNR or RNVR ratings were available and asked for guidance as to how to conduct any recruitment. He was advised to get personnel 'from under the lamp-posts.' On the basis of these two instructions, 'to take up anything seaworthy that has not got a hole in its bottom' and to recruit 'from under the lamp-posts', the Auxiliary Patrol was formed.

Gilbert Owen Stephenson, later Sir Gilbert Owen Stephenson CMG CB KBE DL who, on the outbreak of the war was attached to the Admiralty's Naval Intelligence Division and would later command a fleet of trawlers undertaking patrols from Crete, recalled the extraordinary variety of the personnel acquired for the patrol, from the barrister and the stockbroker in the motor launch to some of the ratings in the trawlers who could not even read a clock. A fair number of trawler skippers were illiterate, yet some took their vessels out to the Mediterranean without being able to use charts at all. The crews manning the trawlers were often also extraordinarily small. They always worked watch and watch, being on duty for twelve hours out of the twenty-four, and when there was minesweeping to be done everybody was on deck.

In November 1914, Commodore CF Lambert echoed Lecky's predicament by warning that men might not always be obtainable in large numbers since the crews of auxiliary vessels were almost exclusively made up of volunteers. He was right. Two months later, crews could not be raised for all the net drifters. For much of 1915, during the first U-boat campaign, this shortage of recruits continued to be a problem for the patrol. In April, Captain TP Bonham, the Inspecting Captain of Minesweepers (who retained responsibility throughout 1914-15 for the requisitioning of fishing vessels, regardless of whether they were to be employed as minesweepers or patrol boats) revealed that the Trawler Section was short of some 2,000 ratings. Many patrol craft were left shorthanded and on one armed trawler there were not enough competent deckhands to steer the vessel.

Regarding communications, Roderick Suddaby notes in his 1971 thesis *The Auxiliary Patrol, 1914-15*:

> The Royal Navy had suffered from a shortage of W/T operators since the outset of the war and, although over 500 men had been sent on a W/T training course by the Admiralty, throughout 1915 auxiliary craft with W/T equipment frequently had to sail without a telegraphist. This manpower deficiency impeded both the numerical progress and the military value of the Auxiliary Patrol.[50]

Lecky noted that at no time did the Auxiliary Patrol include anything but a quite negligible percentage of RN, pre-War RNR or pre-War RNVR officers and men. The two former were required for fleet service and the latter, as noted, were mostly serving ashore as soldiers in the Naval Division. By far the greater proportion of both officers and men was indeed specially recruited 'from under the lamp-posts'. At the end of 1914 there were 635 such officers, a figure which more than doubled a year later to 1,393. Gradually it rose to some 3,000. By the end of 1916 there were approximately 52,000 ratings – a figure which was never exceeded to any degree and which approximately broke down into: RNR 42,000, RNVR 6,000 and RN 4,000 (Pensioners, etc.).

Every armed trawler was commanded by a skipper RNR during the first few weeks of the Auxiliary Patrol's existence, although due to reports of many trawler skippers being incompetent in their new naval role (Rear-Admiral ER Pears wrote that they were 'fishermen ignorant of discipline and the arts of war and devoid of initiative and judgement'[51]), a new system was instituted at the end of October 1914. Thenceforward, two of the six trawlers in each unit would be commanded by RNR officers holding either a Master's or Mate's Foreign-Going Certificate. The appointment of a lieutenant and sub-lieutenant RNR to each unit would, the Admiralty hoped, result in the armed trawlers being much more efficient.

For his part, Captain Humphrey Bowring, the officer in charge of the Dover Net Drifter Flotilla for a time in 1915, observed that skippers did their job well but did not feel the same could be said of the mates:

> The Skippers, taken as a whole, are good competent men, keen and enthusiastic in their work. The Mates on the contrary are mostly unreliable, ill-educated, either quite youngsters or old men, who are evidently in their present position owing to want of ambition or inability to hold a Skipper's certificate.

Yet a mere week before his report, Rear-Admiral Hood had informed the Admiralty that the officers and men of the Dover Drifter Flotilla were working 'willingly and well'.

There was, inevitably, occasional drunkenness and insubordination and some animosity did exist initially between the personnel of the Auxiliary Patrol and the Royal Navy. Many naval officers in 1914 believed that subjection to very strict discipline was the only way fishermen could be transformed into an effective fighting force – an approach which took no account of the highly independent nature of the average fisherman and whose unsoundness was not recognized until early in 1915. Until then, the harsh disciplinary methods of some naval officers aroused considerable ill-feeling among AP volunteer fishermen.

One way of sweetening the pill of monotonous and seemingly fruitless patrol and escort work was the Admiralty's offer of financial inducements. Initially, a sum of £200 was offered to all armed trawlers for each German submarine they captured or sank, a figure raised to £1,000 in January 1915, at which time auxiliary vessels were offered prize money of up to £200 for damaging U-boats and a bounty of £5 for each German mine destroyed. In June 1915, the crew of the armed trawler *Ina William* were awarded £500 for the probable destruction of a German submarine. Records show that the marauder had in fact escaped.

At Granton, Captain James Startin RNR devised various forms of disguise for vessels under his charge. His efforts were rewarded in July 1915 when, as noted previously, the armed trawler *Quickly*, disguised as a small Norwegian cargo vessel, severely damaged a German submarine. A number of other SNOs made their mark during the first eighteen months of the war, such as Captain Alfred A Ellison, the Captain-in-Charge at Lowestoft, who may have been the first naval officer in the war to recommend the use of Q-ships. His own experiments bore fruit in August when *UB.4* was sunk by the *Inverlyon*, one of the disguised armed sailing smacks which he had sent out with the Lowestoft fishing fleet.

In the previous month, a report by Rear-Admiral Ballard highlighted the imperative need for training skippers:

> ...it is not that these men are lacking in courage. Under the supervision of a competent officer they usually do well ... but when left to themselves in responsible situations requiring prompt action they are with a few exceptions not qualified by training or education to show initiative and judgement.

By the end of the year, the men were showing clear signs of being able to carry out naval work reasonably proficiently as long as they had been trained intelligently.

The illiteracy problem greatly complicated the task of improving navigation. The Flag Captain of Admiral Sir Hedworth Meux, Commander-in-Chief, Portsmouth, estimated that no more than a tenth of the skippers and mates in the Portsmouth Auxiliary Patrol knew anything about charts. North Sea skippers, who had always navigated by the lead and fished in company, were particularly backward in this respect. The consequence was that difficulty was often found in maintaining the patrol line or in meeting an escorted ship at the appointed rendezvous. December 1914 saw the worst scenario: a patrol trawler off Scapa Flow caused the *Monarch* and *Conqueror* to collide, putting both battleships out of action for several months.

By that time, several flag officers – including Jellicoe and Beatty – had protested about the unreliability of the trawler crews, who on occasion even shirked their duties. In April 1915, the SNO at Jarrow reported that the skippers in the Tyne Auxiliary Patrol 'do their best to get into harbour on the slightest pretext' instead of treating the patrol of the coast as a serious matter, while the skipper of the Portsmouth Auxiliary Patrol trawler *White Ear* was reported as being an 'unreliable and sly man' who once refused to escort an oiler and who at night would sometimes lurk in the background, 'stopped and with lights out'.

Such skulking had been almost eliminated from the patrol by the end of 1915 following strict supervision by SNOs and RNR officers and the discharge of the worst offenders. The significant enhancement of the efficiency of the Orkneys and Shetlands AP through the arrival of RNR officers had been noted by Admiral Stanley Colville, the shore commander of the area, in December 1914, and, indeed, by Jellicoe, who had been forced to place officers from the Grand Fleet on board the armed trawlers at Scapa Flow to ensure a good lookout was kept. Lambert observed, in the following summer, that RNR officers had 'greatly improved matters' everywhere.

Drifter crews, for their part, generally attracted praise. Captain Valentine Phillimore, Captain-in-Charge of Patrol Area XIV, contrasted the 'zeal and keenness' of the drifter skippers under his command with 'the very indifferent class' of the trawler skippers. The ability of the drifter skippers also impressed Vice-Admiral Dare. So satisfactory were those he had had to place in charge of four of the net drifter divisions at Milford (due to the shortage of RNR officers) that he was able to recommend that all the latter in command of net drifter groups at the port should be released for other duties.

Lecky in his lecture looked back at the men of the improvised navy as a body and found it:

> impossible to speak too highly of their adaptability, their behaviour, their devotion to the interests of the State, and the results of their labours. Life in a muddy rat-ridden trench would seem like paradise to anyone who had to stick out two or three weeks of winter gales in the North Sea in one of these small patrol craft.[52]

Lecky also referred to the fact that the operational work of the Auxiliary Patrol really consisted of every conceivable duty arising in war and listed a number of them:

> ...attacking enemy submarines; protecting coastwise trade; the preliminary examination and search of shipping; protection of minesweepers and other unarmed vessels; examination of areas before the passage of fighting ships or valuable merchantmen; perpetual patrolling; hydrophone work; constant escorting of vessels either singly or in convoy into harbour or through an area; driving submarines within reach of other craft; conveyance of messages; rescue of crews mined, wrecked or torpedoed; salvage; assisting in minelaying operations; watching navigational marks at dawn; guarding mined nets and mined areas; making smoke screens; accompanying and rescuing crews of blockships; landing troops, guns and stores on enemy beaches; landing and recovering agents from hostile territory; evacuation of wounded ...

Of all the numerous tasks listed, it was the 'perpetual patrolling' and 'constant escorting of vessels either singly or in convoy into harbour or through an area' which accounted for most of the AP's time and energy. The respective merits of these duties will be considered presently.

The Boom Defence Service employed many hundreds of generally older fishing vessels and others serving almost exclusively in red ensign (non-commissioned) status. Some were armed to assist them in their protection of the fleet and its anchorages and control of coastal waters. The work of operating defensive booms, typically 40-foot timber balks chained together and stretched across a harbour mouth so as to bar the entrance to enemy torpedo boats, required the constant service of pilot vessels, opening ships, closing ships, and large numbers of tenders, repair vessels, and supply ships in the shape of trawlers, drifters, tugs, and barges. By the end of the war, the anchorage for the Grand Fleet at Scapa Flow – many of whose little-used harbour entrances were closed by block ships – was in the hands of no fewer than 125 BDVs.

Static defence of another kind, namely the setting and monitoring of indicator net barrages, was the preserve of drifters, whose value as patrol vessels was restricted by the limited coal capacity we noted. Few had been requisitioned in 1914 for that reason but in the following year, as noted earlier, they were taken up in large numbers as the indicator net came into widespread use. In western waters, completion of the net defences in the North and St George's Channels was hastened by submarine activity in the Irish Sea. On account of its width, a barrage as such could not be laid in the latter channel but each day Rear-Admiral Dare's drifters shot their indicator nets at selected points. The netted area of the deep North Channel, extending from the Mull of Kintyre on the north-east side to Rathlin Island on the south-west side, became fully operational by early summer and was intended to keep a U-boat submerged until its batteries were exhausted. Forced to surface, it could then be attacked by patrolling armed auxiliaries. In the English Channel, the Dover AP was reinforced in early 1915 by 60 drifters, which laid and watched over several miles of indicator nets on both sides to make the Dover Straits impassable to submarines. The barrage led to a German naval order being issued in April 1915 (and not revoked until December 1916) instructing U-boat commanders heading for the Western Approaches to take the longer passage around the north of Scotland. For the larger U-boats this meant one week less killing time per cruise around that important trade route.

In the month the war broke out, trawlers, for their part, were called on by the Admiralty to patrol the waters around Scapa Flow. Twenty, all armed, performed this duty. Patrolling in general would, however, prove to be an offensive stratagem which ultimately paid poor dividends, although that could not be foreseen in the early years of the conflict. Sheer weight of numbers did nevertheless give patrolling vessels nuisance value against German submarines and increased the chances of important rescue and salvage work being performed (there were cases when U-boats had to abandon an attack on a merchant vessel on account of a patrol vessel's timely appearance in the vicinity. This happened three times in one week in the Milford Haven area alone.)

Captain Phillimore conveyed the futility of aggressive patrolling to the Admiralty in May 1915 stating: 'It is hopeless work looking for submarines and only pure luck when one bobs up alongside a patrol boat.' Hence during the first unrestricted submarine campaign between February and September 1915 the Auxiliary Patrol only accounted for six U-boats. Low speed, poor armament and the coastal, as opposed to the open-sea, area of operation were the main reasons for this low tally.

For patrol vessel crews, sheer monotony was perhaps the worst thing they had to contend with in the form of a constant and usually vain lookout maintained for days at a stretch. In *Pushing Water*, the author, 'RNV', wrote:

> The whole cordon of ships surrounding the British Isles and all the trade routes are doing exactly the same as we are doing, whether they are big or little. We are all 'pushing water'. It may seem an aimless proceeding but, nevertheless, every unit is part of a whole organization working with the most clockwork precision.

Escort and examination duties were less monotonous and yielded better results: Admiral Sir Henry Jackson recorded in a memorandum that between November 1914 and June 1915 not a single escorted ship was lost.[53] Up until September, German submarines managed to sink only a tiny proportion of the numerous oilers and other valuable vessels sailing with an individual armed trawler escort. The immunity from any successful submarine attack enjoyed by troop transports crossing to France was, of course, due to a close destroyer escort, although armed yachts and trawlers played their part.

One inherent difficulty in escort work was the generally slow speed of trawlers relative to that of their charges although, in practice, important ships whose maximum speed exceeded 10 knots were normally escorted by a destroyer or armed yacht, not by a trawler.

Commander AT Stewart RN recalled:

> Trawlers were invaluable for escort work and they could keep up with all the slower types of merchant ships. I recollect sending small convoys from Bizerta which were to be accompanied by trawlers and torpedo boats, but the torpedo boats were told 'if you cannot keep at sea and have to come back, the trawler will take the convoy on', and that is what happened more than once.[54]

Yet many masters in Home Waters were very reluctant to comply with the Admiralty stipulation that their faster vessel should reduce speed to allow the escorting trawler to keep up, for not only did they feel more vulnerable to submarine attack but their vessels become unmanageable at very low speeds. Richmond's successor as ADOD, Captain HV Grant, considered that in bad weather vessels might be better advised to proceed without an escort. High speed was erroneously believed to be the answer to U-boat attacks, a belief unfortunately fostered by the comparatively low speed of most German submarines in 1915. When more powerful types became operational thereafter, high speed was revealed to be an inadequate defence for ships which could not exceed 15 knots.

Escort work greatly stretched the resources of the Auxiliary Patrol. On one June day in 1915, every available armed trawler in the Humber patrol area was engaged on escort duties while in early October that year, Captain Startin relayed to Admiral Lowry the fact that over the previous four weeks the vessels under his command at Granton had spent 1,173 hours on escorting. Only Rear-Admiral Tupper at Stornoway among the SNOs appreciated the strategic benefits of escorting. He wrote to the Admiralty in early July 1915:

> The escorting of valuable ships seems to me to be a good way of utilising Auxiliary Patrol vessels as, in addition to contributing to the safety of the vessel escorted, it also gives the Auxiliary Patrol vessels a better chance of looking for submarines.[55]

The startling fact is that the general consensus of naval opinion dismissed escorting as an ineffectual defensive measure. Captain Ellison at Lowestoft, for example, complained that more time was wasted on escort duties than on anything else, while Admiral Sir Reginald HS Bacon, who headed the Dover Patrol between April 1915 and January 1918, wrote of escorting as 'a continual source of trouble'.[56]

The important task of boarding and examining neutral ships to ensure they were not carrying contraband or operating in disguise also fell to the patrol and could be a thankless one, with merchant vessels (whether through dislike of official interference or, more likely, fear of a submarine attack) sometimes refusing to cooperate, even with warships.

Armament

With the munitions factories operating to capacity to meet the nation's needs for arms for other forces, the Auxiliary Patrol was beset by a serious shortage of guns from the outset. Even as late as August 1915, most of the minesweeping trawlers and net drifters were armed only with rifles, although by then guns were at least available for all the patrol trawlers, even if the majority only carried one 3-pounder or one 6-pounder. Such weapons were inadequate to inflict critical damage to a submarine with a direct hit. A very few were armed with a 12-pounder – hence the near-success achieved by the *Ina William* and the actual success on the very same day by the armed trawler *Oceanic II* east of Aberdeen, which disabled *U.14* by gunfire and sank her by ramming; an attack praised by Jellicoe, in reference to the participating trawler *Hawk*, as 'a fine exploit, typical of the consistently good work of the vessels of the Peterhead patrol' which was 'especially welcome at this time when submarines were very active in northern waters'.[57]

As an emergency measure, the transfer of 65 x 12-pounders from defensively armed merchant ships was approved by the Admiralty in August and arrangements were put in hand for the arming of every minesweeping trawler with a 6-pounder and every net drifter with a 3-pounder.

Assessment and Achievements

There were divergences of opinion regarding the Auxiliary Patrol's effectiveness during the first period of unrestricted submarine warfare. In the month before the dispatch of *U.14*, Jellicoe argued that the lack of success of the Navy's anti-submarine operations could largely be attributed to the low speed, poor armament and inferior wireless communication of the patrol vessels, yet Commander LAB Donaldson, the Chairman of the Submarine Attack Committee, recalled him once generously stating that without the Auxiliary Patrol the Grand Fleet often could not have gone to sea. Vice-Admiral Sir Lewis Bayly, some weeks after his appointment to the Queenstown command, was sceptical of the ability of the existing force of yachts, trawlers and motorboats to improve the submarine situation in the Western Approaches. Naval writers such as Corbett and Marder also had doubts about the effectiveness of the Auxiliary Patrol during the first 18 months of the war.

Yet other writers held opposite views. Sir Archibald Hurd, the official historian of the Merchant Navy, observed that although the auxiliary craft did not sink many U-boats, their mere presence frequently had the vital effect of saving merchant ships which might otherwise have been destroyed, while E Keble Chatterton, with whom Hurd collaborated in his own chapters on the patrol and who was the author of a book on the service, was the staunchest of the AP's supporters. He wrote from experience, for he had himself commanded several patrol craft during the war. Within the Admiralty, vigorous endorsement came from Lambert, the Fourth Sea Lord, who was largely responsible for the patrol's inception and expansion, and also, as we have seen, from his naval assistant, Lecky. Like Lecky, Donaldson believed the Auxiliary Patrol was acting as a real deterrent to German submarines. Noted earlier was the support from Rear-Admiral Tupper commanding the Stornoway Auxiliary Patrol from January 1915 to January 1916, who commented in his memoirs that:

> ...the yacht patrol may not have destroyed very many (U-boats), but they made life difficult for them, and submarines rarely attempted any sort of a fight with one of the ships on the patrol.

The patrol's full potential had not yet been revealed in 1915. Tellingly, however, there was not a single proposal from any naval quarter during that year for a halt to be called to its expansion, an expansion which in fact took place on a major scale in September with the incorporation of minesweeping trawlers which had previously formed a separate command.

Chapter 6

The Horned Killer

Death may come in a terrible form,
Death in a calm or death in a storm,
Death without warning, stark and grim,
Death with a tearing of limb from limb,
Death in a horrible hideous guise:
Such is the minesweeper's sacrifice!
Careless of terrors and scornful of ease,
Stolid and steadfast, they sweep the seas.

From *The Minesweepers* by H Ingamells[58]

Nearly a quarter of a million mines were laid during the First World War by the countries involved and by neutrals protecting their own harbours. Of this number, Britain was responsible for about 129,000, nearly half of them around enemy coasts and in the Mediterranean. The allegation was made by the enemy that it was Britain which first laid a minefield in the middle of the North Sea, a statement industriously circulated and emphasized by Germany and which had, recorded Walter Wood in *Fishermen in Wartime*, obtained wide credence, especially in neutral countries. Attention would be called to the matter in the House of Commons at the beginning of 1917, when Dr Macnamara retorted that: 'It is so notoriously false as to be ludicrous.' It was not, in fact, until the beginning of November 1914 that the first British minefield had been laid.

Germany's policy of wholesale mining in the North Sea and the Atlantic was implemented from the day war was declared, not only to cause havoc to enemy shipping generally but also to lure to their doom any naval vessels pursuing the minelayers. The mines were laid far out at sea on major neutral trade routes and no notice of their existence had been given. Minelaying by Germany accounted for a total of 43,636 mines. Of these, no fewer than 25,000 or so were laid at points around the British Isles – 90 per cent of them by submarines. The remainder were deposited in the Baltic, the Mediterranean and the Black Sea. Allied shipping casualties amounted to a million tons in 586 ships. German naval losses through mines were 148 warships and 36 U-boats.

Both during the war and after, fishing vessels were crucial in combating this menace. Not only did they patrol and sweep the seas for the Navy but they also saved many naval vessels from mines by serving as the ultimate indicators of minefields through their own destruction. We saw earlier how humble were the beginnings of Britain's minesweeping force and how four days after the outbreak of the war, 94 ordinary fishing trawlers had been mobilized and were out at sea sweeping. A further 100 were requisitioned for the purpose within a fortnight and were fitting out. But there would soon be casualties.

A Wolf in Sheep's Clothing

It was in connection with German minelaying that the first shot in the naval war was fired – in response to an alarm signal communicated by a fisherman. On that fateful morning of 5 August 1914, the *Königin Luise*, a small German steamer of the Hamburg-Amerika line which for years had ferried tourists to seaside resorts, was observed by Lowestoft skipper Charles Wright to be throwing objects overboard. The *Eastern Daily Press* for Friday, 7 August, reported that:

> a Lowestoft trawler had been concerned in sending a warship in pursuit of a German mine layer. This we were able to confirm yesterday afternoon. The vessel concerned being the *LITTLE BOYS* of Lowestoft whose skipper is Mr. Charles Wright. She observed, through binoculars, a foreign-looking vessel dropping mines into the sea 30 or 40 miles off Lowestoft and the skipper at once realised the danger and gave information to a warship which passed a little later. The warship at once went in pursuit.[59]

The mines were later found to be so numerous as to constitute an area designated the Southwold Field. The wooden sailing trawler *Little Boys* was one of a handful of vessels at the port owned by one William Brown. Her days had not been without incident. She had, at the end of May 1899, collided with Lowestoft's *Young Jack* (LT 339) which sank, and in January 1902 collided with Belgian trawler O.173 and was damaged. On 16 March 1917, the *Little Boys* would cut away her fishing gear to escape from a U-boat. She was sold to Belgium in 1921 and renamed *Stéphanie Médard* (O.201).

Lowestoft skipper WS Wharton, for his part, later recollected:

> ...we sighted what we thought was one of the G.E.R. [Great Eastern Railway] Steamers which ran between Harwich and Rotterdam.
> My attention was drawn to the Steamer, making a zig-zag course for no apparent reason. We were in company with more Lowestoft smacks, when about 10.30 a.m. we sighted some British Destroyers bound on a S.S.E. course. A few minutes later we noticed two Destroyers alter their course, and open fire with their Bow Guns on the Steamer which we thought was a G.E.R. boat. The Destroyers blew her to pieces and she sank stern first. She was painted and rigged like the Harwich Steamers. We thought at the time that it was two German Destroyers sinking the British Steamer. Next morning, after having finished our night's work we sailed to the Southward when we came into a lot of oil and wreckage, some of which we picked up. We also found two Life Buoys; one was marked HMS 'Amphion' and the other marked 'Konigin Luise'. Two days later we arrived at Lowestoft and handed the wreckage and Life Buoys over to the Customs Officials. We then heard all about the Ship we had taken for an English Ship, and she turned out to be a disguised German Mine-Layer named the 'Konigin Luise' and the two Destroyers which took part in the sinking of her were H.M. Ships 'Lance' and 'Landsail' [*sic*].

The destroyers *Lance* and *Landrail* were the first to open fire on the minelayer, and the *Lance* has the distinction of being the first RN vessel to open fire on the enemy in the 1914-1918 naval war.

Early in the evening before her ill-fated sortie, the *Königin Luise* had lain at anchor in the Ems and did indeed resemble one of the Hook of Holland steamers. Her mission had been to foul the East Swin Channel, one of the channels used by shipping to various harbours and ports in the Thames Estuary, and she had been instructed to proceed rapidly to the Thames and lay her mines as near as possible to the English coast, but only south of Lat. 53 N. *Korvettenkapitän* Biermann, however, had clearly been out in his dead reckoning, as his mines were laid some 12 miles north of the target area. The Germans had hoped to dislocate coastal traffic but above all damage the Grand Fleet; in this they were unsuccessful, since the fleet had moved north several days before.

When sighted the next day by a now-alerted flotilla of British naval vessels, including the new light cruiser, HMS *Amphion*, she was still some 30 miles offshore and travelling at 16 knots. On seeing the flotilla, Biermann jettisoned his mines and headed southward and then south-east, in order to leave British waters. At 11.15 a.m., the flotilla began shelling the steamer, which sent a wireless signal through to the High Sea Fleet that her mines had been laid. By noon, she had been sunk. Her survivors were taken aboard the *Amphion*, yet their hours were in fact numbered, for although this vessel had helped to send the *Königin Luise* to the bottom she was, by the greatest irony, to become one of her first victims by foundering on the new minefield herself – the first British ship for close on 100 years to be destroyed by the act of an enemy.

The Admiralty quickly realized the enormous value of any and every item of information relating to the enemy's activities or, as in the case of Wharton's finds, remnants from sunken vessels. It officially made such liaison worthwhile for fishermen by issuing a notice to this effect which appeared in the *Fish Trades Gazette* on 17 October.

The Revd CH Hicks, attached to the RNMDSF, felt that Skipper Wright should have been able to benefit from these arrangements. He expressed this view in the *Toilers of the Deep* on 15 October, 1914:

> I should be glad of an opportunity of meeting the officer in charge of the Lowestoft base, to whom I have just written concerning the case of the skipper whose information led to the sinking of the mine-laying 'Königin Luise' on the first day of the war. It seems that the Admiralty's reward now offered ought in this case to be retrospective, the good man stating what he saw when HMS 'Laurel' came near, without any thought of personal benefit for himself or members of the crew.

In the wake of the *Königin Luise* incident, the 100 trawlers mentioned earlier were immediately requisitioned and by 21 August had been dispatched to Lowestoft, now a busy naval base. Here, at the rate of six a day, they were fitted out for their new minesweeping duties; from Dover, half a dozen Admiralty trawlers were hurriedly fetched up to sweep a channel shoreward of this minefield (others were moved as far as north-east Scotland, where Admiral Lowry needed them to watch for minelayers in the Moray Firth, where a single destroyer had been available for night patrol work).

E Keble Chatterton vividly recalled the comings-and-goings of this early phase of the war at sea:

Those of us who were at sea off this coast during the first few weeks of war will always remember the amazing amount of traffic – colliers, tramps, even topsail schooners – in one never-ending procession bound to and from the North Sea ports. It was just as if no enemy existed the other side of the horizon.[60]

It was vital that a clear channel should be permanently maintained over the vast area as far north as the Outer Dowsing to the South Goodwins. On 11 August, Captain Ellison at Lowestoft hired 50 unarmed steam drifters to patrol this area in sections to watch for any other minelayers which might be at work after dark. With autumn not far off, there was a growing urgency to guarantee a swept fairway as soon as possible.

The Tyne, Humber and Tory Island Fields

Yet the enemy continued its insidious operations. On the night of 24 August, the 2,200-ton German cruiser *Albatross*, able to carry 400 mines, set off on her mission to foul an area off the Tyne. Escorted by the cruiser *Stuttgart*, she began laying a field of 194 mines about midnight on 25-26 August, in zigzag formation, some 30 miles off the river mouth. An extraordinary finding by the present author, for which evidence is presented in Chapter 8, is that both vessels had substantial numbers of captive British fishermen on board. This point has not been made in any of the numerous and varied sources consulted when researching material for this volume.

Right until the end of the war, the enemy was certain this minefield had been laid some six miles offshore. Once the field's limits were learned, it was decided to discontinue sweeping and concentrate on maintaining a safe channel inshore up and down the coast. So apart from a couple of subsequent exploratory sweeps, the Tyne minefield remained unswept until the end of the war. The *Albatross* would, during the following July, be driven ashore by the Russians onto Gothland. She was subsequently salvaged and interned in Sweden until after the Armistice.

Another recognized German minelayer was the 1,970-ton *Nautilus*, which also carried 400 mines. She left the Ems in the early hours of 25 August, a matter of hours after her accomplice, and made for the Dogger Bank. There she altered course and at midnight laid two legs of mines in a position some 50 miles east of the mouth of the Humber. Both minelayers then returned safely to Germany. In his memoirs, *Germany's High Sea Fleet In The World War* published in 1920, Admiral Reinhard Scheer – who would assume command of the entire German High Sea Fleet in 1916 – recorded:

> By day their operations were covered by a light cruiser and a half-flotilla of destroyers, as mine-layers must be kept out of action if at all possible. Both ships were able to carry out their commission undisturbed and laid their mines accurately at the places indicated. The actual work began at midnight and was favoured by thick weather. On the way back another six fishing-steamers were sunk.

These losses will be looked at later. As for previous victims, he wrote:

> On August 21 the light cruisers *Rostock* and *Strassburg* with Flotilla VI made a sweep in the direction of the Dogger Bank with a view to searching the fishing grounds for English fishing-smacks. They also met enemy submarines, one of which

fired two torpedoes at the *Rostock,* but both missed. On this cruise six fishing-steamers were destroyed which were found, well separated, in a circle round Heligoland, and were suspected of working with English submarines.

These would have been the Boston trawlers *Skirbeck, Wigtoft, Walrus, Flavian, Julian* and *Indian*. Chapter 8 provides more details.

Frequent reference, published and otherwise, was made in those days to the role of German fishing craft not only as spies – before the war and after its declaration – but as layers of mines. This view was contemptuously dismissed by E Keble Chatterton in *The Auxiliary Patrol*:

> It was most unfortunate that politicians, ignorant of seafaring matters, should promulgate the absurd notion that this minefield had been laid by German fishing vessels wearing a neutral flag. This statement caused some amusement among those familiar with the capabilities of trawlers and drifters. You have only to measure off the distance to the nearest German port, and then consider how long it would take a 10-knot trawler to get across, and reckon how few mines she could carry. The conception was ludicrous; the operation would never have been attempted, and the German Government publicly denied the truth of this foolish suggestion; but it showed our state of nervousness and the dominating fear of mysterious hidden-hand work.

Although it was expedient to sweep certain channels through the Humber minefield, it existed, on the whole, until after the Armistice. From this field, as from others, many mines did, however, break free from their moorings during bad weather and would drift in an easterly direction across the North Sea.

Chatterton commented:

> I have often examined the mechanism of one of the Humber mines, and no one can deny that it was beautiful work, of which even a watchmaker would not be ashamed.

These early fields were at least all discovered quickly. Had that not been the case, certain wounded battleships making for the Tyne, Humber or Harwich, following a fleet action in the North Sea, would almost certainly have been sunk, with great loss of life. Small craft had therefore had to be sacrificed for the protection of their bigger sisters.

The long swept lane from the Downs needed to be modified by creating an inner channel from Haisborough to the Inner Dowsing. Thanks to the excellent work of the sweepers, this lane, buoyed all the way, extended by mid-September from the Downs to Flamborough Head, and preparations were being made to continue it as far as Whitby.

Ironically, the enemy did Britain a good turn in laying mines. Once the extent and position of the fields' areas had been ascertained, the policy adopted was not to sweep them up but to leave them intact as a buffer. Had the enemy gone close inshore and fouled the swept channel, then its operations would have had catastrophic results. The risk and danger, especially before submarine minelaying was introduced, were simply too great for the minelayers. Hence the expedient adopted later by the enemy of sowing mines under the cover of a strong raiding force, as at the time of the attacks on Scarborough and Gorleston.

Another German strategy was to sink transports bringing Canadian troops across the Atlantic to England. The first convoy (of 31 transports) left Canadian waters on 3 October 1914 for Plymouth Sound. Targeting it was the *Berlin* of the Norddeutscher Lloyd line, an exceptionally large minelayer of over 17,000 registered tonnage and a speed of about 17 knots. She left the fatherland on the very day the troops reached Plymouth Sound, having erroneously assumed that the transports would come to Liverpool via the north of Ireland. When she herself reached that area, she laid a big minefield off Tory Island. It very soon claimed its first victim – a 5,000-ton steamship called the *Manchester Commerce,* bound for the River St Lawrence, whence the Canadian convoy had started. On the following morning, while the Second Battle Squadron was steaming in the area, the third ship in the line, HMS *Audacious*, struck a mine and eventually foundered.

Because every available patrol craft had been sent to the North Sea – the main theatre of war – within the first few weeks of the war, no one knew of the *Berlin* having been anywhere near the Irish coast. Caught unawares, the Navy immediately ordered four trawler sweepers to leave Milford Haven for Lough Swilly, on the northern coast of County Donegal, where part of the Grand Fleet – with Admiral Jellicoe's flagship – was anchored at the time. Until the minefield was cleared, the ships were effectively blockaded.

It was naturally suspected that the enemy might have fouled the strategic points of the North Channel (the strait separating Northern Ireland from Scotland) and St George's Channel (a channel connecting the Irish Sea to the north and the Atlantic Ocean to the south-west), so two groups of six trawlers, each attended by an armed vessel, were ordered from Lowestoft the day after the *Audacious* disaster. One was to proceed to Larne to sweep the North Channel and the other was to go to Milford to sweep the St George's Channel.

Two additional squadrons of 20 or so trawlers each, with a proportion of minesweepers, were to be formed without delay to scour the west coast and the trade approaches. Six minesweeping trawlers swept from the entrance to Lough Swilly – which was itself patrolled by the armed yacht *Lorna* and six trawlers – to the west and south of Tory Island yet found no mines, only to learn later that these were farther north. The small fleet at the lough entrance was soon supplemented by drifters taken up at Kingstown.

On 28 October Jellicoe, fearing other new minefields might be laid off the anchorage used by the Grand Fleet, ordered Stanley Colville, the Vice-Admiral commanding the Orkneys and Shetlands, to send trawlers to sweep for mines up to within 30 miles of the bases.

The East Coast Raids
Two German raids on the east coast that winter involved the minelayer SMS *Kolberg*. A light cruiser built in 1910, she had been assigned to defence of the Bight area and had, on 28 August, taken part in the Battle of Heligoland Bight. She was one of four light cruisers attached to the German battlecruiser squadron attacking Great Yarmouth on 3 November 1914 under Admiral Franz von Hipper. Little damage was done to the town, with shells only landing on the beach after the ships laying mines offshore were interrupted by

British destroyers. However, 130 were laid and a British submarine was mined when attempting to leave harbour and attack the German ships.

Six weeks later, the *Kolberg* was again laying mines under the cover of a raiding force targeting Scarborough, Hartlepool, West Hartlepool and Whitby. On 16 December, she laid 100 off Scarborough, a couple of which were found by gunboats on the 19th. Half an hour later a Grimsby trawler minesweeping unit brought 18 to the surface simultaneously. Two of the vessels, the *Orianda* and the *Garmo*, struck mines on the 19th and 20th respectively (see page 79) and it was not until April 1915 that the field was finally cleared. Of the 100 mines laid, 69 were accounted for. The heavy losses to shipping, apart from the two trawlers, included seven British and seven neutral steamers, four minesweepers and an armed yacht. On land, the toll of the raid was 137 fatalities and 592 casualties, many of whom were civilians. Public outrage was felt towards the German navy for an attack against civilians – and against the Royal Navy for its failure to prevent the raid.

A memorandum from Rear-Admiral Edward B Charlton detailing minesweeping operations off Scarborough between 19 and 31 December 1914 was published by the Admiralty in a supplement to the *London Gazette* on 19 February 1915. Initially, it reported, there was no indication of the position of the mines, although, owing to losses of passing merchant ships, it was known that a minefield had been laid. Sweeping therefore needed to be carried out at all times of tide, adding greatly to the danger of the operations. Nevertheless, a large number of mines were swept up and destroyed, so that by Christmas Day a channel had been cleared and traffic was able to pass through by daylight.

Some 1914 Casualties

Before mines claimed any fishing or ex-fishing vessel victims in August 1914, havoc was wrought by enemy surface craft (the U-boat had yet to become a major force to be reckoned with).

As early as 7 August, as we saw, the Grimsby trawler *Tubal Cain* was sent to the bottom by the battleship *Kaiser Wilhelm der Grösse*, 50 miles from Iceland. On the 22nd, fellow Grimsby trawler *Capricornus* was sunk by torpedo boat 85 miles east by north of Spurn Point, and between that date and the 26th no fewer than 22 further trawlers were captured and sunk by a German flotilla. The crews were taken off and conveyed to Wilhelmshaven as prisoners of war. Nine of the vessels had been owned by the Boston Deep Sea Fishing and Ice Company Ltd. More details, plus the story of the destruction of the Grimsby trawler *Valiant*, captured off Whitby on the 25th, are provided in Chapter 8.

It would not be long before the Humber minefield was discovered by our fishermen. At 10 p.m. on 26 August, the Great Yarmouth steam drifter *City of Belfast* found a couple of mines in her herring nets some 13 miles north by east of the Outer Dowsing Lightship. Another mine exploded in her nets the next day, so she wisely left them. Three ships foundered in this highly dangerous location in 1914, as did two more in 1916; even as late as April of that year, 35 mines were swept up. Neither the direction nor extent of the minefield was known to us, although a certain area was painted red on the charts and proscribed as a mine area. But this was only on the basis of a guess, supplemented by the known positions of mined vessels and information from the sweepers. Thus three dangerous fields – the Southwold, Humber and Tyne – had been sown off our coasts within the first month of the war. Had they not been discovered early on by fishermen, each of them would have had a far more devastating impact.

The Tyne minefield soon claimed victims. Within four hours an Icelandic trawler had been blown up, a casualty followed shortly afterwards by the loss of a Norwegian steamer and a Danish sailing ship. The drifters *Lottie Leask* and *Doreen* were returning to North Shields with their catch when they sighted, about 27 miles off the Tyne, the Icelander and the Norwegian in distress on the trade route to Newcastle. Both the Selby-built *Skúli Fógeti* and the *Gottfried* were in danger of sinking immediately, having been seriously damaged by the explosion of submarine mines. With all haste, measures were taken to ensure the safety of the crews and 21 were taken off the doomed vessels (12 by *Lottie*, whose herring nets had been cut away to enable the Icelanders to be rescued) and conveyed to North Shields. Her skipper, Jack Crane, and his crew were later awarded £10 by a grateful Icelandic Government. This drifter would be requisitioned in May 1916 and converted to a boom defence vessel, becoming a training ship in the following year, but would regrettably be sunk by the gunfire of *U.39* off Sazan Island (at the entrance to the Bay of Vlora, Albania) on 18 December 1915.

On the news of the sinkings being received, the four trawler sweepers based on the Tyne were sent to the scene, leaving at 5.30 a.m. next day. Two of them, the *Thomas W. Irvin* and the *Crathie*, both of Aberdeen, were sunk. The former vessel, with the senior officer of the group on board, fell victim first. With her port side torn completely open by the blast, she went down in less than five minutes. Three of her crew were lost. The *Crathie* was struck amidships and broke in two like a piece of matchwood. Two men died. Her injured and unconscious skipper, Herbert H Cook, was trapped in the wheelhouse but was mercifully removed from the death-trap by one of the crew. The rescued crews of both vessels were soon reporting for minesweeping duties again and were understood by the *Fishing News* to be forming the crew of the Shields trawler *St. Leonard*.[61]

The Danish vessel which succumbed to the minefield was the *Ena* of Svendborg, whose crew was saved by a British torpedo boat.

The *Thomas W. Irvin* and the *Crathie* were the first fishing vessels on naval service to fall victims to mines. On the same day, 27 August 1914, the Buckie herring drifter *Barley Rig* (BCK 14) also sank off the River Tyne through the same cause. There was a dull explosion just as the crew were about to shoot their nets and she foundered within a few minutes. All her crew of nine were hurled from the shattered vessel into the water. Five of them, terribly injured, were either killed or drowned. The survivors (four brothers by the name of Clark) managed to cut the boat adrift before the vessel went down. Being without oars, they drifted about for two hours before being sighted by the trawler *St. Clair* and landed at Hull the next day. Also brought in was the body of the engineer, known as Charlie, from Fraserburgh.

On the last day of August, the minesweeping torpedo-gunboat *Speedy* was sent, under orders from *Halycon*, with ten steam drifters from Lowestoft to sweep the Humber minefield. On 2 September, the steam drifter *Eyrie* struck a mine, which carried away her stern and sent her to the bottom in three minutes. Six lives – all Lowestoft men – were lost. The next day saw further tragedy. Intending to sweep under the previously-shot nets, *Speedy*, in company with three drifters, was holding one end of the sweep-wire with *Lindsell* (often referred to as *Linsdell*) holding the other. Extra power was provided by *Wishful* and *Achievable* towing her. At 11.00 a.m., after they had been toiling for an hour, *Lindsell* struck a mine aft, near the Outer Dowsing and close to where the *City of Belfast* had had her first uncomfortable experience. The *Lindsell*'s stern was instantly blown off, her bows upended and a few minutes later no trace of her remained. There were five fatalities, including Skipper Woodgate. The *Speedy* lowered her boats and picked up survivors, but the skipper, mate, engineer and two deckhands from the *Lindsell* perished. Presently, at 11.15 a.m., the *Speedy* herself, while engaged in this rescue work, hit a mine, which blew off most of the ship's after part, and she sank to the bottom. One rating was lost. Although the abandonment was a disciplined exercise, with the behaviour of some persons being complimented on, five skippers of drifters anchored some four miles away were censured for refusing to close when ordered (they merely launched their pulling-boats). Apart from the material losses, the toll was 12 men killed and at least three injured, two badly. The wounded were ferried to Grimsby by the minesweeping-gunboat *Spanker* in the vicinity. Due to the blast, her wireless failed.

Among the handful of non-auxiliary vessels which fell victim to mines in September was the *Imperialist*, one of the finest trawlers to sail out of Hull. Built at Beverley in 1911, she was attached to the famous Hellyer line of trawlers. She left for Iceland on 6 September carrying a crew of 12, of whom two would be lost, and was on her way back from a successful fishing trip on the Iceland grounds when disaster befell her. Her skipper, Joe Wood of Hull, had been a very successful fisherman whose name had been well known all along the east coast. Leave to presume his death was granted by the Probate Court on 12 October 1914. The spare deck hand who lost his life was Thomas Jackson, also a Hull man.

One of the survivors, his face disfigured by an abrasion, told a press representative that he was lying down in the forecastle when the explosion occurred:

The forecastle simply tumbled to pieces about our ears and I fell through into the chain locker. I was lucky not be knocked out, and I scrambled on the deck as fast as I could. The boat was going down and I scrambled aft, where I found that efforts were being made to launch the boat. We guessed we wouldn't have time to get it over the side in the ordinary way, and we cut away the lashings. There were five of us in her when the ship went down. As she settled down the small boat floated clear, and we picked the other five up out of the water. Before she sank she turned right over and disappeared like a stone. The last I saw of the skipper was on the bridge, and I reckon when she turned over she smothered him and took him down with her.

Had we not got the boat's lashings cut away none of us would have been alive. We set out to row for the shore, taking our bearing from the moon, and we rowed all night when the *Rhodesia* sighted us and picked us up. We were then about dead beat, not having had bite or sup, while most of us had very little clothing, and we felt the cold. Nobody can have the least idea what it is like getting blown up by a mine unless they have been through it. It's terrible, and I don't want to be in another affair like it.

The mate, J Gibbs, was the last man of the 10 to be rescued, having been swimming about for some time before being picked up, and was utterly exhausted when he was pulled out of the water.

On 13 October, a telegram was received at the Board of Trade Office, Aberdeen, from the naval base at Lowestoft stating that HMT *Princess Beatrice* had not been heard of since 5 October, and that it was feared she must be regarded as lost. The crew was mainly made up of Aberdeen men, including the skipper, and their relatives received information earlier in the day of the fears held by the authorities as to the safety of the vessel. Many of the men's wives had received letters from their husbands at the end of the previous week and hope was still entertained that the vessel might yet return to port. One of the victims of the explosion, James Robert Smith, was an Englishman from North Shields, aged 35 and married with a family. He had gone to Aberdeen seven years earlier and had sailed from the port in several ships, including the steam trawler *Clementina* belonging to Messrs JW Young of Aberdeen.

Another Aberdeen boat, the sweeper *Drumoak*, was reported by Lowestoft naval base as being missing. Her skipper, Robert Ellington, and three other members of the crew hailed from that port. The vessel was in fact mined and had sunk off the Belgian coast. Nine names were printed in the FTG's 'Roll of Honour' as Trawler Section casualties from this vessel, while that of a tenth, Victor Philip Glenister of Aberdeen, appeared in the *Fishing News* on the same day, which reproduced a telegram from Lowestoft listing the crew.

Under the despairing headline 'Three more Grimsby trawlers lost', the *Fish Trades Gazette* of 24 October 1914 reported:

> The *Ajax* has certainly gone, for the Board of Trade announced definitely that she was blown up by a mine on September 2 ... and with such a curt announcement, there appears to be no doubt that the nine members of the crew were all drowned. The other vessels, the *Lord Howick* and the *Oxford*, are both owned by the Consolidated Steam Fishing and Ice Company, the former – an old Blyth trawler – having been absent since September 2 and the latter since September 10, without any word of their whereabouts being reported.

The *Ajax* had indeed been lost with all hands, while the *Lord Howick* had gone down on 14 September. The *Oxford* sank on an unrecorded date but was officially missing from the date recorded above.

There were two vessel victims on 29 October. The Ramsgate fishing smack *Boy Jack*, on returning to harbour, reported the loss in a mine explosion of her sister vessel, *Our Tom*. No trace of the crew of three, Skipper Larkins, Ted Maxted and George Haffenden, had been seen. The other casualty that day was the trawler *Rosella*, which struck a mine when returning from Faeroe.

Luckily, eight of the crew of 10 were rescued by the Shields trawler *Raider*. In early November 1914, the Board of Trade held an enquiry at Grimsby into the circumstances attending the death of William Sperring, skipper, and Peter Petersen, mate. It was shown that the disregarding of Admiralty instructions had been the cause of the sinking of the trawler and the subsequent loss of the two men. The verdict given was that they had met their deaths by drowning through the vessel having been blown up by an explosive mine. It was also proved that the vessel was in the midst of a minefield which the skipper had been warned about prior to leaving Grimsby.

A contemporary writer, Commander EH Currey, recorded in *How We Kept the Sea* the circumstances attending the loss of the drifters *Copious* and *Fraternal*:

On November 2, an enemy squadron appeared off Yarmouth and opened a furious cannonade shorewards but did not succeed in hitting anything except the coast-guard gunboat *Halcyon*, which was slightly damaged. One of the crew of this ship was seriously wounded. A few hours after the departure of the German ships, a British submarine, *D.5*, struck a mine dropped by the retreating cruisers off Yarmouth and sank with the loss of all on board except two officers and two men. Two steam drifters, the *Copious* of Yarmouth and the *Fraternal* of Lowestoft, struck mines about the same time in the same waters and sank. Only one of the crew of the *Copious* out of 10 was saved. Four men were saved from the *Fraternal* and six were drowned. The shooting of this German squadron seems to have been beneath contempt and they were in such a hurry to get back home that they did not even stop to sink the little *Halcyon*, which ship would have been an easy prey for them. ... From the calculations of fishermen who saw the whole affair, some hundred and twenty shots in all were fired. The fishermen in the first instance mistook them for British ships and one man, as they passed close by, waved a friendly teapot at them; to which the German sailors replied by shaking their fists.

The sole survivor from the *Copious* was young Frederick George Read from Yarmouth, who related how the vessel's nets had been fouled by two mines and each one had had to be cut away before the drifter got clear. She had been on her way to Yarmouth with her catch when the final and fatal encounter with a mine occurred. Read had saved himself by clinging to what was left of the wheelhouse until picked up some 20 minutes later by the steam drifter *Primrose* of Lowestoft, which landed him at that port. At a formal enquiry held at the Customs House, it was found that the vessel had been lost through striking a mine and that the loss of life had been unavoidable.

The day after the attack on Lowestoft, the former Fleetwood trawler *Mary*, employed as a minesweeper, went down due to a mine explosion, taking her skipper, William S Greenaway RNR and seven men, with her. In company with two other trawlers, the *Columbia* and our friend the *Driver*, she was attempting to sweep a field off Great Yarmouth, in the vicinity of Smith's Knoll. Her consorts closed and were able to pick up six survivors.

The loss of the Lowestoft smack *Speculator* (LT 1050) formed the subject of another enquiry held on 23 November 1914 at the Customs House. The vessel, missing since 9 November, had carried a crew of five hands, all of whom were lost. In the opinion of the owner, William Lane Jr, who gave evidence, she had been destroyed by a mine. The Collector agreed there seemed no doubt whatever that such was the case.

The Hartlepool trawler *Doris Burton* left Aberdeen for her home port on 21 November and nothing further was heard of her until towards the end of January 1915, when her owners, Messrs RH Davison and Company, received news that the Danish steamer *Avance* had picked up a lifeboat belonging to her.

In the memorandum by Charlton mentioned earlier, the following officers and skippers were specially commended for their services in connection with the sweeping operations off Scarborough:

Allerton	**Skipper William RNTR**, drifter *Eager*, No. 202, kept to his station in heavy weather, also standing by the SS *Gallier* after she had been damaged by a mine.
Belton	**Skipper Thomas B RNTR**, drifter *Retriever*, No 223, kept to his station, marking the safe channel for shipping when all other drifters were driven in by the weather
Boothby	**Lieutenant H RN**, also attached to HMS *Pekin*.[62] When Trawler No. 99 [*Orianda*] on which he was serving was blown up by a mine on the 19th, he successfully got all his crew (except one, who was killed) to safety. Boothby was again blown up on 6 January 1915 in Trawler No 460 [*The Banyers*].
Crossley	**Lieutenant CV RN**, again from HMS *Pekin*. While sweeping on the 19th, three violent explosions occurred close under the stern of his ship, Trawler No. 465 [*Star of Britain*]. He controlled the crew, and crawled into a confined space near the screw shaft himself, discovered the damage, and temporarily stopped the leak sufficiently to enable the pumps to keep the water down and save the ship.
Parsons	**Lieutenant Godfrey Craik RN**, HMS *Pekin,* displayed great skill and devotion to duty in continuing to command his group of trawlers after having been mined in Trawler No. 58 [*Passing*] on 19 December.[63] On this day his group exploded eight mines, and brought to the surface six more, Trawler No. 99 being blown up, and Nos. 58 and 165 [*Boreas*] damaged, all in the space of about ten minutes.
Preston	**Commander (later Captain) Lionel G RN**, on the minesweeper HMS *Skipjack* proceeded at once, on 19 December, into the middle of the area where mines had exploded to give assistance to damaged trawlers. He anchored between the trawlers and the mines which had been brought to the surface and sank them.
Scott	**Sub-Lieutenant WL RNR**, drifter *Principal*, went alongside the trawler *Garmo* in a dinghy, at considerable risk to himself and his boat, to rescue a man as the vessel was floating nearly vertical with only the forecastle above water. She turned completely over and sank a few minutes after he left her.
Snowline	**Skipper Ernest T RNTR**, drifter *Hilda and Ernest*, No. 201, performed his duties as commodore of the flotilla of Lowestoft drifters under Chief Gunner Franklin RN in a most satisfactory manner. He kept to his station in heavy weather, standing by the SS *Gallier* after she had been damaged by a mine.
Thornton	**Skipper George W RNTR**, also on the *Passing*, displayed great coolness and rendered valuable assistance to Parsons in controlling the crew when the vessel had been mined.

Tringall	Skipper T RNTR, trawler *Solon*, No. 66, went, on his own responsibility, to the assistance of the steamer *Gallier*, which had just been mined on Christmas night. It was low water at the time and dark and the steamer was showing no lights, so had to be searched for in the minefield.
Walters	Commander Richard H RN, AMS Staff, who was in charge of the whole of the minesweeping operations during the period.
Wood	Lieutenant WG, RNR, trawler *Restrivo*,[64] No. 48, did excellent work in going to the assistance of damaged trawlers on the 19th and performed the risky duty of crossing the minefield at low water when sent to bring in the *Valiant*, which had been disabled by a mine.

The demise of the Lowestoft smack *Queen of Devon* (LT 83) was witnessed by Harry Howard, skipper of the smack *Sis*. He saw a vessel some three-quarters of a mile away which he was sure was the *Queen*, blown up on Sunday 20 December. She was towing her rig on the starboard side when suddenly he saw her enveloped in smoke. Neither he nor his men saw any trace of wreckage or of the crew when they reached the scene. In David Butcher's *Following the Fishing*, Arthur Collins, son of the skipper bearing the same name, recorded:

> My oldest brother was deckhand on her and he went down too. That happened a week before I was born and I was entered on the roll o'dependents in the Low'stoft Fishermen's Widows and Orphans Fund the day that I was born. My mother said I was the youngest one they'd ever had on their books.

The day before, the former Grimsby trawler *Orianda* referred to above, one of a number attempting to clear the mines laid off Scarborough by the German cruiser *Kolberg*, struck a mine when assisting the minesweeping gunboat *Skipjack* and sank in 10 minutes with the loss of one man. A fellow-GY trawler, the *Garmo*, engaged in the same operation, detonated a mine on the 20th. Six men were killed, including Skipper Thaddeus Gilbert RNR.

In *Daring Deeds of Merchant Seamen in the Great War* published in 1918, Harold FB Wheeler related how HM Minesweeper *Night Hawk*:

> …came into contact with a mine while on duty ridding Scarborough's South Bay of prize packets filled with trotyl which the Germans had flung overboard after their cowardly attack on the North-Eastern seaside resort. The mine-sweeper was from three and a half to four miles off the town when she struck something which the skipper likened to a rubber ball because a deadening concussion followed. The explosion was so terrific that ten seconds later, the vessel had entirely disappeared. Probably the entire bottom was blown to pieces and the poor fellows below fell through into the water with the machinery. The more fortunate members of the crew, including Harry Evans, the skipper, were hurled overboard all drawn under by the suction of the sinking vessel. Five went down with the ship – or rather, what remained of her.

The *Night Hawk* was lost on Christmas Day, 1914. Miss Newnham, of the Grimsby RNMDSF, wrote in the *Toilers of the Deep* lamenting this loss and that of the trawler *Ocana* on Christmas Eve, just as preparations had been made for the men coming home for the holiday. 'We can understand', she stated, 'how deep a shadow has been cast on the festive season.'

During 1973, one of the inshore trawlers working off Scarborough fouled her nets on an underwater obstruction, which broke up before it could be brought aboard. The object was part of the bow of a steam trawler. Some brass letters reading NIGH... confirmed it was from the *Night Hawk*. The find is today in the small museum at Scalby Mills, Scarborough.[65]

1915 Minefields and Victims
Minelaying by Germany continued apace in 1915. No fewer than 480 mines were laid in the Eastern Dogger Bank area yet despite the density of this field not a single British vessel of any size was lost in it. Sweepers disposed of 69 of the mines and the swell of the winter sea probably cleared the rest. A total of 360 mines were laid in the Humber approach and were responsible for the loss of four British and five neutral steamers, plus three minesweepers. The field was defined by May, during which 127 mines were swept up. By the middle of July it was clear.

Fields aimed directly at the Grand Fleet were laid by the auxiliary cruisers *Meteor* in August 1915 and *Möwe* in January 1916. The *Meteor's* 380 mines were deposited by night in the approach to the Moray Firth. The first alert came from a Cromarty trawler making a routine sweep on the morning of 8 August. The destroyer *Lynx* was lost the same day and the sloop *Lilac* had her bows blown off. The offending cruiser was for her part sunk the next day by British cruisers. A channel was cleared along each shore and 222 mines were removed. As a protection against similar attacks, the rest of the field was left unswept but by the time of the final clearance in 1918 it contained only four mines.

By April 1915 the minesweeping forces had expanded greatly and were distributed as follows: Grand Fleet, 6 gunboats, 1 sloop and 9 trawlers; Scotland, east, 47 trawlers; Humber, 6 paddlers, 30 trawlers; Lowestoft (war channel), 47 trawlers; Harwich and Nore, 33; Dover, 12; south coast, 24; west coast, 4; and Clyde, 6 paddlers (fitting out).

Although the havoc caused by submarines attacking fishing vessels is covered in the next chapter, the year 1915 saw an important development in the use of U-boats for minelaying. The Flanders Flotilla commenced these operations then and their mines were first discovered off the South Foreland on 2 June 1915. These were laid by small 'UC' boats, equipped with 12 cylindrical mines with charges of 350 lb of TNT, carried in vertical chutes. The capture of the stranded *UC.5* on 27 April 1916 and its subsequent public display allowed its mechanisms to be viewed in leisurely detail. She was eventually scrapped in 1923. Submarine minelaying imposed a heavy strain on the minesweeping forces at Harwich, Dover and the Nore, these being the areas mainly affected at first. Coastal navigation was greatly hampered by the continuous location of small groups of mines giving rise to an incessant stream of orders for the diversion or stoppage of traffic.

According to the Germans, 648 mines were laid between Grimsby and Dover by submarines in 1915, nearly half of them in the Lowestoft area. From June until the end of the year, according to *British Vessels Lost at Sea* (1919), mining casualties in the North Sea were relatively light among fishing boats, with just eight victims. October and December were even 'blank' months. Among patrol and sweeper vessels, by contrast, the situation was, according to the same source, more serious, with seven losses in August alone, six in October and four in December (the *Carilon* was lost on Christmas Eve and the *Resono* on Boxing Day).

The pages of the *Fishing News and Fish Trades Gazette* reported as missing or lost through mines further vessels not subsequently listed officially, including the *Doris Burton* from Hartlepool, referred to previously, and the *Dovey, Yarmouth, Cassiopeia, Fitzroy, Viceroy, Dominican* and *Perseus* from Grimsby, the latter with the loss of ten lives, including that of the skipper.

Attacks by enemy surface vessels had not ceased entirely. A brace of Hull boats was lost in May, beginning with the patrol trawler *Columbia*, torpedoed off Foreness on the 1st. On the 18th, three trawlers (the *Duke of Wellington, Euclid* and *Titania*) were dispatched by a TBD in the north-west section of the Dogger Bank and their crews taken prisoner.

Grimsby suffered grievously. A detailed list which appeared in the *Grimsby Daily Mail* of 15 December 1915 gave the number of local trawlers and the numbers of crews lost through various causes during the year. No fewer than 55 vessels and 269 lives had been lost. Dependents had been provided for from the compensation fund and in some cases by private charity. The most severe loss of life had been from the trawler *Horatia* on 29 March 1915, when 14 men perished, the *Minotaur* lost 11 hands and three vessels lost 10 men each. In monetary terms, the average value of each trawler had been £4,000.

Mines in home waters claimed only two auxiliary vessels in early 1915; the sweeper *The Banyers* and the patrol vessel *Bedouin* on 6 January and 13 February respectively. Ordinary fishing vessel losses were also light (two in January, none in February and one in March), although May was a black month for sinkings, with the foundering of the *Uxbridge* on the 3rd, the *Don* on the 6th, the *Hellenic* on the 8th, the *Angelo* and *Sabrina* on the 21st and the *Condor* on the 29th.

An April loss was that of the Grimsby trawler *Recolo* in the North Sea on the 26th. An explosion occurred on board in which two men were killed and seven wounded. The vessel foundered shortly thereafter, the survivors being picked up by the Hull trawler *Sebastian*, which conveyed them for medical treatment to a warship. It was not certain whether the explosion was caused by a mine or, as Skipper Gladwell thought, a torpedo. She is, however, officially listed as a mine loss. GF Sleight, JP, interviewed by the *Grimsby Telegraph* on the day after the tragedy, stated that the *Recolo* was the ninth vessel he had lost since the outbreak of the war. She had been a comparatively new boat, being only four years old, and had cost him at least £8,500. The nine vessels had cost an average of £9,000 each. The loss of the *Recolo* was additionally distressing since in a few minutes she would have been homeward bound. When the explosion occurred, she had completed her trip and was making her last haul with a good catch. Every man of the eight on deck was injured by flying fragments. The ship began to founder immediately and it was only with great difficulty that the wounded men managed to launch the boat and escape as the ship sank, taking the second engineer, Fred Smith of Grimsby, with her to the bottom. Fred Aisthorpe of Boston, the trimmer, died of wounds while in the small boat. The crew rowed for six hours in a sorry plight before being picked up.

On 3 May 1915, the *Uxbridge* had a mine in the net when the gear was hauled. As the net reached the side of the vessel the mine exploded and the vessel was so severely damaged that she sank in ten minutes. Her crew of nine, of whom three were wounded, were just able to escape in their small boat and were lucky enough to be picked up by another trawler.

The *Don* was blown up by a mine in the North Sea on the night of 6 May. The skipper, William Carrick and deckhand Stanley Hargreaves were the only survivors of the crew of nine. Two men had been on watch when Carrick went up on deck to make arrangements to haul in the gear, but before a start was made the vessel was struck and lifted out of the water. There was a terrific explosion and he knew no more until he found himself in the water surrounded by a lot of boards. He clung to these and then saw Hargreaves holding onto some other wreckage. His ship had completely disappeared. Although he searched all round, he saw no sign whatsoever of any of the remaining seven men of his crew. As all had been below when the explosion occurred, none of them would have had much chance of getting clear. He kept alongside Hargreaves on the boards, but there seemed no hope of their being rescued. Hargreaves had been injured and was losing a lot of blood and Carrick himself had received a nasty wound on the side of the head. Mercifully, they were seen and picked up by the paddle boat *Devonia* after half an hour and taken below for treatment. The officer in command, having heard the fate of the trawler, made a thorough search of the vicinity for any possible survivors, but there were no signs of life amid all the wreckage. The *Devonia* reached Grimsby the next morning and the men were taken to hospital suffering from injuries and shock.

On 8 May 1915, another Grimsby trawler, the *Hellenic*, was blown up by a mine caught in the trawl. This came from a field which had been laid by the German light cruisers *Stralsund* and *Strassburg* on 17 April. Three of the crew of nine hands were never seen after the explosion. The remaining six, after being three hours in their boat, were picked up by a patrol steamer and landed.

On 18 June 1915, Sir Luke White, Liberal MP for Buckrose in Yorkshire's East Riding, held an inquest in Speeton on a body identified as that of Robert Heritage of Scarborough, skipper of the trawler *Condor*, referred to above, which had been missing since 29 May. RW Crawford, managing owner of the vessel, said it had left Scarborough at 2.30 p.m. on that day and at 10 o'clock that night there was a tremendous explosion. Although this occurred some six miles from Scarborough, the sound was heard on the sea front. Three other trawlers from that port near which the *Condor* had been fishing during the day returned to the scene but found only small portions of wreckage. Heritage's body was retrieved later. Despite being a very powerful swimmer, he had drowned. The jury returned a verdict of 'found drowned from the trawler *Condor*, which was sunk by a mine on May 29, 1915 off Cloughton, near Scarborough.' The coroner and jury expressed sympathy with the bereaved widow and son and other relatives and also with the relatives of the remaining eight members of the crew who had been lost.

The Grimsby trawler *Devonshire* brought into her home port the sole survivor of her sister ship, *Cheshire*, the fortunate man being Walter Dorkin, the chief engineer. Both vessels were owned by the North Lincolnshire Steam Fishing Company, better known as the 'Wold Company'. Dorkin, of New Cleethorpes, owed his life to the fact that he happened to be on duty in the engine room when the mine struck the vessel. The explosion occurred at about 5.30 p.m. in the North Sea on 14 July. Part of the engine room was shattered and he rushed on deck. Directly he reached the deck, the *Cheshire* sank under his feet, leaving him struggling in the sea. He could find no signs of the remaining eight members of the crew and was certain they were all either killed by the explosion or drowned. A deckhand by the name of Kelly, who lost his life, had joined the vessel when it was ready to leave Grimsby on its fishing voyage, fatefully substituting for the deckhand scheduled to sail on her. After swimming clear of the wreckage, Dorkin noticed what appeared to be a buoy and went towards it, intending to cling to it for support. When he got near one of his legs became entangled in some wire and he realized with horror that he was caught in another floating mine. It was an agonizing time, but he never lost his head and fortunately managed to free himself and swim away. The *Devonshire* had been fishing in the locality and fortunately the skipper heard the noise of the explosion. He at once steamed with the vessel in the direction of the sound and discovered Dorkin swimming. The exhausted engineer, who had been struggling for just under an hour, was taken on board her.

Yet the odd vessel was lucky. In July 1915, the RNMDSF monthly, *Toilers of the Deep*, recorded that when the trawler *Aquarius* arrived at Grimsby, Skipper Ringwood reported that a large mine had been found entangled with the trawl boards. As it might have exploded at any moment, he had ordered the crew into the boat for safety. They had waited for a while, but nothing happened. They had returned to the ship and he had then cut away the gear and buoyed the mine so that it could be picked up. Once ashore, he made a sketch of it and passed it to the authorities, together with details of the mine's exact location. [66]

On the afternoon of Saturday, 24 July, the Grimsby trawler *Perseus*, belonging to the Grimsby and North Sea Steam Trawling Co. Ltd, was lost with the whole of the crew of 10 hands. The trawler *Lindum*, arriving at Grimsby on the following Monday, brought in the bodies of John Constantine (skipper), William Pickett (mate) and George Monkton (deckhand). The other bodies were not recovered. The trawlers *Lindum*, *Ventnor* and *Perseus* had been fishing within sight of each other when a powerful explosion was heard. Skipper Staples of the *Lindum* later stated that he thought his own vessel was being shelled by a German submarine. However, he saw a huge column of smoke where the *Perseus* had been and when this cleared the vessel had disappeared – blown to smithereens. The *Lindum* and *Ventnor* steamed to the spot but there were no signs of life among the wreckage and only three bodies were to be found. After recovering these, Staples steamed around the vicinity for nearly an hour in the hope of picking up other members of the crew but none were sighted.

The steam trawler *Tors* of Grimsby was blown up by mines in the North Sea on 30 July with the loss of eight of her crew of 10 hands. The official report stated that she had been struck by not one but two mines, the second one causing her to sink immediately.

Many other ports, of course, sustained losses from time to time during the year. Four fine Aberdeen auxiliary trawlers went down during the last six months of 1915. The *Briton*, built by Hall Russell for the city's Standard Steam Fishing Co. Ltd, had been taken up for minesweeping in February. She was mined and sank off the Longsands in the Harwich area. Of the crew of 15, there were only three survivors. The *Ben Ardna*, owned by Richard Irvin & Sons Ltd and taken up for minesweeping at the outbreak of the war, was mined and sunk off the Elbow Buoy while on duty. Two men died. The *Javelin* was sunk when sweeping in the Thames estuary, in a field probably laid by *UC.6*. Also lost when on naval service was the *William Morrison*. Owned by the Pioneer Steam Fishing Co. Ltd., she was one of several vessels named after one of their skippers. Just two months old, she was mined and sunk near Sunk Head buoy off Harwich. Three ratings were killed.

The outlook at the end of 1915 was far from bright, and in spite of the better design and greater number of its ships the minesweeping service was barely able to meet the strain. Appendix 2c details the ex-fishing vessels hired by the Admiralty which succumbed to mines when on service during that year.

Tributes to Sweepers

Many tributes were paid by the public, the naval authorities and the press in recognition of the hazardous but determined work performed by fishermen and others as minesweepers during this difficult period.

The impressions of a visit to the Grand Fleet by Frederick Palmer appeared in *The Times* on 7 September. In these he stated that:

> In all, Britain has 2,300 trawler minesweepers and other auxiliaries outside of the regular service duty on blockade from the British Channel to Iceland, and in keeping the North Sea clear. Their reservist crews have been most zealous in performing their important part in overcoming the kind of naval warfare which Germany has waged.

All through the winter, these men cheerfully performed their arduous and dangerous work, with no guarantee of safety from submarines despite protection in some cases from armed vessels. Nothing could lessen the risk of destruction from a torpedo discharged from some unseen foe or, above all, from a mine which had perhaps drifted from its field.

After the war, in *The Auxiliary Patrol* (1923), naval writer EK Chatterton acknowledged the part played by humble fishermen in assisting the naval forces:

> It is, indeed, a remarkable tribute to the trawlermen, whether still fishing or enrolled under the White Ensign, that some of the most important minefields were revealed by these seafarers. By this means the lives of ships, peaceable and warlike, were saved over and over again.

And in his 1935 book devoted to the minesweepers, *Swept Channels,* Taffrail (Captain Taprell Dorling) confidently declared:

Ask any man who served at sea between 1914 and 1918 which was the most perilous, monotonous, and bitterly uncomfortable work of the war afloat, that which demanded the greatest hardihood, courage, individual resource, and unfailing good seamanship. The reply, nine times out of ten, and justly, I think, will be: 'The work of the minesweepers.'

Chapter 7

Sea Wolves Roaming

To the German Submarine Crews

Brave men! whose deeds your country's honour blot,
O gallant seamen, who befoul the seas!
Assassins of the deep! We blame you not –
The crime is theirs who set you tasks like these;

Who dare not fight, but keep their battle fleets
Hidden in port, and send you forth to drown
The crews of merchant ships, to match their feats
Of dropping bombs on a defenceless town;

Not you we scorn, but them, your lords, who throw
Your lives like loaded dice in their vile game.
O gallant men, who strike the coward's blow!
O seamen, doomed to prostitute your fame!

SR Lysaght[67]

A number of dramatic successes marked the opening of the Germans' submarine warfare: on 2 September 1914, *U.21* was approaching the Firth of Forth when she sighted the cruiser HMS *Pathfinder*. It took only one torpedo to send her to the bottom, with 259 of her crew of 360. Three more cruisers succumbed within an hour of each other on the 22nd. HMS *Aboukir*, *Cressy* and *Hogue*, anchored off the Hook of Holland, were torpedoed with the loss of 1,462 British sailors. The perpetrator was Otto von Weddigen in *U.9*, whose orders had been to patrol the waters between the Dutch coast and the English Channel. The submarine enjoyed further success on 15 October, sinking the cruiser HMS *Hawke* 60 miles off Aberdeen with the loss of 525 lives, while on the 31st, *U.27* sank the British carrier HMS *Hermes*. For rescues by fishing craft from the cruisers, see Chapter 13.

On 7 October, a U-boat had made its way into the naval anchorage of Loch Ewe, on Scotland's west coast, to which the Grand Fleet had been moved following a torpedo attack – mercifully unsuccessful – by *U.15* against the battleship *Monarch* off Fair Isle, as early as 8 August. The submarine was rammed at that location the next day by the British cruiser *Birmingham*, with the loss of all 25 of her crew. She was the first U-boat loss to an enemy warship in the war.

After further submarine scares, part of the fleet was moved again, this time, as we saw, to Lough Swilly. Scapa, its northern base, would be targeted again later in the year: *Kapitänleutenant* Heinrich von Hennig, commanding *U.18* – a fast boat with a maximum surface speed of 14 knots – overcame the navigational difficulties of the approaches by following an ancient steamer taking supplies into the anchorage. But no ships were home – they were out making a sweep of the North Sea. He had, however, proved that the base was virtually undefended.

It was a trawler which was instrumental in preventing Hennig from taking the vital intelligence back to Germany and returning with a U-boat pack to wreak havoc among anchored capital ships. As *U.18* passed through Hoxa Sound, she was spotted by the armed trawler *Dorothy Gray*, which charged at the submarine, ramming her before she had time to dive. The submarine was further damaged by the destroyer HMS *Garry*. Hennig, trying everything possible to evade his pursuers, was finally cornered by a pack of destroyers and his submarine scuttled. He and his crew were captured. Because nothing more was heard from *U.18*, the Germans assumed she had been caught and destroyed in attempting to enter the Flow and that the anchorage was indeed impregnable. All further plans to attack it were therefore called off. By February 1915, Scapa was ringed by a range of anti-submarine defences which stood unchallenged for the rest of the war – save for a desperate suicide mission in the final hours of the conflict when a German submarine, manned entirely by officers, perished at the harbour entrance.

The enemy sought to attack Britain's economy with a campaign against its supply lines of merchant shipping. In 1915, however, with their surface commerce raiders eliminated from the conflict, they could depend only on the submarine to conduct such operations.

The campaign against commerce began on 20 October 1914 with the scuttling by *U.17* of a British merchant steamship, the *Glitra*, after the crew was evacuated. It was the first recorded instance of a merchant ship being captured or sunk by underwater craft. A number of other sinkings followed. To the Germans, it now seemed that the submarine would be able to secure an early victory where the commerce raiders on the high seas had failed. On 30 January 1915, they took the campaign to a new level by torpedoing two Japanese liners – the *Tokomaru* and *Ikaria* – without warning (Japan was an Allied power). Launching their first unrestricted submarine campaign, they next announced, on 4 February, that from the 18th they would treat the waters around the British Isles as a war zone. In it all Allied merchant ships were to be destroyed – indeed, no ship, whether enemy or not, would be immune.

Yet the German submarine campaign yielded less satisfactory results than the Allied blockade against the enemy, which was preventing almost all trade for Germany from reaching that country's ports. Although seven Allied or Allied-bound ships were sunk out of 11 attacked during the first week of the campaign, 1,370 others sailed unmolested by German submarines. In March 1915, during which 6,000 sailings were recorded, only 21 ships were sunk during the whole month, while in April 23 ships from a similar number went to the bottom. Countermeasures, such as nets, specially armed merchant ships, hydrophones and depth charges, were clearly having an impact.

It was, however, the growing hostility of neutral countries which hurt the Germans even more. Any sympathy those countries may have had for them on account of the British blockade began evaporating with their declaration of the war zone. Their attitude was triggered by the torpedoing and damaging in February 1915 of the *Belridge*, a Norwegian tanker carrying oil from New Orleans to Amsterdam, in the English Channel. This was Norway's first casualty in the war zone. Following the Germans' continued, albeit occasional, sinking of neutral ships, undecided countries soon began adopting a hostile stance when there was a threat to the safety of their own shipping.

A major turning point and massive error was the sinking by a German submarine, on 7 May 1915, of the British liner *Lusitania* en route from New York to Liverpool. Warnings had admittedly been posted in the American port and it must be conceded also that the vessel was carrying 173 tons of ammunition. Yet 1,198 of her nearly 2,000 civilian passengers were drowned, and among the dead were 128 US citizens. The tragedy caused a wave of indignation to sweep across America, yet the US Government clung to its neutrality policy. It responded by sending several notes of protest to Germany. Nevertheless on 17 August, the *Arabic*, which also had American and other neutral passengers on board, was sunk by the Germans. They undertook, following a renewed US protest, henceforth to ensure the safety of passengers before sinking liners, although it was only after yet another liner, the *Hesperia*, was torpedoed that Germany, fearing further US provocation, took the decision to suspend its submarine campaign in British home waters and west of the British Isles.

Fishing Vessels as Targets, April-May 1915

The sinking of fishing vessels began in April and would increase in frequency during the spring and into late summer.

Oberleutnant zur See Johannes Spiess was second-in-command to von Weddigen in the diminutive *U.9* which won the first great naval victory of the First World War by sinking the *Aboukir, Hogue* and *Cressy*. He subsequently described[68] how the sinking of fishing craft became official policy in early 1915:

> On February 4th, six weeks before Von Weddigen took the long dive to the bottom of the North Sea, the Emperor arrived at Wilhelmshaven. He inspected the naval forces and we were all presented to him. At the conclusion of the ceremony, we were informed that the All Highest had signed a proclamation 'declaring the waters around Great Britain and Ireland a war zone.' That meant the opening of the so-called 'unrestricted submarine commerce warfare,' which was to be waged against all enemy merchant ships encountered in the waters that had been declared a war zone. The U-boat was proving itself to be a far more effective weapon than any of us had dreamed. With its success came the idea of a submarine blockade.
>
> ...I took command of *U.9* and off we went on our first cruise, the purpose of which was to play havoc with Allied merchant shipping. *One of our tasks was to drive the great British fishing fleet away from its regular haunt* [author's emphasis]. We captured and sank scores of smacks off Dogger Bank. This was far less glorious than gunning for armoured men-of-war, and less exciting. But it supplied many unexpected thrills, at that.

He then went on to describe his encounter with the Hull trawler, *Merrie Islington*, which will be recounted later.

A foretaste of things to come was described by the Government Secretary, Treasurer and Registrar-General of the Isle of Man (and Admiral Fisher's nephew), Bertram E Sargeaunt, MVO, OBE in *The Isle of Man and the Great War*. On 23 February, a Peel fishing boat was attacked by an enemy submarine. The *Girl Emily* had put to sea at about 4 p.m. and was fishing for cod some 10 miles off her home port when a U-boat appeared and came alongside. The commander asked the skipper, John Hughes, whether he was fishing and when told he was, brought his submarine round to the *Girl Emily*'s starboard quarter. When about 100 yards away, he opened fire. Hughes was at the tiller at the time, and the first shot struck a stanchion barely a yard away from his feet. He was severely wounded in the face with splinters, some of them entering around his eyes and affecting his sight. The U-boat then fired three further shots, which penetrated the bulwarks and the sail of the fishing boat. The Germans then came alongside and demanded the catch of fish.

On another occasion, the date of which is unrecorded by Sargeaunt, a Manx fisherman named Dickie Lee was taken on board an enemy submarine and exhaustively interrogated with regard to certain matters connected with the Island. He was kept on board the U-boat for the whole of one night and was told that after breakfast on the following morning she would be sinking other vessels and that he would be put in a boat belonging to one of them to get back to the Island. This he managed to do in due course. When narrating the story of his imprisonment to the authorities, he stated that during his captivity he was able to observe a chart of the Irish Sea on board the submarine which was 'marked in a peculiar way' and which yielded interesting information.

Lee's experience was one of many where fishermen spent time on U-boats while their vessels were sunk and before being cast adrift. Such was the fate which befell, on the night of 1 April 1915, the first three U-boat fishing vessel victims of the war: the North Shields trawlers *Jason* and *Nellie* and the Milford-registered trawler *Gloxinia*. The perpetrator was *U.10*, commanded by Fritz Stuhr, and the location was about 40 miles from the Tyne.

The first to suffer was the *Jason*, the submarine firing two shots at her from a gun on deck. The fishermen at once took to their boat. The submarine came towards them and ordered them to come on board, as their small boat was required. Stuhr, who spoke good English, said he was going to destroy the *Jason*. 'When did you start to sink fishing boats?' the skipper asked. 'We have orders to sink everything,' replied the commander. 'This is war, and you started it.' When the *Jason*'s men were in the submarine they were treated to coffee, bread, and tobacco. The Germans said their vessel was a new one with a 3,000-mile radius. She carried wireless equipment.

A party of Germans then got into the small boat and went to the trawler, which they sank with bombs. Still keeping the *Jason*'s crew on board and towing their small boat, the submarine then headed for the *Gloxinia*, the crew of which were given five minutes to get off in their boat. The trawler was then sunk.

The crew of the *Jason* were then ordered to return to their small boat, the commander of the submarine saying, 'If I don't see another craft I will tow you to the coast, because I am going to pay the Tyne a visit.' The two crews were put on board the trawler *Rhodesia* and the submarine then set off to attack the trawler *Nellie*, which suffered the same fate as the others. Her crew was picked up by the Lowestoft trawler *Girl Kathleen*. The crews of all three steam trawlers were landed the next morning, Good Friday, at North Shields fish quay.

This initial attack caused an observer to comment wryly in the *Fishing News* of 10 April 1915:

> The German submarines have extended their piratical campaign in a new direction. Fishermen are now included in the category of non combatants who are exposed to the depredations of the enemy's 'under sea boots.' Of this new policy the North East Coast has just had a particularly impressive lesson, for three Tyne trawlers have been sunk off the mouth of the river. The enemy are evidently strong believers in the theory that small fish are better than no fish.

Although Germany had had a relatively feeble force of submarines at its disposal when the war began (only 29 – extremely primitive – submersibles, two of which were out of service for repairs and three not fully completed), another dozen vessels had been added to the fleet when the first unrestricted U-boat campaign was declared in February, although the several submarines that had been sunk must be subtracted from the total. The Germans little thought, however, that the war would last long enough for the boats recently commissioned to be of any use. When this thinking was found to be wrong, they began turning out submarines as fast as they could, but even then there was a lapse after the Battle of Jutland when the yards were occupied with repairing surface vessels.[69]

The commanders knew the potential of their boats all along. In *The Log of a U-boat Commander, or U-boats Westward, 1914-1918*, Ernst Hashagen wrote:

> In the struggle with England the submarine was an important weapon: finally, indeed, it was the deciding factor. Westward we cruised in our boats, throughout the months and years. There stood our enemy, England: there, where the sun sank daily into the sea. In the west, where the Atlantic swell rolled against the rocky shores of the Island Kingdom: there, where the trade-routes lay, were the very arteries of the British Empire: there was the wide and storm-tossed battlefield of the U-boats. Westwards we sailed – always westwards. There, and in battle with England, the fate of Germany was destined to be decided.

Interestingly, no auxiliary fishing vessels were sunk by U-boats in home waters in 1915, although there were two losses in the Mediterranean from that cause (the net drifters *Restore*, sunk by gunfire in the Adriatic on 12 October and the *Lottie Leask* – mentioned previously – dispatched in the same way on 18 December off Albania).

A third Shields trawler was lost in April. The crew of the *Lilydale* arrived home on Friday the 30th and reported that at noon on Wednesday, when 75 miles off the Tyne, they were attacked by a German submarine. The first intimation they had of her was when she fired three shots over their bows at about 500 yards distance. She then approached and the crew was ordered to leave the trawler. They were taken on board the U-boat and some of the Germans boarded the *Lilydale*. The commander pulled down the trawler's ensign and seized her chart and papers. A bomb was placed on board, and five minutes later there was a terrific explosion, and the trawler sank stern first. A patrol boat was seen approaching, and the trawler crew were hastily transferred to their own boats, from which they were rescued. There was running fire between the submarine and the patrol boat. The submarine was at last seen to dive by the crew of the trawler and they saw no more of it.

Four Grimsby trawlers – the *Acantha, Zarina, Vanilla* and *St. Lawrence* – went down between the 5th and the 22nd inclusive with the loss of 20 lives.

The *Acantha* was torpedoed without warning and sunk off Longstone, her crew of 13 being rescued by the Swedish steamer *Tord* and landed at Blyth. The crew took to the boats but, while they were launching the craft on the weather side, several shots were fired at them but no one was hit. After the crew had taken to the small boat the submarine crew continued to fire at them with rifles, and several shots hit the sides, making holes in the gunwales.

Contrast this with the action of the Royal Navy in April 1918. The Commander-in-Chief of the Grand Fleet reported having undertaken a sweep of the Kattegat on the 15th. The Admiralty announcement stated:

> Ten German trawlers were sunk by gunfire, their crews being saved by the British ships. There were no British casualties.

The May edition of the *Toilers of the Deep* commented on this terse report:

> That is the British way – especially the way of the Navy; and we are proud of and thankful for the noble spirit which scorns to wage war on helpless men. There is not a British fisherman who would have acted otherwise.

News of the destruction of the *Zarina* on the 7th was brought to port by the crews of the trawlers *Ruby* and *Pinewold*, who stated that while trawling within sight of a vessel they believed to be the *Zarina*, two German submarines came to the surface. Shortly afterwards a loud explosion was heard, and the trawler in the distance was seen to founder. The two trawlers steamed to the spot and saw a quantity of wreckage, but no signs of the crew of the sunken vessel. The submarines had dived and were not seen again. Evidently, no chance was afforded to the *Zarina*'s crew to take to the boats. Nine lives, including that of the skipper, were lost.

With the destruction of the *Vanilla* and the *St. Lawrence*, the enemy stooped to new levels of callousness and cruelty. The *Vanilla* was torpedoed without warning on 18 April 1915, 53 miles E by S from the Inner Dowsing Light Vessel. As in the case of the *Zarina*, nine lives were lost, including that of the skipper. The following day's issue of the *Grimsby Telegraph* stated that two submarines working in company had been responsible, but their effort to secure a second trawler, the *Fermo*, failed, and the ship escaped after a chase lasting four hours. The skipper of the *Fermo* reported his experiences to the *Fishing News* representative. After seeing the *Vanilla* 'blown into thousands of pieces', he steamed among the wreckage but there was, understandably, no sign of any member of the crew. When only 400-500 yards from the submarine, a torpedo was discharged at his vessel. It failed to strike, however, and then the submarine, turning, made for the trawler as she kept on a full-speed pressure. Yet the *Fermo* always managed to keep clear of her, finally arriving at Grimsby unscathed.

In a piece entitled '*MURDER ON THE HIGH SEAS*, the *Fishing News* of the 24th indignantly declared that the loss of the *Vanilla*, with all hands, would meet with the strongest condemnation throughout the civilized world:

> This outrage against international law was marked by the utmost brutality and inhumanity. ... Every member of the crew of the *Vanilla* was drowned or killed by the explosion, but the *Fermo* escaped the pursuing submarine and brought the news to this country. Such an action as that of this submarine and the action of many others that have attacked merchant vessels and thereby caused the deaths of members of the crew is nothing but murder on the high seas. It is, of course, at present quite useless to protest to Germany or to Germany through neutral countries against such outrages as these. Our enemy at present is a law unto himself, and commits any crime without thinking twice about it if it suits his own book to do so, having not the slightest regard for international law or the usage and custom of warfare. But there is without doubt a day of reckoning to come, and such an outrage as the attack upon the *Vanilla* will, as the Admiralty said in the official statement, be kept in remembrance.

The writer went on to record the contrast between the German and British treatment of fishing vessels captured. No small German vessels had been molested and in none of the cases was any German life lost. In the regular editorial entitled 'Random Shots' in the same issue, the writer expressed the view that:

> So far from deterring these hardy sons of the sea from carrying on their work, the outrages have undoubtedly produced a quiet resolve to avenge the murder of their comrades, with the result that recruiting for the R.N.R. has received a very notable increase. The majority of skippers would welcome the arming of their trawlers with means of defence. Provide them with a gun, and they are confident that all fish of the 'U' species will speedily realise that the North Sea is a most unhealthy place in which to seek a living.

The *St. Lawrence* was sunk 88 miles E. ½ N. of Spurn Point on the 23rd. The trawler *Queenstown* brought in seven of the crew of nine hands. The other two, whose rescue the Germans prevented, had been drowned. Skipper J Hines graphically recounted what had happened:

> We were fishing on Thursday morning when about 11.30 a number of shells were fired at us. We could not see any signs of the enemy, but the weather was somewhat hazy. The shells kept flying all around us, but none of them hit the *St. Lawrence*. About half an hour later I saw a German submarine about two miles away and approaching us. The firing with shells still continued, and again without hitting the trawler. I had given orders to go full speed ahead, but the submarine gradually

overhauled us, and still kept up a shell fire. Altogether I estimated that 50 shells were fired at us, not one of which did any damage to the *St. Lawrence,* but a splinter from a burst shell struck me on the side of the head, and inflicted a scalp wound, which I am glad to say, is not likely to be serious.

As it was clear the submarine was bent upon sinking us, and no opportunity was given to us to get into our boat, except under the fire of shells, I decided to risk our lives, and I gave orders for the boat to be launched. This was done, and seven of us got into it. The third hand, J. Hanson, and a deck hand named P. Rogers, went below to get some lifebelts to put on. We waited in the small boat in order to take them in, but the captain of the submarine waved us away. The shells were still being fired, and we had no alternative but to row away from the trawler. Hanson and Rogers, who had again come on deck, jumped overboard and were swimming towards our boat. I turned it round, intending to pick the two men up, but the submarine again ordered us away and refused to let us pick the two men up. The submarine then went alongside the *St. Lawrence,* and a boarding party climbed on to the trawler. We could see them place bombs on the deck, and with these the *St. Lawrence* was sunk.

The two men were still swimming some distance away, and I made another effort to reach them, but before we could get near enough both men sank and were drowned. After the *St. Lawrence* had been blown up, the submarine went away. We then rowed in the direction where I knew some other trawlers were likely to be, and the *Queenstown* finally picked us up.

It seems incredible, but it is true, that the Germans were shelling the trawler for nearly three hours and never once hit her.

The mate of the *Queenstown*, which had been fishing in company with the *St. Lawrence*, attributed the escape of his own vessel to the fact that it suddenly became hazy, and the submarine could only deal with any particular trawler she had selected. When the *St. Lawrence* survivors were sighted they had rowed about four miles from their vessel.

The Germans issued a denial of the submarine's conduct. An official wireless message issued from Berlin on the 27th stated:

With regard to the sinking of the English trawler *St. Lawrence* on the 23rd inst., *The Times* states that the commander of the German submarine prevented the lives of two of her crew being saved. We learn that the German submarine forced the boat which was attempting to escape, to stop. The crew got into the boats, but three of the crew remained behind. They then made signals to the boat to return for them and sprang overboard, and only one of them was picked up, the other two being drowned. At this time the submarine was 250 metres away and in no way hindered efforts to save them. What *The Times* says, therefore, is slander.

In May 1915, the month of the *Lusitania* outrage, the piracy was stepped up, with a total of 22 trawlers going to the bottom. Hull came off badly, losing no fewer than 11 vessels, and Scottish boats now became victims (four of the six trawlers destroyed were from Aberdeen). Nor were submarines the only perpetrators – four vessels fell victim to a torpedo boat.

On the 8th, the *Fishing News* remarked:

The Germans have tasted fishermen's blood and have found it sweet. At any rate, they are now carrying on a warfare against fishermen with the same persistent ferocity as characterises their inhuman attacks on merchant vessels.

Taking up – not for the first time – the issue of arming fishing vessels, the periodical declared that such a measure would be ineffective 'unless it were done well and the boat were given such an outfit that she would be able to meet the enemy on a fairly equal footing and sink him', otherwise the sole effect of the trawler firing a shot would be that she would be sunk at once and the crew would not even be allowed to save themselves as they were at present by the more decent German captains. Another plan suggested for the mutual protection of trawlers was that they should agree to fish near each other and under the convoy of destroyers or patrol vessels. This meant, of course, that a skipper might not be able to go off alone to his favourite ground, but that was hardly worth doing if he was to be sunk for his pains. By all fishing together with Admiralty armed patrol boats close at hand, some measure of safety might be achieved.

The attack on the Hull trawler *Merrie Islington* on the 6th by *U.9* was gleefully recalled by Johann Spiess since the trawler screened her from a possible attack:

We had sighted a fishing steamer, the *Merry* [*sic*] *Islington.*[70] A shot across her bow, and her crew nearly jumped out of their sou'westers in clambering into their boats and pulling for shore. Why, they were on the beach even before we had time to draw alongside their deserted craft. Our chief engineer and his detail were about to shin up her side, pile below, and open her sea valves, when our quartermaster sang out:

'Destroyer ahoy!'

Ach! What a start that gave us!

A heavy fog hung over the sea, and the destroyer had stolen up on us through the mist. She was heading straight toward us. On she came, charging at full speed. Our old U-boat was not one of the quick kind, and there was no time to dive.

'Starboard engine full speed astern – port engine half speed ahead!' I barked. Mere instinct caused me to do it.

A moment later, and we had slid around behind the hull of the fishing boat. There was a chance in a thousand we had not already been observed. If we could only keep out of view of the onrushing destroyer! The swift enemy swept churning along. As she passed quite near us our boat was completely concealed behind the fishing smack. What luck! She hadn't seen us at all. On she sped and quickly disappeared in the fog. Then we proceeded to sink our prize.

This incident was not the only one of its kind. In another case a Grimsby skipper reported – and his crew confirmed his statement – that a U-boat came up quite close alongside and her commander and crew remained on deck for half an hour in silent contemplation of the fishermen. Not a word was spoken from ship to ship during the whole of the time, no attempt at attack was made, and neither vessel moved. It was a nerve-racking experience, and the fishermen admit that the tension was severe. Afterwards, when the submarine moved silently away, the crew of the trawler concluded that the pirate was taking shelter from something behind the protecting sides, waiting for the passing of a greater danger.[71]

Not all U-boat commanders were inhuman. The trawler *Lucerne*, of Aberdeen, late of Fleetwood, was sunk by a German submarine on 19 May

1915, 50 miles NE by N from Rattray Head. She was making for her home port with her catch of fish and was about 30 miles off Kinnaird Head when she was held up by a U-boat. The captain boarded the trawler and, with a great display of courtesy, ordered the crew to take to their boat. This the crew had no option but to do, but it was at once evident that she was in imminent danger of sinking as she was leaking badly. The captain of the submarine observed this, and took the *Lucerne*'s crew of nine on board his vessel, while he proceeded to the trawler. The submarine then made up to a Danish vessel, the *Urda*, and transferred the trawler's crew to that ship. The *Urda* then made headway for Fraserburgh Bay, and signalled a report to the shore. Pilot boats went out and received the *Lucerne*'s crew aboard, landing them at Fraserburgh, whence the men proceeded to Aberdeen.

Another commander effectively saved the crew of the Aberdeen trawler *Crimond* by a scrap of material he removed from the vessel before sinking it. The trawler was sunk after an hour-long chase on 19 May, 60 or 70 miles east of Wick. A small boat with a torn rag of canvas for a sail and with the master and crew of the *Crimond* on board limped into Wick Harbour after an arduous and perilous voyage. The men had been afloat for 20 hours without any food but would never, Skipper William Morrison acknowledged, have reached land had it not been for the makeshift sail.

The Summer Onslaught

The toll of sinkings among civilian craft, high in May, soared in June to no less than 60 – two a day. Now a disturbing new element entered the picture: the targeting of the humble fishing smack.

In *Business in Great Waters* (1977), John Dyson wrote:

> The diminishing fleets of sailing smacks suffered cruel fates. 127 smacks were sunk in the North Sea, 62 in the Channel and 60 on the west coast, a total of 249, with a loss of fifty-three lives. U-boats did not waste torpedoes but surfaced nearby and sent over a small boat with armed men who laid time charges. The crews were cast adrift in their boats. About 178 smacks were scuttled in this way, 54 by gunfire, 8 by mines, and the remainder by other means such as fire.

The June 1915 victims – all Lowestoft vessels – were lost in clusters, beginning on the 3rd with the *E & C*, 40 miles SE by E from Lowestoft, and the *Boy Horace*, 50 miles SE from Lowestoft. Both these smacks, and indeed all their sister-vessels, were captured by submarine and sunk by bomb. On the 9th, the five vessels *Edward*, *Qui Vive*, *Britannia*, *Welfare* and *Laurestina* went to the bottom. In the case of the latter two, the *FTG* of the 12th erroneously reported that they had been sunk by a Zeppelin, although further research has revealed that these wooden sailing trawlers were captured and sunk by time-bomb. The following day, the last victim of the month, the *Intrepid*, was likewise sunk by bomb, 60 miles SE from Lowestoft. Later in the war, some smacks would be armed and able to reply.

Those little boats were, mercifully, sent to the bottom with no loss of life. The same could not be said for the trawlers *Victoria*, *Arctic* and *Argyll*, from whom six, four and seven men, in each instance including the skipper, died.

The Milford Haven trawler *Victoria* fell victim on 1 June in the Western Approaches. The cruel and heartless assault on the crew by *U.34*, commanded from 5 October 1914 to 11 December 1916 by Claus Rücker, has passed down in infamy. A masterly narrative of this grim episode featured in Alfred Noyes' *Mystery Ships (Trapping the "U" Boat)* of 1916; the incident was also narrated in E Keble Chatterton's *Fighting the U-boats*. Although an attempt was made by the vessel to escape, the skipper and five crew were killed by gunfire. The *Victoria* caught fire and was eventually sunk by explosives 145 miles from St Ann's Head, near Milford. Four survivors were taken on board the U-boat and later transferred to the Cardiff steamer *Ballater* for return to port. An excerpt from *U.34*'s log records the opinion that:

> ...only the captain knew the purpose that the vessel was acting as a guard vessel. The whole behaviour in any case makes it obvious that it was a guard vessel which fulfilled also fishing duties.

The following excerpts are from Noyes' vivid account of the destruction of the *Victoria*:

> She carried a crew of nine men, together with a little boy named [James] Jones – a friend of the skipper. ... They were about a hundred and thirty miles from land when the sound of a gun was heard by all hands. The boy Jones ran up to the bridge, where he stood by the skipper. In the distance, against the sunset, they saw the silhouette of a strange-looking ship. At first it looked like a drifter, painted grey, with mizzen set. But the flash of another gun revealed it as a submarine.

Skipper Steve Stevenson hesitated at first, then resolved to attempt an escape.

> The submarine opened a rapid fire from two powerful guns, and the first to fall was the little lad Jones. The skipper kept steadily on his course, with the boy dead at his feet. But the submarine gained rapidly and continued to pour a devastating fire on the helpless craft. The skipper was struck next and blown to pieces. The bridge was a mass of bloody wreckage and torn flesh. The next shell shattered the tiny engine-room and killed the engine-man. The *Victoria* lay at the mercy of the enemy. The submarine continued to close on her, and kept up a rapid fire, killing the mate and another engine-man, and severely wounding another. The four men who were left tried to save themselves. The boat had been smashed to splinters and they jumped into the water with planks.
>
> Careless of the men in the water, the submarine steamed up alongside the *Victoria* and sealed her fate by placing bombs aboard her. There was a violent explosion, and her wreckage, strewn over the face of the waters, far and near, was the only visible relic of her existence. Not till nearly two hours after this were the four numbed and helpless men in the water taken aboard the submarine.
>
> They were placed down below, and, one by one, closely examined by the commander as to the system of patrols in the neighbourhood. Dazed as they were, and hardly responsible for their actions, they one and all refused to answer their captors. Late that night they were told that the submarine was about to submerge, and, so far as they could gather, they proceeded below the surface for over twelve hours. ... During the night they were given some coffee and a biscuit each, and the wound of one man, who had been badly lacerated by a shell, was dressed by the ship's surgeon. They lay in the semi-darkness, listening to the steady beat and hum

of the engines, and wondering what kind of a miracle could bring them to the light of day again.

On the next morning the [Cardiff] trawler *Hirose* fell victim to the same submarine. She was no sooner sighted than she was greeted with a hail of shot. She stopped and lowered a boat, while the enemy dashed up. The commander of the submarine shouted through a megaphone: 'Leave your ship. I give you five minutes.' The crew complied – there were ten hands all told – and were ordered aboard the submarine, while the *Hirose* was blown up. After being given six biscuits each, the crew of the *Hirose* were put back in their boat. The survivors of the *Victoria* were ordered on deck and placed in the same boat. The submarine steamed away and shortly afterwards dipped.

It was very dirty weather at this time. There were fourteen men crowded in a small trawler boat, a hundred miles from home. A strong gale blew and the rain drenched them. By dint of baling out the water continually, till their arms were numbed, they managed to keep afloat. Twenty-four hours later, at six o'clock in the morning, they were picked up by the collier *Ballater* about sixty miles off the Smalls Lighthouse. Their condition was then indescribable. Soaked through and through, with the boat half full of water, battered to and fro by every wave, they had lost all hope, and were lying exhausted. Their bodies were stiff with cramp, and they were hauled on board the *Ballater* with difficulty.

But there, at least, they found the rough comfort of the sea. Each man was stripped and his clothes dried in the engine-room. Hot coffee and food and blankets kept them alive till they reached port.

But the ordeal had left its mark upon them all; and when examined as to his experiences on board the submarine, the boatswain of the *Victoria* – a man of over sixty years – seemed to be too dazed to give any coherent reply. All that he could remember was the scene on the deck of the *Victoria* before the crew took to the sea; and his description was that of a shambles, where six of his mates lay drenched with blood, some with their heads blown off, others screaming in agony with arms and legs blown off; and, in a chaos of escaping steam and wreckage, the little boy Jones lying dead on the bridge.

The incident was described by the *Western Daily Mail* at the time as one of the most appalling submarine outrages perpetrated in Western and Irish waters amongst small craft. It also noted that a Cardiff trawler skipper later lost his ticket for a number of years for failing to stop and pick up the survivors.

For Alex Clarke of Ilford and his sister Mrs Delia Clarke of Badgeworth, Cheltenham, the event remains a personal tragedy. Skipper Steve Stevenson was their grandfather. Other crew members were also relatives. The grandchildren have some consolation in knowing that a plaque to the *Victoria* and her crew is displayed at the Tower Hill Memorial, London. Some years ago, at the official Merchant Day service they, with Alex's wife, Betty, laid a wreath there in memory of this tragic event.

Only four days after the *Victoria* went down, there was more loss of life yet the crew evaded capture. The steam trawler *Arctic*, whose story was also recounted by E Keble Chatterton in his *Fighting the U-boats*, was 77 miles SE of the Spurn on 5 June when attacked:

She had just completed her fishing when the gear was being hauled for the last time before starting for home. All the men were at the ship's side stowing things for the trip back, when unexpectedly a few hundred yards off, rose to the surface a submarine, and without any warning opened fire. It was as instant as that.

The first shell struck the Skipper, who was leaning on the ship's rail, and he fell into the sea dead before the eyes of his son a little farther aft. The next shot struck two deck-hands who were engaged in dragging the net aboard: they were both killed. Since it was obvious that the German meant to slay them all, the rest of the crew raced aft to get the boat launched, but even while so endeavouring another shot arrived and instantly wiped out the Mate. It was almost miraculous that the other five got away in the boat, for the shells still rained on the *Arctic* till they saw her finally sink under this bombardment. Pulling hard at the oars, the five were glad to notice a misty fog over the water such as one often finds hereabouts when the warmer weather is coming. It was this curtain of concealment which enabled the boat to escape, and after twelve hours she was picked up by the S.S. *Jurassic*.

Shortly after six o'clock on the morning of the 15th, the Hull fish carrier, *Argyll*, bound for Billingsgate from the Dogger Bank with a cargo of 1,520 boxes of fish, was torpedoed without warning by submarine and sunk, a quarter of a mile from the Sunk LV. Seven lives were lost, including that of Skipper Loads. Shattered by the terrific explosion, the little vessel went down almost instantly. Loads' body was landed at Harwich. Only a few days before this attack, the *Argyll* had rescued the crew of five men and a boy from the Lowestoft trawler *Intrepid*. Just a few weeks before the war began, she had taken out to the North Sea one of the very last of the volunteer Missioners who went to the fleets on behalf of the RNMDSF.

Among the trawlers, Scottish vessels fared badly that June. Between the 3rd and 5th inclusive, Aberdeen lost nine vessels. Commander EH Currey recorded, in respect of the *Evening Star, Ebenezer, Strathbran* and *Cortes* on the 4th, that they were sunk by a submarine that they mistook for a schooner, as she had rigged up her periscope and some sort of a spar with a sail arrangement. Their crews were landed in northern ports. The Dundee trawler *Queen Alexandra* was torpedoed without warning by a German submarine when the crew were working their gear. A patrol boat came to the crew's assistance and took them off. Although she tried to tow the trawler ashore, the latter sank when a mile from land.

By the 12th, the *Fishing News* was reporting:

> The submarine activity has been especially marked off the north-east coast of Scotland, for of the vessels that have been sunk, 14 belonged to Aberdeen and Peterhead. To set against the dead loss of these vessels, there is the fact that they are mostly old boats. The Admiralty has commandeered all the better class and newer trawlers, and one result of this was that owners of boats which were very old and could not hope in ordinary times to compete with the newer vessels have tinkered them up where necessary and have been reaping a pretty good harvest.

Scottish waters claimed English victims, too, as in the case of three trawlers destroyed by submarine shellfire off Peterhead and whose crews were landed at that port. The *Persimon* of Grimsby and the *Gazehound* of Sunderland were both sunk on the 5th, while the Hull vessel *Dromio* (*Bromio* in *Fishing News* reports) was destroyed the next day. Its crew was referred to by one officer among their German captors as 'British bitches'!

On the 23rd came a massacre involving both English and Scottish vessels. No fewer than 13 were sunk, all but two between 35 and 50 miles east (predominantly ENE) of Out Skerries, Shetland. The same location claimed two more trawlers on the following day, the *Vine* from Aberdeen and the *Monarda* from Peterhead.

A website devoted to Scottish holidays[72] tells us that Out Skerries, also called the Outer Skerries:

> ...is the name given to a group of three islands in the Shetland Islands of Scotland. The islands are named Housay, Bruray and Grunay. On Housay and Bruray there is a total population of 80 and a bridge connects the two islands. The island of Grunay is uninhabited. On Housay and Bruray, there are shops, a fish processing plant, an airstrip, a primary school and the smallest secondary school in the UK, with a total population of two students. The mainstay of the economy here is fishing. ... A ferry from Lerwick and Vidlin provides a link with the mainland, but you can also fly here. The runway at the airport is gravel and is the shortest runway in the country.

According to *British Vessels Lost at Sea*, no loss of life through U-boats occurred during July (although a total of 26 men were killed through the mining of the *Cheshire, Perseus* and *Tors*, as described elsewhere). Yet the Grimsby trawler *Fleetwood*, not listed in that source, lost a crew member, according to a report in the *FTG* of 17 July:

> A German submarine made another raid on Grimsby trawlers fishing 50 miles from the Humber on Sunday morning [the 11th], sinking the *Syrian* and *Hainton* and subjecting the *Fleetwood* to a heavy shelling with shrapnel. The *Syrian's* crew were rescued by the *Helvetia* and the men from the *Hainton* were picked up after twelve hours by the Hull trawler *Earl*. The *Fleetwood's* boat was smashed by the submarine's second shot, the third completely wrecked the cabin and injured two of the crew, while a fourth, fired after the vessel had hove to, killed a deck hand named Horace George Gedge, a native of Yarmouth, and severely wounded the chief engineer and the skipper's 16-year-old son, who had gone for a pleasure voyage. It was only after the submarine officers had seen the *Fleetwood's* ruined boat launched and sink, and had seen the havoc wrought on the trawler's deck with the dead and injured lying in their blood, that they responded to the skipper's appeal not to drown them like rats The *Fleetwood's* decks presented a remarkable sight, the fore-deck houses rail, fixtures, etc., being riddled and smashed by the bursting shrapnel shells. At the inquest on the deck hand on Monday, the jury returned a verdict of 'Murder' against the crew of the German submarine.

As always, a number of other Grimsby vessels went the way of their sisters, while Hull sustained five losses, all in Scottish waters. They included the *Honoria*, illustrated in Alex Gill's *Lost Trawlers of Hull*, and noted there as one of four trawlers from the port which were lost twice. The first time was in 1901 when she was stranded at Cleveland; three Redcar men endeavouring to rescue her were drowned when their coble capsized. Aberdeen, for its part, lost three vessels. This prompted the *Fishing News* (published in that city) to comment, on 31 July, on how badly the port had fared through losses due to submarine warfare, not only in human, but also economic, terms:

The average trawler costs from £5000 to £8000 to build and equip, and working on an average of £5000 per boat as the value of the 28 fishing vessels lost, this represents the sum of £140,000 to Aberdeen trawl-owners.

A marked feature of both the July and August attacks was the targeting, with renewed ferocity, of the humble smack. In July, with 20 victims, their losses outnumbered those of steam-powered vessels (16) for the first time. All were sunk within a range of 15-35 miles from Lowestoft. They were mainly destroyed in clusters: four on the 12th, four on the 24th, three on the 27th and no fewer than eight on the 30th. *Young Percy* was the only single victim in one day, being captured and bombed on the 28th.

One sinking had features out of the ordinary. When in their small boats, the men of the smack *Speedwell*, destroyed on the 12th, sighted the trawler *Emerald*, which had been abandoned by her crew after being attacked by a submarine. They boarded the vessel, which had her foredeck slightly lifted, and took her into port. Other survivors were not so lucky. The RNMDSF Port Missionary at Gorleston recounted on 22 September how he had not long since visited in hospital a man who had, in the past, sailed in the Mission Ship and had had the misfortune during the war to have been in three fishing vessels destroyed by submarines. All the vessels had belonged to Lowestoft and in the last one the Germans fired on the crew as they were getting into their small boat. They lay at the bottom of it, wanting to get away from their smack that was being shelled. The third hand, named Baker, was trying to scull the boat away when he was shot through both legs. Miraculously, he survived without any medical attention and was eventually operated on after they had been picked up and landed in port.[73]

The list of officers and men who lost their lives from British fishing vessels in the period August 1914 to July 1915, as reported to the Board of Trade, was a stark reminder of the sacrifices made in that first year of war. The listings appeared in the September and October 1917 issues of the *Toilers of the Deep*. In nearly all cases the place of last abode was shown against the name of the victim. Analysis of these listings bears out the comment made accompanying them, i.e. that Grimsby suffered very heavily, with a predominant proportion of victims hailing from that port and the neighbouring locality of Cleethorpes. Specifically, the rounded percentages were 49 for Grimsby and 13 for Cleethorpes/New Cleethorpes, making 62 per cent in all. The figure for Hull was 8 per cent, that for Lowestoft 4 per cent and that for Aberdeen – surprisingly – 1 per cent.

The list was updated to include deaths reported to the BoT during August. It comprised 22 names. With 12 casualties, Grimsby's proportion was maintained, while eight Lowestoft victims were listed.

The only loss of life in that month resulted from the mining, 56 miles E by N from Spurn, of the *Grimbarian* on the anniversary of the war's outbreak, with six fatalities, and another mining on the 23rd, 40 miles N by W from Rattray Head, of the 290-ton Hull trawler *Commander Boyle*, from which three crew perished. This was a new vessel and Skipper Fox was making his first voyage on this, her second trip. These were two of only seven trawlers to be sunk during the month. In the case of the Fleetwood vessel *Thrush*, sunk on the 9th, the crew were in their lifeboat for about 62 hours. A patrol boat was finally sighted about 50 miles from the mainland and the men frantically waved their coats and blankets to attract attention. Even then they were mistaken for a submarine and the approaching vessel had its guns ready trained on them until they were recognized.

No fewer than 29 smacks and one small fishing boat, the *Lark*, were dispatched that August, all within 58 miles of the East Anglian coast. Half a dozen were destroyed on the 6th, 10 on the 11th and four on the 23rd. The crew of one of the latter group, the *Boy Bart*, was reported as having been landed in Holland. The losses of a number of Scandinavian merchant vessels were also reported by Reuters and Lloyds during this month of intense activity by U-boats.

Yet, looking at the bigger picture, the German submarine campaign was not having much of an impact on British shipping. In a lengthy editorial entitled *THE SUBMARINE WARFARE* in the *Fishing News* of 28 August 1915, it was pointed out, with support from statistics published by Lloyd's Register, that 'the damage inflicted by German submarine warfare is of infinitesimal proportions'. Even with its war losses included, the United Kingdom had actually suffered less in the way of depletion of shipping than the bulk of the world outside the belligerents. Another striking fact brought out was that British losses had been more than counterbalanced by additions to shipping, the tonnage in 1915 showing an increase of something like a quarter of a million tons. The writer concluded:

Altogether then no very appreciable damage has been sustained, proportionately reckoned, by the German policy of marine 'frightfulness'. The pretentious 'blockade' of Britain has not resulted, as the Germans fondly and foolishly hoped it would, in sweeping British shipping off the seas or even out of the war zone they were pleased to formulate. The intimidation that lay behind the threat of submarine attack has proved equally futile. It has simply been disregarded, our shipping trade being practically carried on as if German submarines had no existence. There is a cool courage here for which we may justly take credit, particularly in view of the pessimistic spirit so prevalent.

The position of German shipping, on the other hand, contrasted very unfavourably with that of Britain. The total tonnage of German vessels had been reduced from 5,459,000 to 4,706,000 – a shrinkage of no less than 753,000 tons.

Altogether, they have cut a very sorry figure in naval warfare, despite the piratical work of their submarines, and for the present at least their mercantile marine is simply a negligible quantity.

A Welcome Respite

These assertions were of little comfort to the owners and crews of the Lowestoft smacks, whose losses continued into September. Mercifully, however, this was the last gasp of the Germans' much-vaunted U-boat campaign, for nervousness over America's possible entry into the war following her increasing indignation at the lives of her citizens lost in wanton submarine assaults caused an about-turn in imperial policy. On 27 August, the Kaiser imposed severe restrictions on U-boat attacks against large passenger vessels and on 18 September 1915 he called off unrestricted submarine warfare altogether.

So the toll for September was half-a-dozen smacks sent to the bottom within the same general area as in August and with no loss of life (although in distant south Devon, eight miles S by W from Berry Head, Brixham, the smack *Albion* was sunk by a mine with three fatalities, including the skipper). As in the case of the *Boy Bart*, some men were landed in Holland. After rowing for some hours, the crews of the *Emmanuel, Victorious* and the Yarmouth-registered *Constance*, which were sunk on the 7th, 44 miles ESE from Lowestoft, were taken aboard the Dutch trawler *Firano* and landed at IJmuiden the following day.

The U-boat might appear invincible, judging by all the successful attacks against helpless fishing craft chronicled here. Yet during this first year of the war, an appreciable number of losses had been sustained among them. Visiting the Grand Fleet, Frederick Palmer, whom we met earlier, reported in New York that he had been shown:

> …maps marking points where German submarines have been sighted and the results of the attacks on them, classified under 'captured', 'supposed sunk' and 'sunk'. … When the question is asked [of] officers 'How did you get them?', they answered: 'Sometimes by ramming, sometimes by gun-fire, sometimes by explosives, and in many other ways we do not tell.' Officers and men on battleships and armed cruisers are envious of those engaged in submarine hunts, which is regarded as great sport.

Palmer remarked that although the submarines had played a more important part than many had anticipated, the methods of countering their attacks and of destroying them had also developed 'beyond expectations'. Securely ready at its base after initial abortive attempts to seek out German warships, the fleet could steam out to action directly the patrols continually sweeping the North Sea reported any signs of the enemy.[74]

One of the 'other ways' the officers did not tell was bound to have been the stratagem of a trawler operating in tandem with a hidden British submarine to lure an unsuspecting U-boat (the 'tethered goat' scheme). One of the older A, B, and C classes of coastal submarines was used. Submerged, and in telephone communication with the trawler, she would be released for action directly a U-boat was seen to surface. This ploy had first been used successfully on 23 June 1915 when the trawler *Taranaki*, with submarine *C.24* behind it, sank *U.40* off Aberdeen, leaving 29 dead and an unknown number of survivors. The method was deployed a month later, specifically on 20 July, when *U.23* fell into a trap set by HMT *Princess Louise* and the Royal Navy submarine *C.27*. Although 10 Germans survived, 24 were killed. But a price was paid for this complicated tactic the following month. On 4-5 August, the *C.33* disappeared, with the loss of 17 lives, possibly as a mine victim or through some accidental cause, at some stage after slipping her tow from the trawler *Malta* to return to harbour.

On the 29th, the trawler *Ariadne* was towing the submerged *C.29*, when the submarine was destroyed by a massive underwater explosion and again 17 lives were lost. Evidently, the pair had, due to navigational errors, strayed into the German minefield off the Outer Dowsing Lightship. These tragedies apart, the enemy cottoned on to these tactics and they never worked again. What was worse, all British trawlers (whether or not innocent) were now regarded by U-boats as potential Q-ships and treated accordingly.

'Marine traps' in the North Sea were, incidentally, complained against by Dutch fishermen in October 1915 because, 'besides catching submarines, they damage fishing nets'.[75]

A general sense of relief now prevailed in the fishing trade over the respite in attacks from U-boats. Commenting on the 'modified piracy', the *Fishing News* was hopeful that the American/German agreement would mean that a ship-master would no longer feel that the appearance of a periscope was the death-knell of his vessel and that the skipper would find ample time to collect his 'bits of things' before leaving his trawler as a target for the submarine's gun:

...a more comfortable prospect than at present, when the first warning he is likely to get is a shell through his wheel-house.[76]

The outcome was more than could be hoped for. No fishing vessels at all were sent to the bottom by U-boats in home waters in October, November or December. Not until 18 January 1916 would they again be targeted, with the long-suffering smacks bearing the brunt of the attacks. But that was in the future. For the moment, the fishing industry and the families of those who worked in it licked their wounds and took stock of what 1915 had brought them. Looking back on the sufferings of the year in the port of Grimsby alone, Miss Newnham of the RNMDSF reported:

The year 1915 will long be remembered in the fishing port of Grimsby. A year of sorrow and of suffering! Instead of our usual peaceful avocations, our men are wearing the King's uniform, and seeking to protect the shipping by sweeping the mines, and guarding our shores by the patrol-boats. Several of the men were severely wounded, but, thank God, they have made a good recovery. ... Sorrow and suffering on the sea mean the same reflected in the homes; in what degree may be realised perhaps when I say that in 1915 we have lost 31 of our vessels, with all hands!

I fear I cannot describe all the work this has meant in visiting, providing for temporal needs where necessary and in trying to comfort and cheer whenever able.

In the RNMDSF journal *Toilers of the Deep*, nothing but contempt was expressed for those who had brought such needless sorrow to the fishing community and to the nation:

Cowardly and murderous beyond expression has been the conduct of most of the German submarine commanders in the prosecution of the so-called blockade of British shipping, but they have utterly failed to terrorise the men of the North Sea, and some day, when the whole and full truth can be revealed, we shall know how deeply we are indebted to our fishermen.[77]

Chapter 8

Captivity

The slow hours creep and creep,
Till night the day redeems.
Thank God who gives us sleep!
Thank God who sends us dreams!

By day, barbarian Powers
May herd us in their pen;
The night – the night is ours;
They cannot hold us then....

Six prisoners in one stall!
O'er each his blanket spread!
And no man there at all,-
Each on his errand sped.

The gates are open wide, –
Those gates they guard by day;
Through those broad gates we ride, –
Away, away, away! ...

From *Night at Ruhleben* by Joseph Powell, Captain of the Camp[78]

The Germans did not wait for war to begin before taking prisoners. Towards the end of July 1914, when relations with Britain were strained, the harbour authorities at Hamburg, Stettin (as we saw in Chapter 1), Bremerhaven, Lübeck and various other German ports began placing obstacles in the way of British ships leaving for sea. Initially, these were detained on various pretexts, such as the danger of them being sunk through the measures being taken to defend the approaches to the ports. However, this feigned concern did not lead the Germans to warn incoming ships not to enter the ports, so that day by day the number of British vessels in German harbours steadily increased.

Writing in the partwork *The Great War* in 1916, FA McKenzie pointed out:

There were many British people in Germany at the time of the outbreak of war, people who had settled in Germany for business, holidaymakers, tourists, people visiting health resorts, and the like. There were many Germans in England. The Germans in England were given time to leave. Our Government gave them every facility for leaving, and went so far as to permit large numbers of able-bodied men of military age, Army reservists, to get back to Germany from other lands in vessels that came under the supervision of our Fleet. The Germans acted very differently. British vessels in German ports were prevented from leaving some days before the declaration of war. British people, except under special circumstances, were not allowed to leave Germany after war was declared.

Numbers of Englishmen, such as sailors at ports, and visitors, were arrested as spies before the war broke out, and were detained, often without trial. Others were kept under semi-arrest. Even old men in the sixties and seventies who had gone for heart treatment to Nauheim were not allowed to go back until some weeks after the outbreak of war; and on November 6th, all Britons of whatever position were arrested throughout Germany and placed in internment camps.[79]

Britain's fishermen for their part would face wartime perils on the high seas with cheerful resignation but would later find the forced inactivity of internment especially irksome. Most of them would have already suffered the severe shock of being compelled to witness the calculated plundering and sinking of their vessels and the loss not only of their catches but also of many personal effects. Many would return home broken men, after suffering years of inadequate accommodation, hard labour, severely restricted food rations, poor health care and, in some cases, brutality. Their story is one that should be told, not only for its intrinsic interest but because it reveals how one occupational category responded to such circumstances and what attempts were made in their homeland to alleviate the conditions under which they lived.

Many were captured early on, with nearly half the vessels concerned falling victim to enemy surface craft towards the end of August 1914. Later, when U-boats held sway, their commanders often simply left the crews to survive in their open boats, being unable, or unwilling, to convey them to Germany. There were, however, notable exceptions, such as the case of Skipper Alf Rawlings recounted later. The enemy's policy became one of destroying fishing vessels as systematically as possible. The taking of prisoners was low on the list of priorities.

In the summer of 1915, the Board of Trade issued the first of several lists of merchant seamen and fishermen detained as prisoners of war in Germany, Austria-Hungary and Turkey. The total number recorded was 375, of whom 73 were prisoners in Turkey and 17 in Austria. Of those who were prisoners in Germany, 228 were fishermen – four out of five captives. Of the 108 vessels named, 23 were fishing boats, owned by 12 owners.

By the summer of 1917, the list of fishing vessels exceeded 50. The last one recorded by the BoT and in *British Vessels Lost At Sea* as yielding captives was the *Virgilia* on 3 June that year, skippered by the Alf Rawlings mentioned above. The valuable record he has left of his experiences is reproduced in this chapter.

Looking at the bigger picture, the number of fishermen interned in enemy (and neutral) countries was admittedly a tiny proportion (around 1 per cent) of the multitudes of British military, naval and other civilian prisoners held captive during the war. On 1 August 1916, the total number of POWs officially given out by the German Government was 1,646,223, of whom 30,903 were British. Yet these hardy seafarers endured the same hardships and deprivation, hunger and disease, as their fellows scattered across the length and breadth of the *Vaterland* and elsewhere.

In Volume III of *The Merchant Navy*, Archibald Hurd states that by July 1917 the number of captive seamen in Germany had risen to an aggregate of 2,752, besides 71 men held prisoner in Turkey and 41 in Austria-Hungary. Well over half (1,503) were held at Ruhleben, near Berlin, the next highest total being at Brandenburg (670). The notorious military camp of Sennelager in Westphalia is not listed separately in this source. The place would haunt many a fisherman for the rest of his life.

The Board of Trade statistics relating to fishermen captives at that time revealed that, of their number, 138 belonged to Grimsby, 65 to Boston, 26 to North and South Shields and 18 to Hull. There were 222 interned at Ruhleben, 81 at Brandenburg, 13 at Dulmen, 10 at Hameln, two each at Ströhen and Soltan, one each at Karlsruhe and Haveburg, and ten at places unknown – in all 342. Three had died in captivity and 21 had been released.

The First Captives

On 22 August 1914 alone, seven Boston boats – the *Flavian, Indian, Julian, Marnay, Skirbeck, Walrus* and *Wigtoft* – fell into enemy hands. Of these, six were owned by the Boston Deep Sea Fishing & Ice Co. Ltd. and one by Fred Parkes of that port. An eighth vessel, the *Capricornus*, hailed from Grimsby and was operated by the Grimsby & North Sea Trawling Co. Ltd. There were nine crew aboard each vessel, save the *Marnay* on which there were 10, making the total number of men captured 73.

The three days 24-26 August were equally disastrous. No fewer than 15 vessels were captured by torpedo boats, all but three of them (the *Kesteven, Lindsey* and *Porpoise* belonged to the beleaguered Boston Deep Sea Fishing & Ice Co. Ltd.) from Grimsby. The Grimsby & North Sea Trawling Co. Ltd. lost a further three vessels – the *Chameleon, Pegasus* and *Pollux*. Various Grimsby owners sustained the remaining losses. These enemy operations yielded a further 139 captives, so in the space of five days, well over 200 hapless fishermen fell into enemy hands.

Among this number, several have left us vivid accounts of their capture and captivity, prominent among them being RW Kemp, skipper of the Grimsby trawler *Lobelia* and former lay reader in Hamburg for the Missions to Seamen. His story was recorded by Walter Wood in his 1918 book *Fishermen in War Time* and, in less detail, in the *Fishing News*. It is an extraordinary fact that parallel accounts have also been left us by the steward (Arthur Higgins) and second engineer (William Manley) from the same vessel.

Kemp had been at sea for over 40 years, having been master of a vessel since the age of 25:

> I had started from home to earn my livelihood a fortnight before Christmas in 1913, and I worked away up to August 1914, when the war broke out. We had come into port, Grimsby, not knowing what was going to happen, and lay there for ten days before the insurance people would permit us to go to sea. When we sailed it was on condition that we fished within a certain limit.
>
> …We sailed on August 20, and the day before a friend and myself went for a bit of pleasure to a little country place a few miles from Grimsby.
>
> …We went to sea, and he was blown up by a mine and I was taken prisoner by

the Germans and after sixteen months of shameful treatment was sent home a broken man.

...The *Lobelia* was in the nor'-west corner of the Dogger, what we call the Nor'-West Rough, and there were other steam trawlers about. It was fine, calm summer weather, and we were in good spirits, for we had 160 boxes of fish in the fish-room, the result of five days' fishing. We were making another haul and then we were going home.

...It was three o'clock in the afternoon, and we were hauling. We had got our otter-boards up to the gallows and should soon have had the cod-end of the net unlashed when we saw, all at once, ten torpedo-boats and three cruisers, and as soon as they hove in sight we knew that they were Germans.

...One torpedo-boat rushed up – she was like an eel, and must have done forty knots. She came quite alongside and made her bow rope fast to our bow; then, while the German sailors covered us with revolvers, the commander shouted to me and ordered me to produce the ship's papers. That was all he wanted – he bullied and scurried us about, and would not let us stop to get any of our belongings.

...There was nothing for it but to obey, and so we jumped on board the torpedo-boat, and immediately Germans were sent on board the *Lobelia* and put bombs in her engine-room, then the torpedo boat cast off and steamed some distance away, and we saw the *Lobelia* blown to pieces.

...All this had happened so swiftly that I could hardly realise it, then I saw that there were two other fishing crews on board the torpedo-boat, and that these craft were scurrying round destroying all the British fishing vessels that they came across. These fishing vessels were absolutely helpless, and had not the slightest chance of escaping or defending themselves.

...It was only ten minutes after we left the *Lobelia* that she blew to pieces, carrying with her every stick and stone that I possessed – and it was the same with the rest of the crew; and in addition to that our 160 boxes of fish and the fish that was in the net – all that we had worked so hard for – went to the bottom. The Germans were in a hurry and wanted to get the job over, and they made no attempt to do anything but get the ship's papers.

Having done this to the *Lobelia*, the torpedo-boat commander went to another steam trawler – I forget her name, but she was a Grimsby boat – and did the same thing as he had done to us; so we had another fishing crew on board with us, making about forty fishermen in all. We were kept on deck, under an armed guard; but we were allowed to talk amongst ourselves. I must say that while we were prisoners at sea we were treated fairly well, under the circumstances; but once we stepped ashore and got under the military we copped old boots.

We were on board the torpedo-boat for about six hours, until nine o'clock in the evening. I could never find out her number or any marks on her, and I believe she had none; but, as I say, she was like an eel. Her commander was a young man of about thirty-five years, and he spoke very good English, as so many of these Germans do. He began at once to try and find out things, but we told him nothing.

He said, 'You have got no men; but we have got the men and we have got the food.' I remember those words.

The commander asked us a lot of questions about the British fleet and said he wanted to know the reason why we went to war with Germany; but we could say nothing.

The sailors gave us something to eat and drink, and we could talk, and were pretty free on board the torpedo-boat – she was not a destroyer; but soon we were to be more strictly treated, and that was when we were transferred to a cruiser. I suppose we were put on board the cruiser because the torpedo-boat was not big enough to house us.

The cruiser was a tidy size; she had three funnels, but one of them was false.

We were put down in the forehold of the ship, and armed guards were posted over us. There were portholes in the sides, but the dead-lights had been fastened down, so that the only light we had was from lamps. We could not, of course, see anything; but we were kept pretty well informed as to what was going on, and in a curious way, for the pilot came down to see us from time to time and told us what was happening. We knew, because we had seen them, that the cruiser carried a lot of mines on her after deck, and the pilot told us that she was going off to the English coast to lay them. We afterwards heard that she had thrown them overboard five miles off Blyth and off Flamborough Head; then the cruiser steamed away for Wilhelmshaven, with other ships. But the Germans were about as much afraid of their own mines as they were of ours, for we heard the cable rattle, and the pilot told us that we had brought up under Heligoland, where I had been ashore many at time in the old days of the sailing fleets, when the island was ours. I would have liked a peep at it again, but the Germans took good care that we should see nothing, and we were not allowed on deck.

The crew's experiences on board the cruiser were also vividly recollected by Arthur Higgins of Grimsby when he was released from captivity under an exchange arrangement in September, 1915:

After arriving on the cruiser we were treated with the greatest insolence. The captain accused us of having been laying mines, and though we denied this we were disbelieved. We were huddled together in a confined space ... and repeatedly addressed as swine and rotten English.

Skipper Kemp continues:

There we were, crowded below in the forehold of that cruiser, for two days and nights, with nothing but artificial light, constantly expecting to strike some horrible mine and be blown to pieces. But we were even more afraid of going athwart one of our own warships, for that would have put us down the locker. We should not have had the slightest chance of escape, so we were glad when we knew that we had reached the Wilhelmshaven that the Germans are so proud of. What it is really like I don't know – all I saw of it was some tall houses and a lot of shouting women and children who jeered at us and threw dirt and stones at us – two hundred helpless fishermen, who were marched four deep through the street; for the gallant German Navy had sunk about a score of fishing vessels – ten Grimsby and ten Boston – that could not defend themselves, and had made prisoners of the unarmed crews. Some of these craft had been blown up, as the *Lobelia* had been; others had been sunk with shot. On board the cruiser one of the officers – I do not know his rank – had tried to get something out of us about the British Navy; but he learned no more than the commander of the torpedo-boat had done.

We soon learned that the 200 fishermen prisoners had been captured by ten torpedo-boats and three cruisers. They had done the business of sinking the ships, but we did not see all of it, because the trawlers were working over a big area, and most of them were out of sight of the *Lobelia*.

William Manley from Hull would be imprisoned in Germany for over 19 months. On his return, he corroborated Kemp's and Higgins' testimonies to a representative of the *Hull Daily Mail*, but added that half a dozen baskets of good fresh North Sea fish on the *Lobelia*'s decks had been taken aboard the torpedo boat.

On the day the *Lobelia* was sunk, the trawler *Valiant* (GY 1178) sailed innocently out of Grimsby towards the same fate. What happened was recorded by a Dutch crew member, identified only in the trade journal as 'P.V.D. L-', who had been sailing out of Grimsby on an English trawler since December 1913. At 7 p.m. the following evening, they were fishing 10 miles off Grimsby in company with four English trawlers when they were approached by two German cruisers and three torpedo boats. One of the latter (*V.155*) came alongside and commanded the crew to come aboard. They were given a few minutes to pack their clothing and food. As soon as they had left the trawlers, the Germans opened fire and sank the *Valiant* with a few shots.

On board the *V.155*, the men found the crews of two other English trawlers which had already been sunk. Subsequently, the fishermen were transferred to the German cruiser *Stuttgart*. There they found the crew of the *Rideo* (GY 314), who had not been given time to take any clothing from their vessel before she went to the bottom. On board the cruiser, the food they were given consisted of coffee and sour bread and soup, and they were compelled to sleep on planks.

All four trawlers fishing in the neighbourhood of the *Valiant* were also sunk and the men taken aboard the other German cruiser, the *Albatross*. An hour later, the German fleet steamed at great speed in an easterly direction. On Thursday the 27th, at noon, the prisoners from the two cruisers were landed at Wilhemshaven and taken under military escort to the barracks. Later they were placed in gaol. On the Saturday, any crew members who were not English were liberated and given a free ticket to Bremen, where they slept that night on a shakedown of straw at the police station.

Another Dutchman on an English trawler – the *Seti*, sunk on 26 August, the day after the mass sinkings – was one JL Johnson, the only one of their number to be released, on account of his nationality. On his return to England in September, he stated in an interview how the same German team had been at work:

> Early on the morning in question, about 4 o'clock, we were fishing some 80 miles from the English coast when two German torpedo boats, accompanied by the enemy's cruiser *Albatross*, came in sight.
>
> One of the torpedo boats at once approached the *Seti*, and, coming alongside of our vessel, the Germans gave us peremptory orders to leave her as they intended to sink her. We were given five minutes in which to get aboard the torpedo boat before they did so.
>
> As soon as we had got safely on board the torpedo boat, the latter steamed away, and the cruiser then opened fire on the *Seti*, sinking her with two shots.
>
> The night before, about 6 o'clock, we had seen the German warship sink ... Grimsby trawlers ... which were fishing to the westward of us. According to what the German sailors told me, after taking off the crews of these vessels, the cruiser put in towards the English coast during the night and engaged in mine laying. Returning in the early hours of Wednesday morning they fell in with our ship, which remained in practically the same position throughout the night.

The torpedo boat which took us prisoners landed us at Wilhelmshaven about 11 o'clock the same evening (Wednesday), but the cruiser *Albatross* anchored off Heligoland that night, and landed her prisoners at Wilhelmshaven the following morning. We were marched straight from the warships, under an armed escort, to prison, being placed three in a cell.

Johnson remembered that there were 78 prisoners of war on board the cruiser *Albatross*. When ashore at Wilhelmshaven, he said that on the Thursday (27 August) they could hear the firing of big guns as though a battle were in progress. They understood from the Germans that the German fleet in the harbour were putting out to engage the British warships.

To weave together the various testimonies for clarity, a summary tabulation is provided below in respect of the movements and prisoner intakes of the two cruisers *Albatross* and *Stuttgart*.

Date/time	*Albatross*	*Stuttgart*
Mon. 24.8.14, night	Leaves Germany for minelaying operations	Leaves Germany for minelaying operations
Tues. 25.8.14, evening	At 7 p.m. , with 'another cruiser' (*Stuttgart*) and 3 torpedo boats, incl. *V.155*, attacks the *Valiant* and other trawlers.	At 7 p.m. , with 'another cruiser' (*Albatross*) and 3 torpedo boats, incl. *V.155*, attacks the *Valiant* and other trawlers. *Valiant* crew taken aboard the torpedo boat, which already holds two other crews. Receives all three crews, who join the crew of the *Rideo* already aboard. Total prisoners 40 or so.
	At 9 p.m. takes on board 4 crews from a torpedo boat, including the *Lobelia*'s. (*Lobelia* sunk at 3 p.m.). Total prisoners 40 or so.	
	Takes aboard 4 crews from the attacks described opposite. Total prisoners now around 80 (Johnson confirms 78).	
Tues. 25.8.14, midnight	Lays mines off Blyth and Flamborough Head. Flees eastward with *Stuttgart*.	Flees eastward with *Albatross*.
Wed. 26.8.14, night	Anchors off Heligoland all night. At 4 a.m., in company with two torpedo boats, sinks GY trawler *Seti*, whose crew are kept aboard the torpedo boat then landed by it in Wilhelmshaven (11 p.m.).	Anchors off Heligoland all night
Thurs. 27.8.14, noon	Lands POWs in Wilhelmshaven	Lands POWs in Wilhelmshaven

Wilhelmshaven

Wilhelmshaven was the most important strategic harbour in Germany and the main base of the High Sea Fleet. Vast sums had been spent on the harbour works and defences and on transforming it into a magnificently equipped dockyard. As well as two building slips, there were well-appointed basins for completing, fitting out and coaling warships. Barracks, training establishments, ammunition and torpedo depots, and the locks of the Ems-Jade Canal were also located there. The Jade river's navigable channel was so narrow that it could be easily closed by a chain of mines, while the harbour boasted massive locks which, when closed, rendered it completely isolated from the sea. Any vessels within it were thus secured against torpedo attacks. Moorings laid down outside for cruisers and small craft complemented the available accommodation. Long before a hostile force came within range of the harbour's 12-inch and 14-inch guns, it would have had to pass the works at Wangeroog, a small island bristling with guns and dominating the approach to the Jade channel. The colossal sum of £2,000,000 had been spent on fortifying the island.

William Manley recalled:

My first experience when I landed on the quay at Wilhelmshaven was to receive a blow from an umbrella on the head from a woman, who spat in my face and called me 'an English dog'.

Then we were marched to a naval prison to give our names and other particulars. Next, in threes, we were put into cells, the chief engineer (Isaac Dowson), the steward (Arthur Higgins) and myself were placed together in one cell. In that cell, we were confined three days being allowed one hour each day for the purpose of exercise. For breakfast, we had dry brown bread with a cup of coffee without either sugar or milk. After that, from 10 to 11, we had our exercise and at noon we were served with what the Germans called a basin of soup, composed of a few potatoes and what I would call greasy water. There were no signs at all of meat.

In the cells there was no furniture, and we had to eat, as we slept, on the bare floor. For tea, we had again a piece of dry brown bread and more coffee without sugar or milk. That went on for three days and then they took 147 of us, all fishermen, to a place at Emden, where we were all barracked together in a wooden hut and where we were in the charge of sentries with fixed swords, who were continuously knocking us about and insulting us. The guards were changed every four hours and we were closely watched to see that we did not get away. We could not leave the hut on whatever duty without two sentries being in attendance. We arrived at Emden at about eight o'clock in the morning, but we had nothing given us to eat until 1 p.m., when we were given a basin of what they called soup again without signs of meat. Among those with me were Harry Jackson of Hawthorn Avenue, Hull and Lawrence Kenny of West Street, Hull. We had more brown bread and coffee at night for tea, and nothing more than those two meals we had that day. There was no furniture of any sort in the barracks, and we slept upon heaps of straw, which we collected from a building adjoining. About eight o'clock, the next morning we had breakfast – a cup of coffee and a piece of dry brown bread.

For four days we remained in that barracks, and then they took us to a military place called Sennelager, in Westphalia. For that journey, we had 17½ hours in a train, in wagons used as cattle trucks from 1914, from which cattle had been turned.

Robert Kemp recalled being marched through Wilhelmshaven's streets with German soldiers on each side of them and the women and boys and girls shouting at them, and running after them and pelting them and that the prison cells measured about eight feet by five feet – just big enough to cage one man – yet four of them were put in one of the black holes.

> …there was not room to move. We could not lie on the plank bed and we could not sit on the tiny bench, so we just had to be cramped together, talking and sleeping.
>
> For four terrible days and nights we were in these awful cells, our only change being for one hour a day, when we were allowed to go out to a garden – and a blessed change it was to get out into open air and the sunshine and stretch our aching legs. The sentries brought us our meals, which we ate in the corridor outside the cells. If we wanted to get out for a wash or anything we had to ask leave of the sentries.

The Hell of Sennelager
The misery of the dark holes of the lock-ups in Wilhelmshaven was nothing compared with what Kemp and his fellow-fishermen had to endure at Sennelager. Higgins remembered that during the journey they were given no food or drink. After arriving at the camp, they had their clothes taken away and were given blue canvas convict suits to wear.

On the day after their arrival the Germans shaved one side of their heads and one side of their moustaches or beards as the case may be, after which they were marched into the camp square, where hundreds of German people jeered at them as they were paraded before them. However, among themselves they made the best of it and laughed at one another. One engineer, Robert Mann, of the trawler *Rhine*, who was 65 years of age, could not walk fast enough on the parade and was hurried along by the German soldiers kicking him. He would be released around Christmas the following year after he had been removed to the civilian camp of Ruhleben, bringing the cheerful message that all the Grimsby men in that camp were well and had little to complain of. This, as we shall see, was far from the truth and clearly intended to allay the concerns of loved ones and friends.

Almost immediately the men were thrown into the fields, and for three weeks they slept on the grass or, where there was no grass, on bare earth. They had no covering whatever. It was during the daytime that they lay on the ground and slept, because then it was warm and dry, with the sun out. At night, when there were heavy dews, they walked about and tried to keep warm. At the end of three weeks, the rainy season came on and the men got tufts of grass and built little huts, about as big as dog-kennels, and crawled into them for shelter.

Sennelager camp, Higgins remembered, was surrounded by electrified barbed wire. There were hundreds of English and French soldiers there, all of whom were repeatedly being jeered at. For food, doled out in the open, the men were given – after three days – a small loaf of black bread about half a foot long and four inches deep shared amongst three men. The fare was always sparse, mostly black bread and coffee, without sugar or milk, and occasionally a raw salt herring. Eventually, the prisoners were put under canvas. The exposure in the open during the cold September nights had, however, brought on inflammation of both Higgins' eyes and he suffered excruciating pain. He would beg the guard over and over again to let him see a doctor, but no notice was taken. At the end of November, when still under canvas, with only a bag of straw to rely on, the prisoners heard that the American ambassador was coming to inspect the camp. They were taken from the tents to the German soldiers' barracks and when the ambassador arrived he found each of them provided with a bed, with a fire in each of the quarters and good wholesome food. The visitor was surrounded by German staff officers, who took care that none of the men had any private confident conversation with him and he left apparently well satisfied. He was thus hoodwinked, although in no way to blame for the misunderstanding and the prisoners' plight – he had simply had no chance to learn the truth. As soon as he had left, the men were sent back to their tents and had the same miserable food doled out to them. Robert Kemp recalled:

> For dinner we had cabbage-water, the cabbage cut up into little bits. Sometimes a little bit of greasy fat pork was put into the water, but it was only by chance that you got one of those bits, about as big as the bowl of your pipe. At teatime you had coffee again, and then you got the black bread, which had to last you 24 hours, and that was only as big as your fist.

The canvas tents held about 600 men, and there they were packed like sardines. They were forced to lie on the ground, and all sorts of men were crowded together, foreigners and British – far different from the way prisoners of war were treated in England.

Kemp continues:

> Our being at Sennelager was a great time for the inhabitants, especially on the Sundays, when they would come by – Boy Scouts amongst them – and rush up to the barbed wire fences and tease and torment us and do all manner of things. As time went on we got so that we had no clothing, and no soap, and no means of washing our underclothing. Some of the men 'washed' their shirts by scrubbing them with sand. I tried one day, when it was bitterly cold weather, to 'scrub' my shirt by rubbing it on a bit of a wooden platform we had in the grounds, and it froze so hard to the woodwork that I could not get it off.
>
> In the winter we used to go about with our knees through our trousers, and we had no jackets to wear. I never had a pair of stockings or socks for the whole time I was there. My feet were wrapped up in rags, with old wooden Dutchman's shoes.

In December, when the weather became too bitter even for cattle to remain out, the men were transferred to some wooden huts. Three of them had to sleep on two bags of straw and most of it was verminous:

> For the first five or six months we had a cat-and-dog life. The Germans used to hustle us about, kick us, give us a crack with the butt-end of a gun or a prod with the bayonet, and when they were tired of that they would set a big savage dog on to us, a German brute, to hurry us up. The dog used to help the guard when we were hustled along the roadway to the canteen, about half a mile away, to get our dinners. The dog was a sort of man-hunter, and would go for anything. The brute was on a chain, which was held by a soldier, who let him out a certain length; but at times the soldier would slip the chain, so that the dog could fly at a helpless man.

I saw one of our fishermen cruelly torn in the legs by this savage monster, which had a craze for rushing at poor chaps from behind. And you dared not touch the beast or complain or do anything, if you did you suffered for it. The poor fellow that the brute bit complained to the head commander, and there was an enquiry on the job. And what happened? The man got lashed to a tree for two hours in the morning and two hours in the afternoon for complaining. And that was in the wintertime. He is now at home, but he still suffers a great deal with it, and was in hospital in Germany a lot because of the bites and the lashing to the tree. Can you wonder that as a result of such brutal and inhuman treatment men died through sheer exhaustion? They did. Several of our poor fishermen died, and they are buried in Germany – all through privation.

Robert Mann witnessed the incident with the dog, stating that the unfortunate victim of the harsh discipline had been the skipper of the Grimsby trawler *Zenobia* (J Blackmore) but that he had been punished by being lashed to a tree for two hours a day for four days.

Another victim of German brutality was a Grimsby fisherman (unnamed in the *Grimsby Telegraph* report and whose place of imprisonment was not specified) who had sailed for Messrs Letten Bros and who had been in captivity since the earliest days of the war. He was in hospital for nearly the entire period of his internment, having been brutally assaulted by one of his camp guards. His 'offence' (before any order against smoking had been issued) was that he stooped to pick up a half-smoked cigarette. When applying a light to it to enjoy a smoke, the guard struck him on the head with the butt end of his rifle. After that, his injuries necessitated his confinement to hospital, with operations, and the removal of several pieces of bone from his skull.

Kemp continued:

> It is impossible to describe in detail the awful sufferings of a prisoner of war. Before I was captured, I was an all-round athlete. What I have since gone through I would not have believed possible. Many Englishmen are suffering acutely from rheumatism or the results of fever. The daily drudgery and the bullying breaks down the proudest spirit. No insult is bad enough, and to the English especially the hatred is intense. In the camp, the Germans repeatedly posted up on news of great victories. At the time of the Scarborough bombardment, we had an awful time. They print a paper called *The Continental Times*. It is printed in English and was distributed to us. In big type we read: 'Britain no longer rules the waves. Britain hauls down her flag. For the first time in 100 years, Britain's shores have been bombarded. We, the Germans have done it!' And then followed an account of the raid. The stories we read in this paper made most of us believe that England was having a terrible time, and it was, moreover, very depressing. I fully believed on my way to England that I should find it half desolated, for we had been assured over and over again that the cities and towns were in ruins.

At nearby Paderborn camp, the men were similarly starved of unbiased news; Alfred Moore of Grimsby, captured on the *Seti* in August 1914 and released on age grounds in December 1915, stated they were never allowed to read a newspaper and thus remained in total ignorance as to the events of the war. When he left the camp, he was not allowed to take anything away with him, not even a scrap of paper.

The North Sea. This was the centre of sea power, where Britain's fishermen risked their lives daily against the elements and a remorseless foe. (Leyland, 1917)

A splendid 'real photograph' postcard, showing Scottish fisher girls hard at work in Scarborough; in the background, work is proceeding on the construction of the pier entrance. (Author's collection)

The Kaiser at the helm of SMS *Hohenzollern*. The caption reads *OUR HELMSMAN – OUR FUTURE LIES ON THE WATER*. The card was posted from Germany on 28 October 1905 to an address in Longsight, Manchester. On the reverse, the recipient wrote '*Kaiser Bill on his yacht*' and, at the foot of the picture, '*How do you like this?*' (Author's collection)

Herrings ready for dispatch at Campbeltown, near the Mull of Kintyre, Argyll. It was not only on the east coast and Islands that the 'silver darlings' were an important means of livelihood. (Author's collection)

Great Yarmouth, an important herring port, with serried ranks of drifters moored at the quay. (Author's collection)

Part of the fishing fleet in Lerwick Harbour, Shetland. It is easy to imagine this collection of drifters as the nucleus of a vital auxiliary for the Navy. (Author's collection)

The Crystal Palace in south-east London as depicted on a postcard sent on 5 January 1912. It would become an important training centre within a few years. (Author's collection)

Recruitment poster for the First and Second Brigade of the Royal Naval Division. (Via *www.royalnavaldivision.co.uk/*)

Admiral Sir Roslyn Wemyss, First Sea Lord, with Commodore Sir James Startin RNR, inspecting the guard of honour formed by men from the Armed Trawler Fleet, Granton, Scotland. (IWM Ref Q18975)

The crew of a British
armed trawler
drilling at Granton.
(IWM Ref Q18973)

The crew of a British
armed trawler
receiving gun
instruction at Granton.
(IWM Ref Q18974)

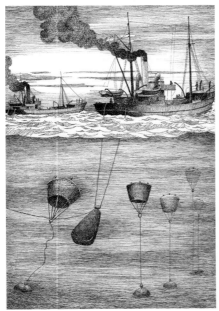

Illustration showing the
way a pair of minesweeping
trawlers used a weighted
wire rope stretched between
them to catch the mooring-
chain of mines and drag
them up from beneath.
(Drawn by Neal d'Enno)

Admiral Lord Charles Beresford (1846–1919) devised a scheme for employing trawlers on minesweeping work.
(Author's collection)

Punch magazine brings home to its readers how vulnerable fishermen and their vessels were to marauding U-boats. From the issue dated 14 July 1915.
(Author's collection)

First Trawler Skipper. (to friend who is due to sail by next tide). "ARE YE TAKIN' ANY PRECAUTIONS AGAINST THESE SUBMARINES, JOCK?"

Second Skipper. "AY! ALTHOUGH I'VE AYE BEEN IN THE HABIT O' CARRYIN' MY BITS O' BAWBEES WI' ME, I WENT AN' BANKIT THEM THIS MORNIN', AN' I'M NO TAKIN' MA BEST OILSKINS OR MA NEW SEABOOTS."

First Skipper. "OH, YOU'RE A' RICHT, THEN. YE'LL HAE PRACTICALLY NAETHIN' TAE LOSE BUT YER LIFE."

MINES EXPLODING IN THE SWEEP.

Mines exploding in the sweep.
(Drawn by Neal d'Enno)

The harbour, Lowestoft. The port became a major centre of minesweeping operations. (Author's collection)

A steam drifter shooting its nets. (Smith's Dock Co Ltd, Middlesbrough)

A steam trawler at work. The diagram shows the trawl warps and the method of dragging the great net on the bottom of the sea. (Smith's Dock Co Ltd, Middlesbrough)

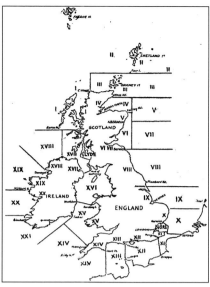

By December 1914, the British Isles were divided into 21 Auxiliary Patrol Areas for administrative purposes. (Chatterton, *The Auxiliary Patrol*)

The sinking of the minelaying steamer *Königin Luise* and the English cruiser *Amphion* in the Thames estuary on 5 August 1914, as depicted on a German postcard used in November 1915. Artist: C Schön, Berlin. (Author's collection)

Originalskizze.
Handkolorit (imit.)

Untergang des Minendampfers „Königin Luise" und des englischen Kreuzers „Amphion" vor der Themsemündung.

Anxious Mother. "COME AWAY, WILLIE! YOU NEVER KNOW WHEN THOSE GERMAN MINES MAY GO OFF!"

Fishermen's wives apparently knew a little about mines! From *Punch* dated 6 October 1915.
(Author's collection)

The caption to this German postcard reads 'Sunday, 9 August 1914. The English cruiser *Amphion* was sunk by a mine laid by one of the Hamburg-Amerika Line steamers, *Königin Luise*, in the Thames estuary.' (Author's collection)

Sonntag, den 9. August 1914. Der englische Kreuzer „Amphion" wurde durch eine vom Hapag-Dampfer „Königin Luise" in der Themsemündung gelegte Mine zum Sinken gebracht

Courage and skill overcame the mine peril: exploding infernal machines brought to the surface by trawlers.
(Partwork *The Great War*, Eds. Wilson & Hammerton)

M.L.'s GOING TO THE ASSISTANCE OF MINED TRAWLER.

Motor launch going to the assistance of a mined trawler.
(Drawn by Neal d'Enno)

Smacks at sea. A fine broadside view by George V Burwood (1845-1917) of LT 292 *Golden Oriole*, sunk by a mine in 1915.
(Courtesy Lowestoft Maritime Museum)

THE MINE PERIL IN HOME WATERS.

MINES & CLEAR CHANNELS IN THE

AUTUMN OF 1915.

Mine Areas
Headquarters of the Auxiliary Patrol Areas in Red.

By the autumn of 1915, the precise locations of a number of enemy minefields had been clearly established.
(Committee of Imperial Defence, 1922)

'All's well!' The men of a minesweeper greet a destroyer in wintry weather in the North Sea. Artist: FJ Mortimer FRPS.
(Partwork *The Great War*, Eds. Wilson & Hammerton)

Submarine in the North Sea – On watch. A German postcard produced as a 'Welfare Card' for the Imperial Association for the Support of German Veterans. Copper engraving by Professor Willy Stöwer.
(Author's collection)

A dramatic depiction by a German artist of the destruction of the three English cruisers *Aboukir, Hogue* and *Cressy* by *U.9* on 22 September 1914.
(Author's collection)

The captured minelaying U-boat *UC.5* photographed on the Thames. The 'exhibit' drew thousands of onlookers.
(Author's collection)

German submariners being rescued by the destroyer *Garry* on 23 November 1914. The *U.18* had been rammed by the trawler *Dorothy Gray* off the Scottish coast. Artist unknown.
(Partwork *The Great War*, Eds. Wilson & Hammerton)

The crew of the British steam trawler *Strathearn* (hired 1915-19) on her way to the fishing grounds. On one of her trips she had a narrow escape from a submarine which chased her. A 4-inch shell smashed her wireless cabin and severely wounded one of the operators.
(IWM Ref Q18963)

An unhappy group of fishermen now prisoners of war.
(*Toilers of the Deep*, December 1915)

A bird's eye view of Ruhleben drawn by GF Morrell and showing the camp in good detail.
(Author's collection)

Aerial view by GF Morrell of Smyrna and region. Fort Yeni Kale ('New Castle'), bottom left, was severely damaged by our battleships on 5 March 1915 and several subsidiary batteries were silenced. (Partwork *The Great War*, Eds. Wilson & Hammerton)

The Dardanelles, showing the Narrows. On these waters our minesweeping trawlers came under murderous fire from both shores (the letters marked against the forts are those referred to in Admiralty dispatches).
(Partwork *The Great World War - A History*, Ed. FA Mumby)

The bulldog bays at the moon. How one German humorist viewed Britain's ambitions in the Dardanelles in April 1915.
(Redrawn by Neal d'Enno from the contemporary *Illustrated War News*)

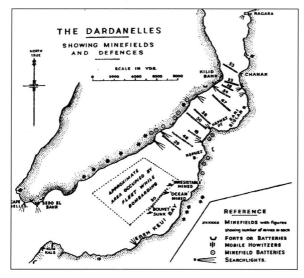

Map illustrating the numerous obstacles facing minesweepers at the Dardanelles. (From *Swept Channels* by Taffrail)

Landing artillery on the Gallipoli Peninsula. A 155-mm gun on a lighter is being towed ashore by a trawler at Seddul Bahr. In the background is the *Euryalus*, which assisted in the landings at Cape Helles and would survive the war. (Mary Evans Picture Library)

A 155-MM. GUN BEING TOWED ASHORE ON A LIGHTER AT SEDD-UL BAHR: LANDING ARTILLERY ON THE GALLIPOLI PENINSULA.

HMT *Lord Wolmer* on service in the Dardanelles. Built in 1911 in Middlesbrough, she was sister-vessel to *Lord Wimborne*, whose varied duties are described in the text. Both boats were hired by the Admiralty from Grimsby's Consolidated Steam Fishing & Ice Co. (IWM Ref SP2370)

The Adriatic Sea, where Scottish drifters would see more action than they bargained for. (EK Chatterton, *Seas of Adventure*)

Sweeping the Channel by J Alfred Newsome (1989) depicts trawlers labouring on their dangerous yet vital duties with great realism, although the artist has not used specific requisitioned or Admiralty vessels as his models. (A Gill, *Lost Trawlers of Hull 1835-1987*, 1989)

Leaving the sinking *Lusitania* – a scene superbly portrayed by artist Fortunio Matania. Fishermen played an important part in rescue operations, saving hundreds of lives at many locations. (R Ballard, *Exploring the Lusitania*, 1995)

The front page of the *Daily Sketch* of 4 January 1915 reporting the *Provident*'s amazing rescue.
(Author's collection)

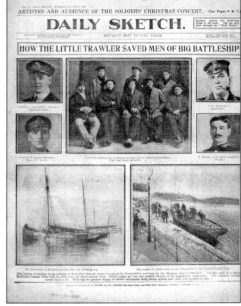

Women and children first! The rescue of *Lusitania* survivors by an Irish fisherman. Drawn by Christopher Clark for *The Sphere*, 15 May 1915.
(Author's collection)

Labour at Sennelager was punishing and no sustenance was given to the prisoners, as Kemp well remembered:

Some of the prisoners used to have to go to work trench-digging, pulling roots of trees out of the ground, and so on. I did the root-pulling, but I got nothing whatever for it. We used to drip in the warm weather. All our food was drink, drink, drink. There was no stayable food all the time I was there, and if it had not been for the help from good friends in England we should certainly have starved altogether. ...

For twelve months out of the sixteen during which I was a prisoner we never saw a knife, fork or spoon. We had to walk about half a mile for our dinner, such as it was, and stand in a crowd, like a mob, to get it. When we had had the stuff served out we used to scoop it up the best way we could, with an oyster shell or a bit of tin, or anything else that we were lucky enough to pick up from the ground.

The following item from the *Fish Trades Gazette* of 15 May 1915 makes interesting reading at this juncture. It is headed *Dainty German Prisoners:*

MR SUTHERLAND also asked the Under-Secretary for War what had been the result of the experiment in allowing Scottish herrings as an optional article in the dietary of German prisoners; to what camps this option had been given; and whether steps were to be taken with a view to extending the option.

MR TENNANT: The experiment in the issue of Scottish-cured herrings as a dietary for German prisoners of war was carried out at Dorchester Camp in March last. The commandant reported that the fish was not liked, and that a large percentage of it was thrown into the refuse tubs. Experiments were made with cooking the fish and serving it with mustard sauce, but while the sauce was appreciated, the fish was not consumed. The English method of cooking was not liked.

In the circumstances, and for disciplinary reasons represented by the commandant, it was decided to discontinue the issue of these herrings.

To describe the discipline at Sennelager as harsh would be an understatement:

We used to have to form up in the morning, and if you did not keep exactly straight in line you got punished. They would make you run round a pole with half a dozen bricks on your back, or dig the ground with a shovel, with the same burden. And they used to go through a form of inspection with you, forcing you to be stark naked, no matter what the weather was like. ... Some of our chaps were a bit obstinate, and they got the worst punishment. The Germans were all push and drive, and if you didn't show yourself willing to do just as you were told, and turned sulky, well, shoot them – that was the order. I saw two or three Belgians and Frenchmen shot for just this offence, turning sulky and refusing to obey orders. There was no sort of court-martial or trial about it; they were shot where they stood. A very common punishment was to lash the men to trees and make them work with the load of bricks on their backs, as I have described – the Germans were rare boys for that sort of business. At Sennelager there were only 200 British fishermen prisoners of war, but there were 2,300 Russian, Belgian and French prisoners, all civilians, some of them burgomasters and so on. And they were rough 'uns too, some of them; but that was no excuse for the terrible punishments which the Germans carried out.

George Benjamin Abbott of Grimsby was only 15 when captured from the trawler *Cancer* on 22 April 1915. Taken to Wilhelmshaven by torpedo boat, he and the rest of the crew were transferred for quarantine detention at the *Stadtvogtei*, or city bailiwick, prison in Dircksenstrasse, Berlin, which was not so much a prison as a place of detention in a kind of model lodging house. The crew of the Aberdeen trawler *Glencarse* were also interned there in April 1915 and recalled it was very clean and equipped with central heating and electric light. Abbott remembered there being a lot of prisoners there:

> …some well-to-do, and I used to clean out their cells for 25 pfennigs (about 3d). For food we had a slice of bread a day, coffee, fish-soup, made of herrings – bones and all – but never any meat.

After six weeks he was moved to Ruhleben Camp, four miles away.

Like the men from the *Cancer*, the crews of two other trawlers (the *Euclid* and the *Titania*) sunk on the same day – 18 May 1915 – were taken to Wilhelmshaven aboard the same torpedo boat destroyer. These 27 men were detained in Berlin for several weeks then likewise sent on to Ruhleben Camp.

A Racecourse near Berlin

The main camp for civilian prisoners in Germany was at Ruhleben, where strong and substantial racing stables were turned into prisons. As the race-course had been reclaimed from the Spree and Havel, it would become a swamp in wet weather, with mud and water up to four inches or five inches deep, so that everyone had to wear clogs.

A number of loose-boxes, each intended for one horse, were on the ground floor and made into compartments for four, five or more men. Those housed in them were comparatively well off. Above the boxes were badly lit and poorly-ventilated lofts, measuring some 260 feet long by 30 feet wide, with sloping roofs. In each loft were placed 200 men and there they had to live and sleep. A description of life in these lofts, given by an unidentified returned prisoner, was reproduced by McKenzie in *The Great War*:

> These lofts, built for storing hay, have undergone no alteration for the accommodation of men. The ventilators are four in number, two on each side; they measure each one foot square exactly, and let the rain in when open. There are also four very small windows on the sides; but as they are only twenty inches off the ground, it is impossible to open them during the night as men have to sleep close against them. The wall in which these windows are set being only three feet high, it will be seen at once that the loft is permanently dark, and that the inmates live in perpetual gloom, being unable to read either by day or by night. In the evening, after sundown, the lofts are illuminated by a half-dozen eight candle-power electric lights. This light is sufficient to move about by, but not for any other purpose.

Another prisoner, whose account was published in *Toilers of the Deep*, testified:

> Never shall I forget climbing the outside wooden staircase up the loft of Barrack 6, and entering a low loft – so low, that we hit our heads. It was almost pitch dark, and there was absolutely no accommodation of any kind, just the dirty bar boards.

We dumped our bags down and went out to receive an armful of dirty straw, which had earlier been used by Russians for three months, and was full of all sorts of curious objects, such as old sausages, bones, etc. This was our bed upon which we slept for about a week, after which we received sacks in which to put the straw. That straw was never changed as long as we were in the camp.

Straw later became scarce, and later arrivals had to be content with shavings, which made a much harder bed.

The food supplied to the men was the same as that supplied in most of the German prison camps. There were slight improvements here and there or variations according to the locality but the following was the general ration.

Early in the morning the men were served with a cup of 'coffee' made from burnt barley, without milk or sugar. During the morning the day's bread – made from rye and potatoes, dark, heavy and unpalatable and with no wheat or flour in it – was issued, in a quantity so inadequate that, as one prisoner said, a man could eat three men's daily portion at one meal. The noonday meal consisted of a dish of soup (bean, cabbage or barley), its usual bad quality being a major source of complaint. It was sometimes putrid, sometimes full of maggots, and sometimes spoiled in preparation. It might contain a little piece of meat, usually horseflesh, sometimes preserved pork. It took even hungry British prisoners a long time to be able to tackle the meat, the amount of which varied with the camp. Whereas in some camps every man obtained a small piece, in others the prisoners cheered when any man in their party got some in his soup, so few came their way. In the evening, the men would get either some coffee or similar dishes of soup. The quality and quantity of food were at their worst at the beginning, this being in part attributable to scarcity in Germany and in part to the Germans being too confident of victory to care about consequences. Some improvement was made later on, but it was generally true that the prisoner who had nothing but his German rations with which to maintain life, lived in a state of semi-starvation.

Every morning, the prisoners had at first to form up in each barracks and march along to the kitchens for their coffee, and wait there often in the rain or snow, maybe for two or three hours, before their turn came. During the day, some were employed with different work – in erecting sheds or barbed-wire fences, or cleaning out the camp. The guards placed over them had apparently unlimited powers of punishment, which they used very freely.

Gradually, this great community of Englishmen of almost every class and circumstance began to evolve its own organization. To alleviate the lot of the sick in the camp, one prisoner – a London coal merchant – asked the authorities to let him have a house that he could turn into a hospital. This he organized with great efficiency and many men doubtless owed their lives to him.

Another Englishman, Joseph Powell, was made captain of the camp. After a time he took entire charge of the food and of the camp organization, naturally under the supreme control of the German authorities. He appointed different committees and departments, including a watch and works department for maintaining order in camp, a kitchen department for all questions concerning prisoners' food and a canteen department for the control of the camp canteens. The book about life at the camp, *The History of Ruhleben: a Record of British*

Organisation in A Prison Camp in Germany, which he co-authored with Francis Gribble and which was published in 1919, has deservedly become a classic.

Educational classes were opened. The prisoners started a monthly magazine. The poorer men tried to earn a little from the more prosperous by opening barbers' shops, offering to clean shoes, cobbling and the like. The community could not have been more varied in composition. As McKenzie wrote:

> Here were hundreds of men taken without warning, most of them, from their wives and families – professional men with their careers broken; financiers, all of whose schemes had stopped, ... working men ..., the mechanic who had been sent over to finish a job in Germany just before the outbreak of war; the photographer who had visited Germany to complete his collection, and who had narrowly escaped being shot as a spy; ... the master who had just started his summer holiday with a long-anticipated tour down the Rhine; the son of English parents who had lived in Germany so long that he had come himself to look like a German – all were there.

Internment outside Germany

Lieutenant TW Moore, RNR, Secretary of the Imperial Merchant Service Guild, was reported in *The Church and the Sailor* of November 1915 to have received authentic information regarding the current conditions of British merchant seafarers interned in Turkey. They were apparently well in health with the exception of one named Andrew Hutton, who was being well looked after at the Seamen's Hospital, Smyrna (present-day Izmir, the country's second-largest port and third-largest city – see Chapter 9). The internees were, however, becoming very weary of their confinement, especially since, being troubled very much with vermin, they could get no proper rest night or day; the heat only made matters worse. They dreaded the thought of another winter in Turkey, being all more or less short of clothes and therefore felt the cold weather keenly. With the kindly assistance of the US Ambassador, the Guild had been able to send substantial sums of money out to these prisoners on two occasions, and was doing all it possibly could to alleviate their distress. A brief account of 20 months' imprisonment in Austria by Boston deckhand William Doughty following an attack on drifters in the Adriatic is given in an endnote in Volume 2. Internment in neutral Holland was a far milder experience than anything we have seen so far.

The training of the Royal Naval Division and its brigades has already been described. In October 1914, some 1,600 members, composed of men from all positions – university and public school men and men from the Royal Fleet Reserve, Royal Naval Reservists, RNVR and many others – were interned in that country after their plucky endeavour to support the Belgian Army in Antwerp.

1 and 2 Naval Brigades had reached the city during the night of 5-6 October. In the retreat to the coast, 1 Brigade crossed the Dutch frontier, having lost their way in the darkness and were, in accordance with international law, detained for the rest of the war. Although the fortress at Antwerp was not saved, Field-Marshal Sir John French, Commander-in-Chief, later claimed that the force under General Paris did:

...delay the enemy for a considerable time and assisted the Belgian Army to be withdrawn in a condition to enable it to reorganise and refit, and regain its value as a fighting force.[80]

Despite the disastrous beginning, the Division survived the bitterness and controversy to be reorganized and flung into battle again at the Dardanelles and thereafter to be once again reorganized and sent to France, where it became part of the Army, and added Arras, Passchendaele, Cambrai and the Ancre to its battle honours.

Accounts of life in Groningen Camp, in the far north-east of the country, were periodically reported in *The Church and the Sailor*, by the Missions to Seamen's representative, the Revd HH Coryton. In one issue, he wrote that their Dutch friends were 'most sporting' and mentioned that among the motley internees were brothers-in-arms from Yorkshire who had joined Kitchener's Army, plus a good sprinkling of marines.

Groningen, a town of about 80,000 people, stood in a very desolate part of Holland. The Royal Naval Brigade Camp, dubbed HMS *Timbertown,* was about the size of an ordinary first-class county cricket ground and located just outside the town. It was composed of several large huts, one row of which was turned into a series of workshops where the men were able to do a certain amount of carpentry, boot-making, etc. Other huts were used as a post office, a general office and a sick bay.

In February 1915, an anonymous correspondent wrote to the editor of *The Navy* magazine that the Groningen internees were well and had passed an enjoyable Christmas as far as circumstances permitted. Describing the occasion, Coryton reported that 4,000 letters and over 2,000 parcels had been received, as against the normal respective figures of 3,000 per day and 6,000 parcels per week on average. Only 12 men were sick in hospital. The men naturally felt their enforced detention keenly, as their lives had become rather monotonous, but in spite of their disadvantages they paid heed to the Scout Law, 'Keep smiling and whistling at all times'. The Dutch authorities, he added, had shown every consideration.

From other sources we know that the men were allowed a certain amount of liberty – inside their confined area – and the Dutch provided them with a ground for football and took them out every day for long route marches in order to keep them physically fit. During these marches they had a guard of mounted men, infantry and bicycle corps members. However, internees were, under certain restrictions, allowed to go out of the camp by signing a kind of undertaking not to endeavour to escape. Safely guarded parties were even permitted to attend the Groningen swimming bath and bioscope fairly regularly.

Occasionally, a communication from a fisherman was published in Britain. One returnee wrote:

Through the hands of the Almighty, we got safely home again, with the exception of our men interned in Holland and 360 in Germany, prisoners.

Another, interned at Groningen, was grateful for being remembered with material comforts:

> Just a line to thank you for the things you sent me. It is very kind of you to send me them – they will come in nice and handy, as it is very cold over here at times. …. I am thankful to you for writing to my wife. I know she is thankful to God for bringing me out of Antwerp to this place. Here we all are and cannot do anything: but it is not our fault. We did what we were sent to do …. I know you are well acquainted with a lot of fishermen. There are only two or three here from Lowestoft that I know – their names are C. E. Clarke, W. J. Tuttle and C. Rice.

From the camp, one of two lady helpers, a Miss Hatchell, quoted an internee stating:

> Every day is the same. The route march (7-8 miles) in the morning, football in the afternoon and the concert or lecture at night – there is nothing fresh to tell.

In May 1915 there were over 1,500 men there, men who, she remarked, '…have come from the very jaws of death'. A daily service at 7 a.m. was attended by some, while subjects studied included languages, shorthand and music. Some were producing a camp magazine, others were making a garden. Surprisingly, knitting classes were held every afternoon, with mufflers and socks being made for the minesweepers and the prisoners in Germany. There was a company called the Follies, which gave excellent entertainments from time to time in the Recreation Hall, plus there were musical societies, and working parties of all kinds. Life there was not wholly dull or monotonous, and everything was done to make it less so.

A visiting correspondent from *The Times* in late 1915 reported that the food was not inadequate and that the men were more comfortable and on the whole better off – except for the consciousness that they were prisoners – than were our new soldiers on Salisbury Plain. So far from demanding sympathy, the camp took pride in its independence and self-sufficiency. Parcels of 'comforts' and other gifts from friends outside to individuals were a private matter and undoubtedly always welcome; but for the camp itself, as a unit, it had nothing to ask of England. Old books or newspapers for its library and reading-rooms were acceptable; but beyond that, its only appeal to people at home was: 'Keep your money and help for the men in the firing line. We're all right!'

More about the life in captivity of our fishermen is recounted in Volume 2 of this history.

Chapter 9

Eastern Mediterranean Fireworks

The Isle of Imbros, set in turquoise blue
Lies to the westward; on the eastern side
The purple hills of Asia fade from view,
And rolling battleships at anchor ride.

White flocks of cloud float by, the sunset glows,
And dipping gulls fleck a slow-waking sea,
Where dim, steel-shadowed forms with foaming bows
Wind up in the Narrows towards Gallipoli.

Introduction to *From 'W' Beach* by Geoffrey Dearmer[81]

Despite Turkey's long-standing friendship with Britain and British officers having effectively managed that country's navy for some time prior to the war, Germany insinuated herself into Ottoman affairs and her influence came to prevail. One of the early means employed to achieve this was the gift to the Turkish navy of the battlecruiser *Goeben* and the light cruiser *Breslau*, although neither would play any significant part in the war, being bottled up for most of it in the Sea of Marmora.

It would later transpire that a secret treaty between the two nations had been signed on 2 August 1914. Churchill wrote in *The Great War*:

> All this time we were deceived. We were forced into a war with Turkey which ulti-
> mately became of enormous magnitude. Greece was thrown into inextricable
> confusion. Serbia was over-run. Bulgaria, joining hands with her recent enemies the
> Turks, became our foe. And Roumania, when she finally came in isolated upon the
> allied side, suffered the direst vengeance at German hands. A more fearful series of
> tragedies has scarcely ever darkened the melancholy page of history.[82]

In late October, a Turkish squadron, working with Rear-Admiral Wilhelm Souchon of the German navy (who had commanded the *Goeben* and *Breslau* and had been appointed commander-in-chief of the Turkish Navy on 15 August), bombarded Russian ports in the Black Sea.

This was swiftly followed, on the 31st of the month, by a British Admiralty communication to all ships: 'Commence hostilities at once against Turkey. Acknowledge.' On 3 November, Admiral Sackville Hamilton Carden, commanding British naval forces in the Mediterranean, carried out his instruction to bomb the outer Dardanelles forts at long range. Two battlecruisers, the *Indefatigable* and *Indomitable*, shelled the batteries on the European side at

Sedd-el-Bahr and Cape Helles, while two French battleships fired at the Asiatic batteries at Kum Kali and Orkanieh. The forts were considerably damaged and there were several hundred casualties among the Turks and Germans manning them. Yet the attacks were not followed up and their chief result was to draw attention to the importance of the region to the Allies.

Carden would be bombing these – and other – forts again, three and a half months later, following the decision to force a passage through the Dardanelles to Constantinople. This was partly in response to an appeal to the British at the end of 1914 from Russia, who badly needed some action to distract the Turks. Not only would pressure be taken off her but, if a successful campaign could be mounted, off the Army on the Western Front as well, since Germany would have to divert resources eastwards. The resulting Gallipoli campaign – an attempt to open a route to Russia via the Black Sea and take Turkey out of the war – lasted eight months. It cost 213,980 British Commonwealth casualties, apart from heavy losses among old naval ships, and ended in the evacuation of the peninsula. An important consequence of its failure was that Russia was cut off from its foreign markets.

Carden was initially successful in his plan for the systematic destruction of Turkish fortifications along the Dardanelles but he was relieved of his command in early March 1915 due to failing health and replaced by Admiral John de Robeck.

The other part of Carden's plan called for extensive minesweeping operations. Here trawlers were assigned a pivotal role, although it must be said that, due to the conditions under which they laboured, they were not the right choice for the task. In principle, the battleships, cruisers and destroyers could, with the mines cleared, get close enough to the forts to disable them. Yet the trawlers, constantly under fire from the shore-based guns and howitzers and restricted by the strong currents to a speed of no more than three knots, could not really be effective The mission was little short of suicidal and many a valiant fisherman understandably rebelled against it.

Norman Wilkinson, the renowned artist, wrote:

> The work of the trawlers in the Dardanelles demands special mention. The men running these vessels are in the majority of cases elderly, and the ships themselves were never intended to come under fire; yet these men have constantly been in very hot places, and have gone there knowing what was in store for them.[83]

Other prominent eyewitnesses would write in praise of the men and their vessels, notably correspondent and author E Ashmead-Bartlett. But first, a look at this fleet leaving England to join battle far from the North Sea and other familiar waters.

The Sweepers' Nightmare
On 19 January 1915, the Admiralty urgently arranged to collect 21 minesweeping trawlers – seven from Grimsby and 14 from Lowestoft – for dispatch to the Dardanelles. They were first coaled and provisioned at Devonport, whence 13 set out on their journey under Commander William

Mellor in the trawler *Escallonia*. The remaining eight followed a few days later, after attention to certain engine-room defects.

On 3 February, the first trawlers began arriving at Gibraltar and left for Malta the next day. They arrived there four days later and were fitted out for the perilous work ahead of them. So important had fishing vessels become that, according to a telegraph from Carden, the Dardanelles campaign could not begin until these craft had arrived. All 21 trawlers had assembled at the island by 21 February, four having sailed for the Dardanelles on the 15th and another four two days later.

More trawlers would soon be required and on Monday, 15 March, the Admiralty ordered the naval officer in charge of Lowestoft to send 30 of his fastest trawlers to assemble at Falmouth en route for Lemnos. They left their east coast base on the Wednesday. In this group was the unnamed writer of a valuable, lengthy and detailed record of trawler operations in the Aegean, covering the period mid-April 1915 to mid-March 1917, and identified from research as Arthur Henry Craven. The notes of this pensioner petty officer, which were never intended for publication, came into the hands of the editor of *The Naval Review* quite by chance and were fortunately published.[84] Here are some early entries:

> Outward bound March 17th, 8.a.m., St. Patrick's Day. – Joined 703, Lord Wimborne, Lieutenant Gowthorpe, R.N.R. (untrained). Commander Higginson, who had been at the [Lowestoft] base, was in command of 30 trawlers and mine sweepers. Sailed from Lowestoft with a tremendous noise of steam whistles for the Dardanelles at 9.30 a.m.
>
> March 19th. – Heavy passage. Arrived at Falmouth. Was to have leave before sailing, but the trawlermen, like at Lowestoft, made their tongues wag where they were going, that Commander Higginson was wise to clear out of it, as no doubt many spies were about.
>
> March 20th. – Sailed for Gibraltar. Rough passage. Had to fall back for the misfits that kept breaking down. Commander very seasick most of the way. After five days arrived Gibraltar a.m., coaled, and proceeded to Malta. Visited E. 14, E. 15; know all the crews.
>
> March 25th. – Arrived Malta to get fitted out with armour plating on winch and wheelhouse; dockyard could only do six at a time.

A detailed diary was also kept covering the period 17 March 1915 to 12 April 1917 by Aberdonian James Clarke, who also left Lowestoft on the 17th on the Aberdeen trawler *Loch Broom*.[85] Sweeping is mentioned but accounts of humdrum, sometimes unpleasant but always vital, duties – often performed under fire – predominate.

A further insightful record was left, again in *The Naval Review*,[86] in the *Narrative of Mine-Sweeping Trawler 448, manned by Queen Elizabeth – The Landing at "Z" Beach, Gallipoli*. Trawler 448 was the *Fentonian* of Grimsby.

Exactly a month before Craven reached Malta, the earlier trawlers had begun their task of sweeping at the entrance to the Dardanelles, covered by a division of battleships accompanied by destroyers. Within two days they had swept a distance of four miles from the entrance of the Straits but no mines had been found. So far, so good.

However, when the sweepers approached the Narrows the difficulties began. Here, where a strong current ran down towards the Dardanelles Straits, the enemy had laid line after line of mines between the European and Asiatic shores, protected by batteries and searchlights. On 1 March, a bright moonlit night, the trawlers valiantly swept to within 3,000 yards of Kephez Point, but when they were abreast of the Suandere River they were the target of such a fierce bombardment from the enemy's batteries that they were forced to retire, covered by a smoke screen from the destroyers. Luckily there were no casualties. Carden telegraphed the Admiralty to report that the sweepers were doing excellent work.

The trawlers tried again during the night of 6-7 March, protected by the light cruiser HMS *Amethyst* and destroyers but were once more driven back. On the night of 10-11 March, again supported by *Amethyst* plus HMS *Canopus* and two picket-boats fitted with explosive creeps, seven more trawlers (*Escallonia, Avon, Manx Hero, Syringa, Beatrice II, Gwenllian,* and *Soldier Prince*) made their way up the Straits and, notwithstanding the enemy's heavy fire, succeeded, together with the picket-boats, in getting above the minefield, their intention being to sweep down with the current. Gunfire from the protecting vessels had meantime been unable, however, to extinguish the searchlights and batteries guarding the Kephez minefields.

In the hellish pandemonium which ensued, with all the vessels under heavy fire from 6-inch guns and weapons of lesser calibre, two trawlers were struck by shells and a couple of men were wounded. Only one pair of sweepers succeeded in getting out their sweep. A couple of mines were exploded but the *Manx Hero* of Grimsby was too close to one of them and blew up. Although she sank, the crew was picked up. This gallant rescue, which took nearly 90 minutes to accomplish, was performed by Captain Robert Woodgate and his crew in another sweeper, the Hull trawler *Koorah*.

Woodgate, during a visit to England, described the incident:

When we were up in the Dardanelles, there was what we call three groups – one, two and three – and each group had to go up, one at a time. The vessel I was in belonged to the second group. The night we were going to make the final dash in the Dardanelles, up to the Narrows, we went, no lights up, everything covered in. They let us get right up to the Narrows, and as we turned round to take our sweeps up, one of our number was blown up. Then they peppered us from each side, from one and a half to two miles. We heard cries for help. I said 'We shall have to do the best we can and go back and pick up.' There was no waiting, no saying 'Who shall go?' As soon as I called for volunteers, three jumped in [boatswain Joe Abbott, Tom Thompson and Bob Strachan]. I kept the vessel as close as I could to shelter them. I did not think any would come back alive, but no one was hit, and I said, 'Now we'll get the boat in.' Just as we got the boat nicely clear of the water, along came a shot and knocked it in splinters. I shouted 'All hands keep under cover as much as you can!' and I got on the bridge and we went full steam ahead.

I could not tell you what it was like, with floating and sunken mines and shots everywhere. We got knocked about, the mast almost gone, rigging gone, and she was riddled right along the starboard side. One of the hands we picked up had his left arm smashed with shrapnel. That was all the injury we got. When we got out, the Commander came alongside and said 'Have you seen any more trawlers?' I said 'Yes, we've got the crew of one aboard, the *Manx Hero.*' We were the last out, and I can tell you, I never want to see such a sight again![87]

Woodgate managed, despite the powerful searchlights and fierce fire, to steer his vessel to the northern shore. The *Daily Mail,* in a review of the splendid work of the minesweepers under immense difficulties, stated that Woodgate's gallantry had probably not been exceeded by any during the war.[88]

The tragic vessel's sweeping partner had been the Milford trawler *Gwenllian,* whose skipper, Captain Robert M Limbrick, wrote to the owner, Morgan Howell:

I am bound to let you know that your little Gwennie has had a six-inch shell through her port side, and a pretty fine hole it made, but we are patched up again. The shell came in about six inches below the bulwarks ... and never hurt the mate, who was at the winch at the time. So were lucky for once. ...if I could only get home, I think I would walk it. ... I was in the North Sea for six months, but I have been through more here in less than five minutes than I went through there in the whole time – four mines exploded, sweeping partner blown up and a shell through you in that time will want a bit of beating.[89]

On the following night another group of trawlers, consisting of the *Restrivo, Vidonia, Star of the Empire, Frascati, Fentonian, Strathlossie* and *Strathord,* renewed the attempt but met with similar misfortunes. The defenceless vessels understandably retired from the piercing rays of the searchlights and the intense shelling. E Keble Chatterton remarked that 'The fishermen had been asked to do the Navy's job, and had no more succeeded than if the Navy had been sent to catch fish off Iceland.'[90] Archibald Hurd commented, in Vol. II of *The Merchant Navy*:

Throughout the whole war these fishermen and their R.N.R. officers were never frightened of mines or submarines, which they attacked with the greatest possible gallantry whenever they encountered them; but it was quite another matter to take these men straight from the North Sea and turn them, ordinary fishermen, into conspicuous targets for field-guns and forts. No harder or more dispiriting a task was ever set the vessels of the Auxiliary Patrol throughout the war than that of sweeping the Dardanelles Straits. The dice were so loaded against them that the sweepers had no chance. To have been successful the operation required very fast craft fitted with efficient gear, and very highly and specially trained crews; moreover, the work had to be done by day, if at all. As it was, the sweeping was carried out by night by slow trawlers handicapped by the current, whose officer and men were inexperienced and had never before been under shell fire.[91]

The Times commented 'No more nerve-racking work can be conceived than that of the slow process of sweeping for mines under the fire of the batteries from the shore.'[92]

Roughly half (115) of the original trawler crews, unwilling to continue sweeping under heavy fire, took the option to return at once to England, where they performed excellent work. 'Some brave stalwarts', commented the unsympathetic Roger Keyes[93] in *The Fight for Gallipoli*, 'insisted on staying to wipe out the past, and they seized every opportunity of most gallantly doing so.' Among them was Skipper Alfred Swain of the Grimsby trawler *Escallonia*, who achieved recognition in the form of a DSC for his minesweeping services, as did Skipper Alfred E Berry of the trawler *Frascati*, likewise from Grimsby. Berry was also commended for good service on the beach at Suvla and his participation in the evacuation. The two vessels were remnants from the original force of 21.[94]

Keyes recorded that among the volunteer crews, a great number came from the battleships *Ocean* and *Irresistible* and all who could be spared from the *Inflexible* during her lengthy refit. Numbers far in excess of those required were available and 'splendid crews were selected'. Even so, Kephez could not be reached. An attempt – by daylight this time – was made on 18 March, the day of the great concerted attack, by the *Restivo* and five sister-vessels and although one pair got out their sweep, they could make no headway to Kephez owing to the fire from howitzers and field guns. Tragically, an unexpected minefield was run into that day by the French *Bouvet*, the *Inflexible*, *Irresistible* and *Ocean*. All but the *Inflexible* sank. Two other French casualties were the *Suffren*, badly damaged by shellfire, and the *Gaulois*, beached in the Rabbit Island group nearby but later refloated. The major assault was called off despite being close to success; the Turks were running out of ammunition. The two senior commanders in the Mediterranean, de Robeck and General Sir Ian Hamilton, decided on a land campaign. A major factor in this decision was the enormous loss of life on the *Bouvet* – over 600 men, including the captain. Little happened in the several weeks pending the arrival of the land forces.

Smyrna: a Mini-Dardanelles

The *Manx Hero* was not the only Grimsby trawler to be lost in action in March. Just two days earlier, on the 8th, the *Okino* sank with the loss of 10 men and the survival of five others. But this happened many miles away from the Dardanelles.

The vast vilayet of Smyrna covered no less than 21,000 square miles. Its numerous islets, bays, coves and creeks, afforded safe anchorage to many a vessel – and lay at Germany's disposal. The waters of the wide Gulf of Smyrna became a very narrow channel at Sanjak Kalesi before extending again into the horseshoe-shaped natural harbour of the populous city.

The plan to smite Smyrna from the sea was devised as something of a feint. It would cause the Turks uneasiness and make them withdraw some of their forces away from the Dardanelles and, more importantly, prevent the vilayet becoming a base for U-boats.

Hence, on 2 March 1915, the Admiralty sent Vice-Admiral Richard H Peirse, commanding Allied naval forces on the Suez Canal, a telegraph ordering him to proceed from Egypt in his flagship the *Euryalus* and bombard and destroy the Smyrna forts as a matter of urgency. He would have at his disposal two battleships temporarily detached from the Dardanelles, the *Triumph* and *Swiftsure*, as well as five minesweeping trawlers, *Okino, G.M., Beatrice, Achilles* and *Renarro*, the Russian light cruiser *Askold*, one destroyer, and the seaplane-carrier *Anne Rickmers*, a former German merchant steamer. Her captain, LB Weldon, would be the author of *Hard Lying – Eastern Mediterranean, 1914-1919* (1925), in which he left a recollection of the trawler skipper who transferred him and his crew to the *Euryalus*:

> The skipper of this trawler was a bit of a character. He was a typical North Sea fisherman, over sixty years old, and a fine specimen of a man. There he was in his little wheel-house, dressed in exactly the same kit as he wore in the North Sea – two jerseys, muffler and sea-boots. He explained to me that he always had to have a thin man at the wheel as otherwise two couldn't have fitted into the wheel-house. He was a fine old boy with a wife and eleven children at Grimsby, but 'doing his bit'. I asked him how he liked it, and he replied, 'It's orl right, sir, but I would like to be able to 'it back.' In those days the trawlers were not armed.

Fort Yeni Kale, which controlled the narrow Sanjak Kalesi channel and which had to be captured or silenced if any surface vessel was to get through into Smyrna Harbour, was bombarded for a whole hour by the battleships under perfect conditions on 5 March at a range of 14,000 yards. This was too far away for the stronghold to make any reply. Nor was it able to when the distance was closed to 10,000 yards and the assault repeated.

Following this excellent start, four of the trawlers, under cover of the battleships, set forth the next morning to sweep through the minefield. This was an opportunity for the Turkish guns to speak. Despite their inaccuracy, the trawlers, under fire for 40 minutes, had to be withdrawn.

A sweeper from Brixham later recounted:

> Their shells fell anywhere but on our ship. Some pitched so close to us that the splashes nearly swamped our decks. How we came through untouched was a miracle. Had we been under British artillery instead of Turkish we could never have come out alive. ... We had our sweeps ready to shoot out when we were signalled to retire. ... One shell would have smashed any one of the sweepers.[95]

The big ships, now at 8,000 yards, fired at the batteries again for an hour, although the *Euryalus, Triumph* and trawlers all suffered some damage.

Operations were resumed on the 7th, when all the batteries that could be located were shelled by the squadron. The battery of field guns and searchlights at Chiflik, to the south-west of Yeni Kale, were destroyed by the *Triumph*, although she was hit the next day. When night fell on the 8th, both battleships fired at the searchlights, keeping them dimmed so that the channel was actually swept by the trawlers to within 3,000 yards of Yeni Kale. But there was a price to pay – the *Okino* foundered on one of the mines. Lieutenant Geoffrey T Whitehouse RNR, the trawler skipper Weldon had met and three others were saved. At a memorial service held next morning on board the *Euryalus*, Captain Weldon was relieved and delighted to see his acquaintance. He had been in the water for an hour and a half before being picked up.

Captain Henry James of the Milford trawler *G.M.* later recounted what happened.[96] The trawler contingent from the Dardanelles included the *Beatrice* from Hull, which was the sweeping partner of the *Okino*. They had completed a sweep, and the *Beatrice* had slipped the sweep wire. She was proceeding back to the fleet, leaving the *Okino* to heave in the wire. The latter vessel then followed, and had been steaming about five minutes when she was blown up, sinking in about two minutes. One of those saved was a Milford man, Fred Ingram, second engineer, of Milford Haven. He had just been oiling the engines when suddenly the dynamo was hurled from its place and flew past him into the bilge. This was the first sign to him that something had happened, and he rushed on deck, only to see that the ship was doomed. He jumped overboard and, being a strong swimmer, was able to take his lifesaving collar from his belt, inflate it and fasten it round his neck. He managed to cling to some wreckage, and after struggling in the water for three and a half hours was picked up by the picket boat. For volunteering to do his utmost to stop the stricken *Okino*, Ingram was awarded the DSM. The *Beatrice* received a shell on the fore side of the funnel; part of the missile penetrated into the stokehold and a piece of shrapnel struck the chief engineer, William Holland of Milford Haven, on the head. He was later operated on and recovered.

The *G.M.* herself was also under heavy fire and with her partner, the *Achilles* of Grimsby, led the fleet in the attack on the Smyrna forts. 'How we came out of that corner, I do not know', said the skipper. Shells and shrapnel were bursting all around, but there were no casualties. All the ships were continually under fire, and although they were hit repeatedly, the missiles did not strike the vital parts. There were remarkable escapes. One trawler was struck by a shell aft, which went through the bunkers and the fish room, cutting the main stanchion, then through 25 tons of ballast and out through the bow. In another case the shell went clean through a trawler from side to side. James' subsequent experiences in the Dardanelles were not, he recalled, so exciting as at Smyrna, although they were always dangerous.

The Smyrna operation ended in a curious way. Force was producing no results so diplomacy was tried. A truce was called and the Vali was called upon to surrender unconditionally and destroy all forts and batteries, as the fall of Constantinople could not be long delayed. The British Government, he was told, had no intention of becoming involved in military operations here. This bluff failed, for, on the 13th, the Vali declined the terms. The truce was therefore terminated the next day. Peirse went back to Egypt and the *Swiftsure* and *Triumph* returned to the Dardanelles, where they arrived in time to take part in the great push on 18 March.

Strangely, the objective at Smyrna was achieved, for our guns had threatened so formidably and our sweepers had so nearly approached the narrow entrance that the Turks, fearful that we might conquer the city and port, sank several steamers at the narrows in Sanjak Kalesi channel in a blocking operation. On 2 June, a blockade of the port would be declared and would be maintained by a destroyer and various other craft, including a couple of trawlers and two motor gunboats of the Royal Naval Motor-Boat Reserve, commanded by RNVR officers. Smyrna was never used again from that month to the end of the war.

At the Dardanelles, major changes took place in April. By the 7th the Commander-in-Chief had discontinued minesweeping inside the Straits, as he felt the result did not justify the risks. 'In short', remarked Chatterton, 'the volunteer crews of trawler men, Royal Naval Reserve and Royal Navy had been able to effect little more than the fishermen themselves.'[97] The mines remained unswept until the end of the war, so the fleet never penetrated the Narrows. Military action began and predominated, with the Navy now supporting the Army.

The Landings, 25-26 April 1915

In these operations, trawlers again played a vital part. In the first landing, north of Gaba Tepe, which was carried out under the orders of Rear-Admiral CF Thursby, the squadron included 15 trawlers; and 14 trawlers formed part of the squadron which carried out the landing at the southern extremity of the Gallipoli Peninsula under the orders of Rear-Admiral RE Wemyss. At 'Y' Beach the King's Own Scottish Borderers were transferred from the transports to four trawlers. These, towing boats alongside, proceeded in line abreast to positions from which the troops could row ashore in the small boats. Royal Marines followed astern in a further four trawlers. A couple of trawlers also assisted at 'W' Beach, while at 'S' Beach, four trawlers convoyed by *Cornwallis* brought in the South Wales Borderers, who then landed in cutters. Half a dozen other trawlers swept Xeros Bay, where a feint was made of landing, at midnight on the 24th-25th under the protection of HMS *Doris*. It should be mentioned that a number of French trawlers operated in the Dardanelles, in the landings, at Morto Bay and in minesweeping operations.

For about a month prior to the landing, the unnamed writer of the *Narrative of Mine-Sweeping Trawler 448* had been in command of that Grimsby vessel, which he had manned entirely with ratings from his own ship, the original crew of fishermen having returned to England. While the Army was assembling, she was employed off Cape Helles in sweeping the whole area, which was afterwards occupied by the transports.

One day he carried out a test of the number of men that could be embarked in a trawler, and succeeded in stowing 535 quite comfortably, with nobody down below. Each man was fully equipped with food, ammunition, etc. for three days. He also found room for the machine guns and entrenching tools. With this number on board he was able to proceed inshore, with boats in tow, anchor, and land the men.

Of that memorable Sunday the 25th, he wrote:

We weighed at 2.30 a.m., and steamed slowly across towards the Gallipoli peninsula. Meanwhile, the covering ships had come round via the north of Imbros, and were about two miles ahead of us. *Queen, London*, and *Prince of Wales* each carried 500 Australian troops, who were destined to form the covering force. ... The weather conditions were perfect, calm as a mill-pond, pitch dark, with a slight mist. As near as I can judge it was about 4.10 a.m. when the first boat-load landed. The story is already well known how the Australians leapt over the side, fixed bayonets in the water, and charged the beach. I made my first trip in just before 5 a.m., when I was sent in to pick up the empty boats and tow them out to the transports. The enemy's guns were fairly busy about this time, and a lot of shrapnel were bursting near the inshore line of transports; later, as it grew light, the destroyers opened fire and apparently silenced them.

...Having completed this preliminary reconnaissance we returned to the transport anchorage, and the remainder of the forenoon was spent in going round the various ships to hasten the disembarkation of troops and small-arm ammunition. I towed in several lighters loaded with .303, and also two barrel piers in sections. ... I spent the remainder of the afternoon landing guns and ammunition. It was during one of these trips that my first casualty occurred. We were under a fairly heavy fire whenever we went within three-quarters of a mile of the shore, as shrapnel were bursting intermittently, with, every now and again, some rapid salvoes. Also there was a continuous shower of bullets; ... it was one of these [snipers' bullets] that killed my stoker petty officer, who was on watch at the time and had come up on deck to help the seamen in slipping the horseboats. ... Just as I was going to anchor [at the beach], I found that my opposite number – trawler No. 49 [*Frascati*] – had run ashore; so I got a wire across to him and for a couple of hours tried to get him off. This method having failed, I went away and found an obliging destroyer, who did the trick in about two pulls.

The beach by night was one of the weirdest sights I have ever seen; everywhere there were lights and flares, screened from view in front and on the flanks, and the whole hillside was picked out in lights, shining to the rear from the dug-outs and shelters; and, on the move the whole night long, were the stretcher bearers, and the men carrying up the supplies and ammunition. All along the foreshore men were unloading lighters, and at one end the wounded were being embarked....

About 10 p.m. a large lighter full of wounded was brought out by a steam cutter, and left alongside me to wait for a picket boat; as none arrived after a quarter of an hour or so, I got under weigh and took them out myself. I had to go very slow to avoid bumping the lighter more than necessary, and it was about 1.30 a.m. by the time I got inshore again and anchored. ... I was [later] given two more boatloads of very severely wounded officers and men. ...I spent nearly the whole day landing artillery and ammunition of all sorts.

Admiral de Robeck wrote:

> I should like to place on record the good service performed by the vessels employed in landing the second part of the covering force: the seamanship displayed and the rapidity with which so large a force was thrown on the beach is deserving of the highest praise.[98]

The Loss of the *Triumph* and *Majestic*

In May, tragedy struck twice in three days at the Dardanelles following the arrival of *U.21* (Otto Hersing) from Germany via Cattaro. The sudden appearance of enemy submarines on the scene doubled every difficulty. From the 22nd, all transports had to be dispatched to Mudros for safety and from that date onwards, men, stores, guns, horses, etc. had to be brought 40 miles from that port on the island of Lemnos in fleet sweepers and other small and shallow craft less vulnerable to submarine attack.

These precautions did not help either the *Triumph* or the *Majestic*, both of which fell victim to Hersing. On the 25th, the pre-dreadnought *Triumph* of 1904 was torpedoed and sunk while firing her guns in support off Gaba Tepe, midway between Suvla Bay and Cape Helles. Her loss was witnessed by Chief Skipper Donald McBain Craig RNR, in charge of an Aberdeen trawler, who steamed straight for the spot on hearing of the tragedy. He was so near the stricken battleship that he was ordered by a destroyer to go astern lest his vessel be drawn down by the suction. Craig steamed about and succeeded in rescuing a large number of the sailors from the water. As the mighty ship took her last plunge, the survivors on the trawler dock raised their caps and paid their old ship its last farewell by giving three hearty cheers. Craig,[99] who would be awarded the DSC for this and other work at the peninsula, told the *Fishing News* in early January 1919 that prior to the evacuation there were a large number of Aberdeen trawlers engaged in operations at the Dardanelles. He was by no means the only member of a trawler crew to assist in the rescue operation. Craven's entry for 25 May reads:

> Turned at full speed inwards to rescue, prepared life-lines and floating material, turned boat out. *Triumph* got list of 10 degrees. Heaps of men clinging to torpedo nets, many jumping into the water. *Triumph* heeled another 7 degrees. Stopped on her port beam, sent boat away with two men; many men swimming towards our trawlers. T.B. *Chelmer* put her bows under *Triumph*, stern walk, another trawler approaching, 719, *William Allen*. Commenced hauling men out of water, tossed oars overboard to the men; I had pulled about four men on board, last one young officer, lots of men screaming for help. Could see a good many losing their heads. Relieved by this young officer, I, at great personal risk, dived in among the batch of screaming men; I had great difficulty to get the men under control.

He retrieved a number of bodies ('I dived under after five, who were lifeless, got them in boats'). Indeed, not all the men he rescued survived:

> There were three men I had rescued getting sewn up, who were buried at sea; four men came to me and thanked me for saving their lives. I had saved about a score or more. ... My trawler had saved 104, and discharged them to *Lord Nelson* flagship.

Craven was awarded the DSM for his actions. In his entry for the 27th, he complains:

> Imagine a battleship at anchor, and no sign of a steam pinnace or picket boat with a gun patrolling around her, which would have been protection under the circumstances. They say she had only one active service seaman on board. Half a dozen trawlers patrolling the mouth of the Dardanelles; not one of them with a gun, only method to sink submarine is to ram. Even if our 30 trawlers were sent for sweeping they certainly before leaving England should have been fitted with some guns.

Hence it came as no surprise to him when the inadequately protected *Majestic* of 1895, while stationed off W Beach at Cape Helles, also fell victim, at around 6.45 a.m. on the very day of the above entry, to Hersing's U-boat. The torpedo tore through the anti-torpedo nets, striking her and causing an enormous explosion. She began listing to port and in nine minutes had capsized, with the loss of 49 men. Luckily, there was plenty of help available from a number of vessels; the destroyer HMS *Chelmer* alone rescued over 500 men. The diarist, for his part, went off in *Lord Wimborne*'s dinghy with the cook and picked up seven survivors.

In his entry dated 3 July, he wrote '*Majestic* would not have been sunk had net drifters been here'. He had already referred, on 27 May, to the need for more destroyers and net drifters.

On the impact of the arrival of U-boats, he noted:

> ...for six weeks from sinking of H.M.S. *Triumph* the situation completely changed, all that was on the sea was trawlers and fleet sweepers to feed the peninsula. T.B. destroyers were kept at it and must have covered many a mile, drawing the enemy's fire, etc.

Drifters in Support

So much has been written in this history about the work of trawlers at the Dardanelles that operations by drifters have been overshadowed. With German submarines operating, radical steps had to be taken to protect the bombarding ships. The prompt decision was therefore taken to send out 30 net drifters from England. These vessels, half a dozen of which were armed with a 3-pounder apiece, set out from Poole in the early hours of 5 June with nets, indicator buoys and 14 days' coal, reaching Gibraltar on the 13th, whence they continued eastward two days later. In addition, 20 more trawlers were taken up.[100] They were sent to Falmouth, where each was armed either with a 3-pounder or a 6-pounder gun; extra accommodation was provided for the crew, the ventilating arrangements were improved and wind sails were provided to adapt them for service in the heat of the Aegean. By the 9th, this fleet had started for the voyage south. As for the net drifters, Craven recorded their arrival on 2 July. On 11 September, he noted:

> Net drifters with nets out patrolling at various points, 703 and 288 [*Dinorah*] protecting drifters when nets are out, moving in outer circle, in opposite direction, when too rough for nets, drifters patrol around Stratie Island. Continued patrolling, keeping a constant chain of escort for transports, submarine not seen.

He recorded that on the 26th drifters sank four enemy mines floating southeast, about half a mile from Stratie Point and on 1 October remarked:

> Seems strange, a good bluff, where the net drifters are about they seem to scare the submarines away ... where our guns are firing on peninsula.

Another four mines were sunk in early December, when the diarist wrote that:

> ...drifters had scared the submarines away, at least have not seen any lately.

The trawlers, of course, did their share of anti-submarine work by patrolling, as recorded above. Clarke wrote on 25 May: '...had orders to go on patrol as a submarine scare was expected and kept on patrol all night.' They remained on patrol for the next three days. On 9 July '...trawler 705 [*Avon*] sighted a Submarine and started firing at it but I don't know if he got it or not it was about one hour before he got any help so I think he got off.'

Maids of all Work

Other trawler duties were mentioned in the December 1915 issue of the *Toilers of the Deep*, quoting the correspondent, and future Dardanelles historian,[101] Ellis Ashmead-Bartlett:

...they have carried thousands of tons of stores from the bases to the beaches, and transported thousands of officers and men and thousands of sick and wounded to and from the islands to the hostile shores.

The campaign would have been impossible without the immense number of trawlers and drifters ... The lot of their crews is a hard one. They must go out in every kind of weather, and are often kept busy for 16 hours out of the 24. They have to go right into the beaches, and are constantly exposed to the enemy's shell fire. Some are officered by sub-lieutenants, but the majority carry the skippers who handle them in the North Sea, in the Channel, and off the West Coast.

Few have any conception of the amount of work accomplished by these craft. In fact, it would have been almost impossible to have kept the Army supplied without them.

Clarke's trawler, for example, heaved up anchor on 9 October and 'went to T327 [*Northman*] to relieve him and left for Imbros at 7 a.m. and returned to Anzac at 7.30 p.m. with Beef and Bread 20,000 rations'. The same load was carried daily until 31 October, except on the 27th, when the weather was too bad to land the rations, while the only variation in cargo was on the 14th and 20th, when the beef was replaced by frozen mutton. Food was only one item of cargo, of course. On 16 September, *Loch Broom* arrived at Mudros and took on board 400 officers' kits and took them alongside the steamer *Japanese Prince*. Men worked all night to unload the cargo. The delivery of mails, often to other trawlers, was also a frequent duty, while on 12 November the vessel left Anzac for Imbros at 6.45 a.m. for 160 bags of coal.

Clarke's recollections frequently relate to duties in connection with the wounded and the dead – 'not a grand job but somebody has to do it' (31 July). On 28 June he had been pleased to record 'we are finished with the hospital ship for a time as we take it in turns, and it is not a very fine job, we buried 33 altogether for the short time we had it'. The crew would be relieved again on 1 September by Trawler 340 [*Loch Esk*] and on 14 September by 327. On 23 August they had orders at Gaba Tepe to take on burial duty and relieve 281 [*Yarmouth II*] for repairs. On the following day they went to 362 [*Beatrice II*] with their mails and then alongside the hospital ship *Devanha* to wait for five bodies to bury. However, they put their foot down when the ship asked them to sew them up and put weights on them 'as it is not a very pleasant job'. Four days later, they were collecting wounded all night. There were so many that three other trawlers were called in to help. On 7 September, *Loch Broom* took 149 sick and wounded to Imbros.

On a more agreeable note, Norman Wilkinson devoted a chapter of his *The Dardanelles – Colour Sketches from Gallipoli*[102] to the work of the trawlers and described a trip made in one of them, engaged in general ferry work, from Kephalo to Helles via Anzac and from Helles to Rabbit Island and Tenedos and back:

Every morning on starting, the skipper knew the ship would come under shell-fire at Anzac almost without fail, as the anchorage is commanded by the Turkish guns, and any sign of movement, or of ships arriving or leaving, invariably brought its accompaniment of shells. I gathered from him that this had been his daily lot for four months.

He was a fine type of North Sea skipper, and took everything as it came with a stoicism which was admirable. He didn't like it – nobody does; but it was his job, and there was an end of it!

...we were close into Anzac beach, and had anchored preparatory to a picket-boat coming off to take our mails, etc. Four other trawlers lay close to us engaged on various duties. The Turks ... now turned their attention to us, and it must be said that nothing is much more unpleasant than to be confined in a very small vessel at anchor with no protection but the thinnest sheet-iron. Their first shot at us was shrapnel, and the range not bad. Shrapnel is, I think, the most spiteful sounding of all shells ... However, after this trial-shot the enemy turned to high explosives. ... Some of them were certainly closer than I care for, but having a camera and a feeling that, after all, things were very much in the hands of Allah, I thought the moment seemed opportune for a photograph.

Anzac was, he wrote, 'a most forbidding spot' and apart from Helles was the only part of the peninsula occupied by the Allies. After a brief stop at Rabbit Island, they reached Tenedos, 'one of the most flourishing of the islands in the vicinity of the Dardanelles', used by the British and French as an aeroplane base. The picturesque harbour was surrounded by quaint buildings, with an ancient fort dominating the whole (Clarke, homesick, remarked in his log: 'This place is like old Torry I only wish it was, but it is not.'). A short stay there completed their business. The return journey to Helles and Kephalo was uneventful.[103]

A regular service of trawlers was arranged between the various islands and beaches, so that within 12 hours, from 7 a.m. to 7 p.m., one could journey from Imbros to Suvla Bay, Anzac and Helles, leaving there at 5 p.m. for the return to Imbros. Or the reverse route could be taken. Every day the trawlers did this round trip, picking up officers, men and stores en route.

The trawlers frequently performed their duties under fire, so much so that one C Nelson, the chief engineer on a Grimsby sweeper, wrote in a letter: 'We are getting quite used to shrapnel flying about, and take it quite naturally.'[104] Clarke testified: 'Was ordered to go and work Transport, 53. Plenty of shelling, trawler 281 got three shells through her but none of the crew are hurt' (19 May); 'got the news that a minesweeper chap was killed in his bunk with a shell on the 705' (22 May). On 26 May, Trawler 448, wrote our unnamed diarist, was ordered by *Queen* to land as much as possible of the transport *Anglo-Egyptian*'s cargo; she started off by collecting a dozen or so horse-boats and big lighters, which she placed alongside, and then towed them inshore as fast as they were loaded. She carried a large number of donkeys and mules, and she took those in first, towing on each trip four horse-boats, each holding 15 mules. The ship was lying a good two miles from the shore, so the trips were long, and picking up the horse-boats at the start was rather a lengthy process 'as a trawler is not an extraordinarily easy ship to handle, and all the work of securing, etc., had to be done by my own ship's company of five seamen'. They were met by a heavier fire on that day than on any other day of the operations; a good many of the ammunition boxes were punctured by shrapnel bullets and the trawler was hit all over the place. It was found that the roof of the wheel-house would not keep out the bullets, although the sides seemed quite safe. By the end of the afternoon, 448 had cleared the transport of nearly all her ammunition and as the shellfire had eased somewhat she carried on again with the mules and donkeys and lighter loads of fodder, etc.

The entry for the 28th records:

> We were very glad to see a squadron of six trawlers arrive this morning, as up to the present there had only been the two us on the job, the third trawler being reserved for Red Cross duties. ... The new arrivals had been taking part in the feint at Bulair, where boats had been towed inshore, but no actual landing had taken place. They were part of the second batch of trawlers, just sent out from England, and were manned by their ordinary fishermen crews.

Clarke again: 'one of our crew got a few pieces of shell into his side' (3 June); 'Still bullets and shells flying about[;] they fired on Achi Baba from Dardanelles side today and an Aeroplane dropped some bombs at Anzac.' (31 July).

Fierce fighting took place in August; on the 10th he wrote:

> Salvar [Suvla] Bay is a new landing place we had taken on Friday, August 6. All day we can hear nothing but the booming of guns and the crack from the rifles, and see the bursting of shells on the Battle field as a great and heavy Battle is in full swing, and here we lay looking on with thousands of bullets flying about us, watching all that is going on, as we have a good view of the land.

On 2 September, *Loch Broom* was lucky not to have been hit by 18 shells which dropped very close to her and the crew missed a big attack on the 24th which began as they came away. Tragedy struck Trawler 327, however, on 3 October:

> Heaved up anchor and went to 362 and 327 with mails and heard that one of the 327 deckhands got struck below the heart with a bullet and died before they got him to the Hospital Ship, he belonged to Yarmouth and left three children.

Evacuation and the Beckoning Aegean

The months of bitter fighting at Gallipoli have been described in numerous publications, both by men who were there and by historians. Only the briefest references to land-based operations have been possible, or indeed desirable, in this study – which it is hoped will remedy the neglect of the role of fishing vessels and their fishermen and naval crews in that theatre of the war.

As 1915 drew to a close on the peninsula, it became abundantly clear that, due to a combination of circumstances, the campaign had no future. Plans were therefore drawn up for evacuation. This exercise, resulting in barely a casualty, ironically proved to be the most successful of all the operations at the Dardanelles.

The last words on this affair rightly belong to the diarist from the *Lord Wimborne*, whose notes have come to occupy a unique place in the specialist literature of trawlers in the Great War:

> We have left with honour, for they have not drove us off. The object of these operations, no doubt, has held the Turks and prevented the invasion of India and Egypt, which should prove to be a menace to the German plans in time to come.

The military should have taken full advantage and pushed with vigour at the beginning, when first landed, when the ships gave them such good cover; they dallied and waited too long, Australians were ready to advance on the third day, although lost most of the officers. 'Suvla' was certainly bad leadership and muddling; supports and reliefs were straggling about the beach, no one seemed to understand what to do.

I should think ever since the submarine put in an appearance and scared all our ships with heavy guns away, we lost the peninsula. Turks took every advantage of the ships' absence, and brought heavy guns on all the beaches. Soldiers lost their stamina and funked, through lack of experienced leaders; trawlers and fleet sweepers were saviours. Had there been another 50 destroyers to protect and keep battleships covering the peninsula all the time, no doubt it would have told a different tale.

The trawlers dispersed to new duties in the Aegean and other parts of the Mediterranean and did valuable, if monotonous, work. Home seemed further away than ever. Clarke expressed the mood of most of the crews at the end of December 1915 when he confided to his log:

That finished another year with the navy blue I wish it was finished altogether fed up, 1915.

Chapter 10

Mare Amarissimo

A Drifter off Tarentum

He from the wind-bitten North with ship and companions descended,
Searching for eggs of death spawned by invisible hulls.
Many he found and drew forth. Of a sudden the fishery ended
In flame and a clamorous breath known to the eye-pecking gulls.

Rudyard Kipling, from *Epitaphs of the War* (1914-18)

For many fishermen, a great number from Britain's far north, the Adriatic was indeed a 'most bitter sea', a sea of suffering, bravery and death.

Kipling's Roman 'Tarentum' is, of course, our present-day Taranto, a port which served as an important base for the drifters serving in the Adriatic. Indeed, it was a stronghold of the Italian Navy in both world wars and, with its arsenal and shipyards, remains a major naval base. Rear-Admiral Cecil Thursby, who took command of the British Adriatic Squadron in December 1915, reached the port with a division of battleships three days after Italy – partly to gain territory – declared war on Austria-Hungary on 23 May 1915 (only in August 1916 did she declare war on Germany).

It was realized from the very outset how vital it was that the Austrian and German submarines based in the heavily-defended, deep-water shelters of Pola (today's Pula) and Cattaro (Kotor) had to be denied access to the Otranto Straits, and therefore beyond. Pola's large natural harbour had been Austria's main naval base since 1859 and was a major shipbuilding centre while the Montenegrin Bay of Cattaro, one of the most indented parts of the Adriatic, served as the home port during the hostilities of the Austrian Fifth Fleet, consisting of pre-Dreadnought battleships and light cruisers.

On the Allied side, Brindisi was the base of the British Adriatic Fleet and the centre of Italian naval operations in the Adriatic. These were supported at the port, and from the Greek island of Corfu, by the French *Armée Navale*. On the coast of Albania, Valona (Vlore/Vlonës), one of the country's oldest cities and her first capital from 1912 to 1913, had been invaded by Italy in 1914 and would be occupied by her until 1920. The port was strategically located at the mouth of the Adriatic and was the closest to the Italian port of Bari across the water. Durazzo/Durrës, Albania's second largest city and capital of the country from 1913 to 1920, was occupied by Italy in 1915 and by Austria-Hungary in 1916-1918. It was captured by the Allies in October 1918.

Enter the Drifter Fleet

The threat to the Allies in the Adriatic and Mediterranean came not from the Austro-Hungarian fleet, which was by and large content to remain within the shelter of its bases, but from German and Austrian U-boats. Part of the counter-submarine strategy was for as many fishing vessels as were available to be stationed in the Straits and use their nets in exactly the same way, as we will see later, as in the Dover Straits, to enmesh U-boats seeking to pass south and out into the open Mediterranean. Supported by destroyers based at Brindisi and Valona, the operations of the barrage would be covered by aircraft.

U.21 had reached Cattaro on 13 May 1915 by sea, although before then other submarines had arrived at the Adriatic overland for re-assembly. From June onwards, the marauders became increasingly active. The decision to send drifters out from England was taken at the end of August and 60 of them were got ready (their names are recorded in Appendix 4). The preparations and journey were recorded by E Keble Chatterton in his *Seas of Adventure*:

> [When] on August 30, 1915, ... the Admiralty, in response to the Adriatic situation, ordered twelve ... drifters from Poole, twice that number from Dover and another two dozen from the Penzance-Falmouth area, the 60 were forthcoming as easily as if they were threescore of loaves. ... In charge of this latest flotilla Commander J. O. Hatcher, R.N., was appointed, with Lieutenant-Commander M. E. Cochrane, R.N., as second, together with a number of young divisional officers from the Royal Naval Reserve.
>
> ...Already at 1 p.m. [on 31 August] the first seven drifters under Sub-Lieutenant Adams, R.N.R., steamed off down the harbour, past St. Anthony lighthouse, with cheers and a military band playing 'Auld Lang Syne' to encourage them from the shore at Pendennis Castle. Five hours later Commander Cochrane's division of seven more shoved off, speeded by the same cheering, the same band, and the same tune. No departure could very well have been more expeditious, but the humorous side of naval warfare showed itself from the moment he stepped aboard. Of luxury there was none, of essential comfort very little, though the carpenter had done what he could with hammer and saw. As to the fishermen crew, one glance sufficiently showed that this was a funny war anyway. No naval officer expected drifter men to be all smartness and spotless in their uniforms, but collectively the *Remembrance*'s crew presented a severe shock to their new captain. 'The skipper,' Commander Cochrane tells me, 'was distinctly "oiled"; the mate was a man of 60 years, and wore a bowler hat; the cook was blind drunk in his bunk; and no one could find the frying-pan. I also discovered that of my personal fresh provisions six tins of condensed milk, two loaves of bread, two cakes, one lb. of butter, and thirty new-laid eggs had been stolen. The weather was rotten, blowing hard, with heavy rain squalls.' Could any voyage have begun under less hopeful conditions?[105]

Commander Hatcher had once served in the Merchant Service and had entered the Royal Navy on the Supplementary List. When the war began, he had been sent to the trawler base at Grimsby, where, Chatterton tells us, 'by sheer personality, unlimited energy, and driving force, he always managed to extract order out of chaos and defeat any obstructionist.' Lieutenant-Commander Cochrane had actually retired from service ten years before the war but had rejoined and was stationed at Devonport, living ashore. Life aboard the *Remembrance* and, once in the Adriatic, the *Clavis*, would be quite unlike anything in his previous experience. The journey was rough and the units were at times unable to keep together; for a time the *Lily Reiach* mysteriously disappeared, although she turned up again later. On the seventh day out from Falmouth both divisions steamed safely into Gibraltar and began coaling. Next day, the Penzance contingent arrived, followed a few hours later by the Poole drifters. Hatcher's units turned up on the 10th, thus bringing all 60 drifters up to strength.

Chatterton observed:

> ...each of these small steamers within a few short weeks was to improve beyond all recognition; to render most brave and patient service; whilst such crews as *Lily Reiach* carried were to crown their brave efforts in glorious death.[106]

By the 25th, following adaptations at Taranto where the ragged armada was placed under Thursby in HMS *Queen*, the first two divisions (for so they would be organized) were sent out to lay their anti-submarine nets across the Otranto Straits. Before the year was out they would be joined, following a request from Thursby, by another 35 of their sisters, taken from Poole and Milford where they had been serving. By the beginning of January 1916 another fifty had come out from England. Others would follow.

Who were these men from the 'wind-bitten North' who manned them? The *Fishing News* reported:

> When they came to the Mediterranean, the difference of the sea and sky surprised them but they immediately understood. They sail about ... as if they were only off the east coast of Scotland. They hobnob and fraternise with the Italian sailors. They walk about with them, talk to them, and hold conversations with them. What language they speak nobody knows but that they must be able to understand each other is certain as they spend hours together.[107]

James Bone, of the *Manchester Guardian*, went out to see the drifter fleet three years later. It made a memorable impression on him:

> My first view of the Scottish drifters ... was at evening in a creek in an island famed for loveliness and luxury. The colour of the sea and sky and hills surpassed even the violence of the picture-postcards of the place that the men send home. Little boats with coloured sails crept out laden with strange fruit, and the whole island with its yellow hills seemed like a haven of rest. Two familiar hard-lined little ships came puffing along the creek, throwing black trails of smoke into the golden air. How often had one seen these boats grinding out of the Fife ports, or lying off the Forth, or bucketing into Grimsby. Here, in this golden scene, they looked very alien, and as we came nearer, two tow-headed men in their shirt sleeves, sitting by the funnel, staring listlessly at our boat and the wonderful scene before them, spat into the water and yawned, and settled down again. The little boats, the weary men, with all the signs that a Scot could read of Scotsmen and their ships, seemed unutterably lonely and irreconcilably alien in this brilliant setting. We had heard much from high naval authorities, Italian and British, of the remarkable endurance and courage of these men in their long three years' service in the Ægean and the Adriatic seas. Their lives have been exceptionally hard, even as things go in this war. They serve six weeks on the barrage and in coaling and practice, and are then

in harbour for five days, where their rest is broken by harbour duty. They are out in all sorts of weathers throughout the year, and there is much sudden bad weather and many bitter cold nights in these waters. The majority of the boats are employed on work which entails ceaseless vigilance and strain of the nerves over long periods, a new sort of work, particularly exacting to these active and rough-and-ready fishermen.[108]

Describing his experiences to the 39th Annual Meeting of the RNMDSF, Chief Skipper HJ Goldspink, who won the DSC and a number of foreign decorations, told his audience:

> I remember when I got out to the Adriatic we did not understand anything about naval work, but the Captain lined us up and said, 'I want you skippers to remember that you are warrant officers in His Majesty's Service, and to go back and put on brass buttons. (Laughter.) You are going to have a gun on board, and you have to look out for Fritz; I am sending so many of you in groups, and you will be detailed off.' They put us through our drills and our Act of Service – we knew about Fritz who had been sinking our fishing crews. We said, 'Give us a gun and we don't fear Fritz, but we didn't like those "Chocolate soldiers" floating about.' (Laughter.)[109]

An allusion, clearly, to mines, the use of the term being doubtless specific to drifter crews at that time and place. The men had good reason to fear them, for the U-boats which infested these waters laid them strategically and in goodly numbers. They claimed their first drifter victim within a few months, although the first casualty to the drifter fleet would be the *Restore*, after only a fortnight on duty, and the weapon of destruction would be gunfire from a submarine.

Meanwhile, the little warships would play an important ancillary role assisting the Allies in offshore operations. On the last day of November 1915, the Serbian army began its pathetic retreat through Albania towards the sea and from then until the end of February 1916 the drifters performed admirable and vital duties under very hazardous conditions. They assisted in the evacuation of the army and thousands of refugees and were present at the landing of Italian troops at Valona. They were always there to assist disabled ships. On 4 December 1915, the Italian transport *Re Umberto*, carrying troops to Valona, struck a mine off Cape Linguetta. The drifters *Evening Star* and *Lottie Leask* (concerning which more below) happened to be in the vicinity and drew alongside the sinking vessel. Before she went down, over 500 soldiers were able to swarm onto their decks using the ropes which had been thrown across to them. With the men safely across, the drifters managed to chop these away minutes before the transport disappeared. The fact that any lives at all were saved was, wrote Admiral Thursby, 'due solely to the courage and gallantry displayed by the skippers and crews of these drifters'. But they would be made to pay.

The First Victims
At 8.00 a.m. on 12 October 1915, the former Lowestoft drifter *Restore*, under Skipper George R Catchpole RNR, was in a group of drifters to the SW of Saseno (Sazan) island preparing to take up their stations. A small vessel, which

proved to be a U-boat (*U.39* under submarine ace *Kapitänleutnant* Walther Forstmann), made for her and although the drifter fired signal rockets and flares and steamed towards the island, the submarine continued to close. Opening fire when about two miles away, Forstmann hit the vessel after several rounds. The shell exploded in the engine room, where it claimed two victims. The crew abandoned ship, allowing the enemy to close and sink her. She went down in three minutes. After attacking three other drifters, the U-boat steamed northward towards Cattaro. Skipper Catchpole was criticized by the ensuing Court of Enquiry for leaving the vessel without checking to see if anyone was still alive in the engine room, while Midshipman William Hargreave RNR, who was in charge of the division, was admonished for failing to engage the submarine. Thursby ordered that the Articles of War be publicly read to him, emphasizing the requirement for officers to do their utmost to engage an enemy in sight (this despite the fact that most of the drifters carried only small arms). The positive outcome from this incident was that by 13 November all the Adriatic drifters were armed.

Forstmann claimed another English drifter victim that year in an incident which bore similarities to the loss of the *Restore*. On 18 December, the former North Shields vessel *Lottie Leask* was sailing for Valona to rejoin her group after a refit period at Brindisi. In the failing light, at 5 p.m., when she was some 20 miles NW of Saseno Island, a surfaced U-boat was seen, closing from the starboard quarter (the skipper believed there were two but this claim was not substantiated). The drifter altered course and, while zigzagging, attempted to engage with her deck gun. Indeed, she fired five rounds, although resistance ended when she was struck on the port side and stopped by further hits. As previously, Forstmann closed and sank the boat after several shots. The crew had by then abandoned ship, taking to the boat. They, too, were censured by the Court of Enquiry, which held that they had abandoned their vessel too quickly and could have offered more resistance. Yet just a fortnight earlier, this drifter had, as we saw above, performed a heroic joint rescue from an Italian ship.

The men from the *Lottie Leask* are also remembered for their adventurous escape, surely one of the most remarkable of the war. After rowing about for the whole of one night in their small boat, they landed on a sandy beach on the Albanian coast and stayed that night at a shepherd's hut; the shepherd took them to a monastery where they were welcomed and given food and a room. Fearing capture by the enemy, they walked on all night through the swamps and continued marching all the next day (the 21st). They slept that night on the hillside but on the following day met some Italian soldiers who gave them biscuits and directed them to an Italian camp. Leaving there at daybreak, they came to a second camp, and finally marched with 100 Serbians to Valona, where, that evening, they boarded a transport, the SS *Myrmidon*, and stayed on it for several days. Finally on 28 December, 10 days after *Lottie* had sunk, they reached the drifter base at Brindisi, to the astonishment of their fellow-fishermen and officers.

Volume 2 takes up the story of the Adriatic drifters and includes an account of a fearful massacre of the vessels and of the circumstances under which the first fisherman in the war to win a VC earned his award. Also included in the volume is a record of service by fishermen and their vessels in a region which could not be in greater contrast to the Adriatic – the waters off the coastline of Russia's Far North.

Chapter 11

Channel Guard

Scores of workers, stern endeavours, forged a weapon for the war,
For the special operations never entered on before.
Thus the fighting force at Dover grew to manhood from its birth,
Waiting for the time when proudly it would show the world its worth

From *L'Envoi*[110]

The Dover Patrol, one of the key naval forces during the conflict, operated over a vast and busy area covering some 4,000 square miles, on waters extending from the North Foreland to the Scheldt and from Beachy Head due south to the French coast. Dunkirk was a satellite of the Dover Command. It was vital that the Channel trade route be kept open for legitimate traffic and closed to the U-boat.

No fewer than 147,674 individual movements across the Dover Straits by transports, troopships, hospital ships and large numbers of miscellaneous vessels took place between 5 August 1914 and 11 November 1918. One and a quarter million tonnes of materials were shipped, almost half of which was ammunition of every calibre, while the approximate number of troops transported both ways reached 16 million.

Dover and its Patrol

The port of Dover was ill-prepared for war, despite work on a great naval harbour being carried out from 1897 to 1909. Neglected in favour of Rosyth as a warship base, it lacked a repair dock and barracks for sailors. Changes were soon made when war was declared, however. The Sixth Destroyer Flotilla came to be based at the port, whose entrances, albeit badly-designed, were made torpedo-proof by sunken vessels and strengthened boom defences. On 1 August 1914, those entrances were for the first time swept continuously all night by searchlights. On the following day, two trawlers ('the first comers of a famous and glorious company', wrote JB Firth in *Dover and the Great War*) appeared to take up their new war duties. Ordinary Cross-Channel services to and from Calais and Ostend were immediately suspended for the duration and Dover became instead the port of departure for troops and stores to the Continent. Dunkirk became its corresponding base on the French coast.

The Straits would be the busiest sea lanes anywhere during the war. 'It was', wrote W Macneile Dixon in *The Fleets behind the Fleet*, 'more like a maritime fair. Never was there such a bustle of shipping since the world was made.' Yet so vigilant and thorough was the work of the patrol that of the enormous number of mercantile vessels passing through, only 73 were lost through various causes – torpedoes, bombs, mines, gunfire and aircraft.

Dover's reputation as a harbour had been, and remained, notorious among those who had to use it. Several years before the war, Captain Taprell Dorling (better known as the prolific naval author 'Taffrail'), described it, in *Swept Channels*, as 'the last haven of refuge that the Almighty had ever made'. As for the plunging and swaying trawlers he saw in the port, he marvelled: 'Heaven knows how those on board them lived, ate, slept or did anything!'

When Belgium was overrun, the influx of refugees into the port was enormous. Their arrivals were recalled by Lieutenant-Commander Stanley Coxon RNVR (pseudonym 'A Dug Out') in his wonderfully vivid *Dover during the Dark Days*. On one occasion, no fewer than 4,500 Belgians found themselves in small steamers alongside the Prince of Wales Pier. Commander Edward RGR ('Teddy') Evans[111] described the scene in *Keeping the Seas*:

> The mine-sweepers, who had been toiling until 3 a.m. arrived at the pier and quickly grasped that the poor Belgians were without food and any sort of comfort. They were, in fact, so crowded together that there was standing room only on board the vessels that carried them. I do not know the exact reasons for their being retained on the little steamers, perhaps it was on account of the capture of thirty spies which were found secreted amongst the refugees; anyhow, it is to be presumed that there was cause enough for the delay in landing these poor people. Rigg, with his mine-sweeper skippers, firemen, boys and lined old mariners made it their business to do what they could for the unfortunate Belgians, and they had the whole forty-five hundred of them fed and tended between 8 a.m. and noon. This was a wonderful feat when we consider that the total complements of the eight small mine-sweepers did not exceed a hundred men. They gave all their provisions, all their money and practically everything they possessed. A stream of billies full of cocoa and tea made its way from the trawlers to the refugee ships. Rigg went the round of the hotels in search of milk for the babies and children. He collected buck-etfuls, which he brought to the pier in his motor-car. When I say collected, I mean literally commandeered it, for this officer and one or two men who were with him simply carried the buckets into the hotel dining-room and emptied the jugs of milk they found on the tables!
>
> The cheerful and willing assistance rendered by the mine-sweepers did no end of good amongst the refugees. ... Fortunately, the weather was perfect, otherwise these poor people would have been in a moderate hell. Commander Rigg removed one poor woman from the steamer and took her to the Lord Warden Hotel, where she gave birth to a child after her arrival. Men, women and children had been standing on board for forty-eight solid hours.[112]

The Commander he refers to was Lieutenant-Commander WG Rigg, whom he described as 'not the least picturesque character in the Dover Patrol'. Originally appointed as Mine-Sweeping Officer, Dover, he had left the Navy and was a District Inspector of the RNLI when war broke out. On rejoining, he was given four old trawlers which arrived at the port straight from the fishing grounds, having discharged their fish cargo at Milford Haven en route. They arrived empty and, save for rusty old trawling wires, had no appliance whatever. Yet within four days they were actually sweeping. Evans recollected the names of two of them – the *Falmouth* and *Abelard*.[113] Although at the time of Rigg's appointment the Dover area was considered impossible to mine on account of the strong tides for which it was infamous, these four vessels were always in evidence ensuring the entrance to the harbour was safe. In fact no mines were laid by the enemy in the area in 1914, but it was only a matter of time before they did. Accordingly, the port acquired a scanty supply of the auxiliary vessels becoming increasingly available through Admiralty requisitions and was able to perfect its minesweeping organization.

The duties of the Dover Patrol were of vital national importance. It had to guard the great route to France, the main artery of our Army on the Western Front, from attack by both U-boats and surface craft (a task successfully achieved, for not one British transport with troops on board was assailed by the enemy) and it had to close the Straits against enemy submarines – a goal which would not, however, be achieved until 1918.

Drifters joined the patrol early on. A contingent of lightly-armed vessels assisting the Examination Service based at Ramsgate as protection against a surprise enemy attack was supplemented by a small force arriving in February 1915 from the north-east fishing ports assigned to tending large-meshed wire drift nets to entangle submarines and make them surface. By June 1915, the number of non-Examination drifters, supported by three yachts, would reach its maximum of 132. On arrival, the drifters and trawlers had no wireless apparatus at all but, by the end of the year, one in six had been fitted with a transmitter. Hydrophones, for all their limitations, were also provided. Each trawler was armed with a 6-pounder high-angle gun, a 7.5-in howitzer and two depth charge traps. Royal Marines, each armed with a rifle, were used on drifters as a stopgap measure, but were sent back to their depot during April 1915, being immediately replaced by 20 Newfoundlanders and 40 Canadians, who would remain with the patrol for more than six months under training before being returned to Canada.

In due course, the trawlers and drifters respectively became Channel Patrols in their own right. The Drifter Patrol, separate from those protecting shipping off Ramsgate and the Downs, was originally under the command of Captain Humphrey W Bowring, later replaced by Captain Frédéric G Bird. Both were made Companions of the DSO in 1916. The netlaying drifters were organized into divisions under an RNR sub-lieutenant or lieutenant, there being about half a dozen drifters in each. Attached to it was an armed yacht, usually commanded by a naval officer, which took full responsibility for operations at sea.

On the trawler/minesweeping front, Dover had eight or so trawlers sweeping under Rigg's command by the end of 1914. The area had been swept assiduously despite the dreadful weather prevailing at the end of the year and despite no mines having yet been found. They would even engage in minelaying activities, the first field being laid between the east Goodwin Sands and Ostend.

The Trawler Patrol was placed under the control of Captain W Vansittart Howard DSO, who also headed the Dover minelaying section. Its functions were traffic route protection, escort duties and minesweeping. Although the force would come to number 255, the maximum number of trawlers ever available at one time for duty was 66. This figure was rarely reached in practice since, owing to collisions, to mined vessels not being at once replaced and to three or four usually being absent for long repairs, the patrol was always short of its proper complement. The minesweeping trawler allocation was soon increased to 84, and these worked with 18 paddle minesweepers and 12 motor launches, while 350 officers and 3,000 men joined this service. The second-in-command was Lieutenant Arthur Buckland, an officer of formidable courage with many years of minesweeping experience.

Initially in command of the force which grew to become the Dover Patrol was the Admiral of Patrols, Rear-Admiral George A Ballard, based in Harwich.

In October 1914, Rear-Admiral Horace Lambert Alexander Hood (1870-1916) took over, although his tenure would be brief. When the war began, he had been Naval Secretary to the First Lord, whom he accompanied to Antwerp. Churchill, fervently in support of bombardments of the Belgian coast, reacted to Hood's view that these were useless and wasteful of ammunition unless backed by military cooperation by ordering him to strike his flag forthwith. Demoted to the command of a small force of obsolete cruisers patrolling the Irish coast, Hood was later – on Churchill regretfully conceding that he had been unfairly assessed – given the command of the Third Battle Cruiser Squadron. He lost his life in the Battle of Jutland and was posthumously awarded the KCB.

His place was taken by Admiral Sir Reginald Hugh Spencer Bacon, who recalled:

> At the outbreak of war the Dover Flotilla formed part of the East Coast Command, with Harwich as headquarters. Its chief function was to prevent German ships breaking through and passing down Channel. It soon became apparent that Dover and the Narrows of the Channel were destined to become of greater importance. The Dover area was, therefore, made a separate command. ... I was summoned to London in April, 1915, to see Mr Churchill, who asked me to take command of the Dover Patrol.

Bacon had been the first captain of the battleship *Dreadnought* and had retired from the Navy in 1909 as Director of Naval Ordnance. From 1910 to 1914 he was managing director of the new Coventry Ordnance Works. He returned to active service on the outbreak of the war and accepted command of the Royal Marine heavy batteries in Flanders. He would be the author of a number of books.[114]

When Bacon took over, the Admiral's staff at Dover consisted of two flag-lieutenants, a secretary and two clerks but all that would soon change. He was, before long, sending his first signal to the Admiralty requesting improved facilities, weapons and, in particular, wireless apparatus. In his *Concise History of the Dover Patrol*, he divided the periods between 1915 and the close of 1917 (when his command ended) into five epochs characterized by definite changes in the patrol's work. Initially, drifting nets to catch submarines was the main activity (April 1915 – August 1915), then bombarding the Belgian coast (August 1915 – March 1916); abandoning drift-nets, laying the first barrage off the Belgian coast and maintaining a daily patrol in sight of Ostend and Zeebrugge (April 1916 – October 1916); preparing for further bombardments of Zeebrugge and Ostend, laying a net barrage from the Goodwins to Dunkirk and planning for a mine barrage from Folkestone to Griz-Nez (October 1916 – March 1917); and finally, laying a second barrage off the Belgian coast, patrolling daily right into the winter, and establishing the Folkestone to Griz-Nez mine barrage, plus bombarding Zeebrugge and Ostend (March 1917 – January 1918). All the time, of course, the patrol was sweeping up and laying mines and protecting transports and other vessels.

At the end of 1917, Bacon was transferred to the post of Controller of the Inventions Department and in the following September was made a full admiral; he retired six months later.

His place was taken by Vice-Admiral Roger Keyes, whose name will forever be associated with the gallant attack on Zeebrugge and Ostend on St George's Day 1918 and, less universally, with the effective strengthening of the Channel Barrage. The raid on Belgium had first been proposed the year before by Sir John Jellicoe but was not formally approved until February 1918 when Keyes devised a plan for a blocking operation to hamper the exit of German ships and submarines.

Concerning the patrol and his predecessor, Keyes generously recorded in his *Naval Memoirs* (1935):

> The activities for the Dover Patrol were immense, and Admiral Bacon had built up an enormous organisation which carried out its daily duties with great regularity and efficiency ... The vessels of the patrol numbered over 300, including large and small monitors, the light cruiser 'Attentive', Flotilla leaders, destroyers, P-boats, trawlers, drifters, minesweepers of various types, MLs, CMBs, and submarines. On a normal night it was possible to concentrate above the minefield four of the older destroyers or P-boats, burning searchlights, 14 trawlers, burning flares, at least 60 drifters, about four motor launches, and two large minesweepers.[115]

Belgian Coast Bombardments

Lieutenant Gordon S Maxwell RNVR recalled, in *The Naval Front*, how many and varied were the tasks given to the patrol more or less from the outset. It might virtually have been termed the left flank of the British Army, for in the first October of the war, during that critical period when the Germans were making a bid for the coast ports as far as Calais, the naval forces under Hood stemmed the enemy advance and held them up at Nieuport, from which point they never advanced.

Lieutenant George HP Muhlhauser, on the yacht *Zarefah*, remembered those early days in his vivid *Small Craft*:

> In December, 1914, a bombardment of the Belgian coast east of Nieuport was planned, and we were sent over, with a group of trawler mine-sweepers to clear a passage for the battleship which was to fire. This sweep was by no means an easy job, as it had to be done at night, the German guns along the coast preventing any work in daylight. On the 13th December we entered Dunkerque with six trawlers. ... In the evening, Lieut. Curzon R.N.R., and the skippers of the remaining five trawlers came on board for instructions, and were told to sweep next morning as far as they could go to the eastward without drawing fire. Later on when it was dark, if they had survived, they were to form up astern of us, and to follow past Nieuport, and for about two miles along the coast.

Next morning we left harbour at 7 a.m., and passed through the Roads, the Zuidcoot Pass, and on towards Nieuport. … At first everything went well; the trawlers steamed along, and tried to look as much like fishermen as possible, and we began to hope that they would get up to Nieuport before their character was realized. But the wily Boche was only waiting for them to get well within range before opening fire. He probably knew quite well what they were about, and inferred that a bombardment was contemplated. As soon, therefore, as they were near enough he opened up with two guns to drive them away, and prevent them from sweeping up any mines that might be there. The trawlers had no choice but to clear out, and promptly slipped the wires, hove them and the kites inboard, and ran for it. Shells burst ahead of them, astern and alongside, but none was hit, though the men on deck were drenched by the spray thrown up, and a few splinters struck the ships. Ten minutes put them out of range, and we all returned to the Roads to wait for darkness before making our next attempt.

That attempt was successful, with a strip about a mile wide being swept against huge odds: German guns lined the sand-dunes for two miles along the coast just three-quarters of a mile away, searchlights were a threat and a TBD could easily have been sent from Ostend, eight miles away. Next day, the battleship HMS *Majestic* arrived for the bombardment and the trawler sweepers and a few other vessels steamed round to form a submarine screen. Luckily, the response from the shore guns was feeble.

Hood wrote that the presence of the ships on the coast soon caused alterations in the enemy's plans. Less and less of their troops were seen, while more and heavier guns were gradually mounted along the sand dunes fringing the coast. The British were assisted in these coastal attacks by a flotilla of French destroyers – indeed, on one occasion, Hood led the fleet into action flying his flag on the *Intrépide*.

The first sortie by Bacon, dubbed 'Fred Karno' by Evans (and by tradition since), was directed at the harbour and defences of Zeebrugge. It took place on 23 August 1915. The force was made up of HM ships *Sir John Moore*, Lord Clive, Prince Rupert and the best part of 100 other vessels and auxiliaries. All the objectives selected were damaged or destroyed and the results were 'markedly successful'. Stanley Coxon recalled the departure of this heterogeneous band:

It was a curious medley of a fleet and consisted of one old-fashioned battleship, several monitors and cruisers, a large force of destroyers, a spotting-balloon ship devoid of masts, a cross-Channel steamer converted into a floating sea-plane base, together with a huge flotilla of trawlers, drifters, armed yachts and motor-launches. The work done on that occasion was exceedingly effective, for we more or less caught the Hun napping. On the 15th the dose was repeated, but in the short interval we found that the defences had been enormously strengthened, and, though effective fire was opened and our casualties were nil, the result of this second bombardment was not altogether satisfactory.

The part played by drifters in the first raid was vital, for the only protection the fleet had was the 16 protective miles of nets laid by them on three sides.

There were further raids in the ensuing months. In the attack on Ostend (6 September), extremely valuable assistance was rendered by the auxiliary craft.

Assaults were then made on Middlekirke, Raversyde and Westende (19 September), Knocke, Zeebrugge and other targets (24, 26, 27 and 30 September) and Zeebrugge (3 October), followed by miscellaneous attacks (6, 12, 13 and 18 November).

During the operations, total British casualties numbered 34 killed and 24 wounded. Three vessels were unfortunately lost: HMD *Greatheart*, sunk by a mine on 24 September; HM Armed Yacht *Sanda*, sunk by gunfire on 25 September;[116] and HM Mine Sweeper *Brighton Queen*, sunk by a mine on 6 October. The drifter went down after she had barely left Dover, striking one of the mines laid two days earlier by *UC.6*. Skipper William Davidson RNR and seven of the crew were killed.

Paying tribute in his report to the Admiralty to those who took part, Bacon made special reference in his dispatch of 12 January 1916 to the efforts of the fishermen, among others, during the operations:

> Their lordships will appreciate the difficulties attendant on the cruising in company by day and night under war conditions of a fleet of 80 vessels, comprising several widely different classes, manned partly by trained naval ratings but more largely by officers of the Naval Reserve, whose fleet training has necessarily been scant, and by men whose work in life has hitherto been that of deep sea fishermen.
>
> The protection of such a moving fleet by the destroyers in waters which are the natural home of the enemy's submarines has been admirable, and justifies the training and organisation of the personnel of the flotilla. But more remarkable still, in my opinion, is the aptitude shown by the officers and crews of the drifters and trawlers, who in difficult waters, under conditions totally strange to them, have maintained their allotted stations without a single accident. Moreover, these men under fire have exhibited a coolness well worthy of the personnel of a service inured by discipline. The results show how deeply sea adaptability is engrained in the seafaring race of these islands.
>
> It is to the excellent work done by the destroyers under Commodore C. D. Johnson, M.V.O., and the drifters under Captain F. G. Bird, that I ascribe our immunity from loss by submarine attack. The mine sweepers, under Commander W. G. Rigg, R.N., have indefatigably carried out their dangerous duties.

In the list of Officers Specially Recommended appended to his dispatch, Bacon mentioned, among others, Skipper Laurence Scarlett RNR of HM Drifter *Hyacinth*, who on 'September 25th, off Zeebrugge, exhibited great coolness in action, remaining and completing his task [of safely getting all the nets and net-mines aboard] although exposed to heavy gun fire.' He was awarded the DSC. This vessel, together with her sister *Fearless*, rescued some survivors under those terrible conditions. Reference was again made to Captain FG Bird of the Dover Drifter Patrol, who was 'in personal charge of the drifters during five of the major attacks, and contributed materially to the success of the operations'.

Minesweeping and Other Tasks

The Dover area had been strewn with mines since the spring of 1915. After June, a far greater danger had to be dealt with – the night time mining of the trade route by submarine minelayers. In response to this development and other enemy minelaying activities, the Dover sweepers swept a distance equal to twelve times round the earth over the next two years. Fishermen were not the only ones to engage in these operations but they were specifically mentioned by Bacon, who commented that the work:

> ...had to be mastered by fishermen in sluicing tides, in quite considerable seas, often in thick and misty weather when the land was not visible, when instinct alone could help them to estimate their position.[117]

During 1915, the whole of the traffic routes had to be swept daily by the trawlers and he took steps at once to fit out as many as possible for the purpose. This activity dovetailed perfectly with guarding the traffic line, since each pair of boats could sweep its own section of the route once in each direction then, after covering a double band of the route in this way, haul in their sweeps and go on with their usual traffic duties.

On 31 October, when Rigg was out with his sweepers, two merchant ships, the Norwegian *Eidsiva* and the British *Toward*, blew up. The yacht *Aries* rescued several survivors and transferred them to attendant trawlers but was herself mined and sunk. A gale blowing from the south-west accompanied by a mountainous sea made sweeping impossible. The sweepers stood by the dangerous area and regrettably the Grimsby trawler *Othello II* was blown up off Leathercoat while waiting to sweep. The only survivor among the crew of 10 was a signal boy, pushed out of the wheelhouse by the skipper as she sank.

The first mines laid by the enemy were placed in groups of six, and later on in groups of 12. However, the numbers became random – and the work greatly increased – once the enemy realized, by the resumption of normal duties, that such clusters had been cleared. Time was then often wasted in searching for mines which had not been laid.

Whenever numbers permitted, 24-26 trawlers were stationed, one mile south of the traffic route, between the South Goodwin Light Vessel and the western limit of the patrol off Beachy Head. Each unit of six was under the command of an officer in a wireless trawler stationed at each of the rendezvous (the South Goodwin Light Vessel, Folkestone Gate, and the Royal Sovereign Light Vessel). Two trawlers were additionally stationed at Boulogne for sweeping the entrances at daylight each morning and two at Dunkirk for sweeping from the Dyck Light Vessel and the secret man-of-war route. These vessels remained on station for four consecutive days and nights. For four days, 26 of the trawlers were nominally resting, coaling, provisioning, and changing boiler water.

Bacon tells how protection of the traffic line against German submarines consisted of pairs of armed trawlers from three to five miles apart, with old type destroyers at every 25 miles to support them. Patrolling on the sea side of the traffic line, these formed 'a most efficient hedge' against attack. U-boats loathed the patrol vessels and their depth charges 'much as a cat dislikes a terrier' and when they sighted our trawlers they took care to give them a very wide berth.[118]

Nets, and later the barrages, were the main defence but 'catches' were meagre until 1918. One early victim, on 4 March 1915, was *U.8* (confused in one online source with *UB.8*), which was trapped in nets, forced to surface and scuttled under gunfire from HMS *Gurkha* and HMS *Maori*. The crew was rescued.

The story of the Dover Patrol continues in Volume 2.

Chapter 12

The Enemy Above

Hail to thee, high-flier
Who with generous heart
Pourest out thy fire
Over earth's dim chart
In sundry spasms of well-premeditated art!

Like a monstrous bird
Overseas thou comest;
Melodies unheard
Through the heavens thou hummest,
And bombing still dost soar, and soaring ever bombest.

From *To a Zeppelin*[119] by 'O.S.'

Airships got off to an inauspicious start in Germany. The prototype *LZ1* (LZ denoting *Luftschiff Zeppelin*, or 'Airship Zeppelin') first flew on 2 July 1900 over Lake Constance but the flight lasted for only 18 minutes before the machine made a forced landing on the lake due to a technical problem. Although two further, and successful, flights were made later that year, potential investors remained unconvinced and the machine was dismantled and sold for scrap.

Despite their imperfections and vulnerability to attack and to the elements, airships began to be produced again from 1906 for civilian, military and naval use. While a number of army Zeppelins would be involved in raids over Britain, attacks would predominantly be carried out by naval airships, of which just one – *L3* – existed on the outbreak of the war. Great faith was placed in these machines, despite the loss of two sisters: *L1* had been forced down into the North Sea in a thunderstorm on 9 September 1913, drowning 14 crew members (this being the first Zeppelin incident with fatalities) and *L2* had been destroyed just over five weeks later by an exploding engine during a test flight. The entire crew had been killed. For its part, *L3*, which first flew on 11 May 1914, completed 24 reconnaissance missions over the North Sea and participated in the first raid on England. It was destroyed by its crew after a forced landing (due to engine failure) in Denmark on 17 February 1915.

The Allies were nevertheless aware that Zeppelins could pose a threat and from the very outset targeted the airship sheds. Since Germany had very few light cruisers, which were traditionally used for reconnaissance, airships were viewed by its navy as a cheaper and, in theory, less vulnerable alternative.

The First Wartime Sorties

After three machines were lost in the first month of the war in daylight raids over heavily defended areas, the German army abandoned airship operations but the navy, with its battle fleet blockaded in port by the Royal Navy, mounted a night bombing offensive which was to be the first aerial strategic bombardment campaign in history. A reluctant Kaiser had finally bowed to pressure from the German Admiralty and given his consent for Zeppelins to be used in attacks against England.

Until that happened, fishermen living on or near the north-east coast could, in theory, take some comfort from the *Fishing News* columnist's assurance in the issue dated 24 October 1914:

> I do not think that the good folk need worry one little bit about an invasion by the air. Zeppelins may come, to say nothing of *Taube* and *Albatross* aeroplanes, but I am sure that our north-east villages, attractive though they may be, will not appeal to the German bomb droppers.

Since, however, Zeppelins were handicapped on a number of missions by poor visibility and unfavourable wind conditions, they did in fact jettison their bombs at such times miles from their true targets in their erratic flight, both on land and over the sea (as some of our fishermen were to find out).

A house in the fishing port of Great Yarmouth boasts the distinction of being the first in Britain to sustain damage by a Zeppelin. It was at 8.30 p.m. on Tuesday, 19 January 1915, that the airship flew in low and dropped a string of bombs on the town. Two people died when one of the bombs exploded in St Peter's Plain and 16 people were injured. St Peter's Villa (now called Merlin Villa) took the full blast which demolished the front of the building completely. The occupant, a Mr Ellis, escaped with minor scalp wounds. A plaque was erected above the front door by Yarmouth Archaeological Society.[120] The targets had in fact been the Humber and the Thames and the raid was carried out by three Navy Zeppelins (*L3*, *L4* and *L6*), although *L6* had to return early with engine trouble when still 90 miles away from the English coast. This was the second setback in a fortnight for its commander, *Korvettenkapitän* Peter Strasser, the highly active Commander of the German Naval Airship Division, since his first raid on 13 January had been frustrated by bad weather. On this second raid, *Kapitänleutnant* Hans Fritz in *L3* was carried far south of his intended landfall and decided to raid Great Yarmouth, which he reached at 8.20 p.m. Releasing a parachute flare, he began his attack from 5,000 feet, dropping six HE and seven incendiary bombs. The second airship, *L4*, crossed the coast nearby but became hopelessly lost. Its commander later claimed to have attacked fortified places between the Tyne and Humber but had in fact bombed sundry Norfolk villages and dropped the bulk of his bombs over undefended King's Lynn.[121]

In its issue dated 23 January 1915, the *Fishing News* again considered Zeppelins, speculating on their role in modern warfare in general and in the raid on Yarmouth in particular. By that time, a fair amount was known about these machines, evidenced by the details of the debate as presented to its readers:

There have been in this country lately two schools of thought with respect to the Zeppelin. One party has regarded it as the most formidable instrument of modern warfare, and looked for an invasion of this country by this type of craft with the greatest misgiving. The other school affected to deride the Zeppelin. It was too clumsy, too unwieldy, too good a target, and too much affected by weather conditions to have much success in an attempted invasion. The first school pointed to the destruction done at Antwerp for justification of their theory; the second called as their witness the *Arethusa* and the *Undaunted*, which easily drove off a Zeppelin attack off Cuxhaven.

There is much to be said for both points of view, but it would be unwise to take too confident a view of the Zeppelin's lack of capabilities for harm. In this raid on Yarmouth at any rate they have at least demonstrated their ability to cross the North Sea and to do grievous damage. Germany has, or had some time ago, about 30 Zeppelins. Their advantage over aeroplanes is that they can remain in the air for a much longer period. A continuous flight of at least 24 hours can easily be undertaken.

Arriving in the Tyne on 9 April 1915, the crew of the North Shields fishing vessel *Grecian Prince* reported an unnerving experience with a Zeppelin. They had been fishing 35 miles N by E of the river, at about 6.40 p.m., when they saw one coming slowly towards them. It descended as low as 150 feet and must have been about 400 feet long. The trawler's crew, who were dragging their nets at the time, could distinguish some of the men on the airship and saw three men lazily walking about on the veranda or platform. The fishermen thought they were taking observations before deciding on their final course. The Zeppelin then manoeuvred about until it passed completely over the vessel and another North Shields trawler, the *Rhodesia*. Darkness was by now just beginning to fall. Understandably, the men on these boats found this experience highly stressful and were greatly relieved to see the huge machine setting off again on its course, WSW to the Tyne, without molesting them. Regrettably, it was only a matter of days before the *Rhodesia* was lost, as she was wrecked on 19 April near Stornoway.

The Blyth tug *Jupiter*, returning to its home port, reported encountering a Zeppelin in the North Sea some miles from land. This account was published in the same *Fishing News* (of 17 April) as that describing the experience of the North Shields trawlers. The skipper heard the sounds of engines overhead and observed the airship; it chased the tug for some time and descended so low that it appeared as though it would touch the masthead. On two occasions the *Jupiter* was able to elude pursuit – once when she ran into a hailstorm and once when the Zeppelin was hidden behind a cloud. The tug was in a precarious position, however, since the captain was afraid to stoke lest the vessel's whereabouts be revealed. Suddenly, however, the airship sailed away landwards and he later saw the flash of bombs and could hear explosions.

Skipper Trevor of the Grimsby trawler *Etruscan* saw a Zeppelin in broad daylight, at about 4 p.m. on Wednesday 14 April while fishing in the North Sea. It appeared to be heading towards Blyth, and indeed an airship did pass over the town on that date. The trawler was positioned at about 100 miles NE by N from the Humber. As in the other sighting, the dirigible was flying at about 300 feet. Several trawlers were fishing in the vicinity and, on approaching these, the machine descended to about 200 feet. It was obviously observing the vessels closely and did so for about 20 minutes. Looking through his binoculars, Trevor distinctly saw the Zeppelin's number, which he was positive was 19. However, *L19* – an airship which would have a much closer encounter with another Grimsby trawler early the following year – did not make its first flight until 27 November 1915. It was in all probability *L9*, which crossed the coast at Blyth. Eerily, the Zeppelin made no attempt to interfere with or speak to any of the trawlers, and after completing its observation it rose and finally disappeared in a NNW direction. The mate of the vessel also thought they could have taken a good shot at her if they had had a gun. They kept the airship in view for a long time, although eventually she rose so high that she ultimately became the merest speck. The conditions were particularly favourable for her, as the light was exceedingly clear and there was only the slightest breeze blowing.

At 12.20 a.m. on 16 April 1915, two Zeppelins came up the River Blackwater and dropped four bombs at Maldon, near Lowestoft. One machine passed over Southwold a quarter of an hour later and dropped three bombs when north of the town, disappearing in the direction of Lowestoft. Shortly after 1 a.m., it was sighted off the port (see below) and passed over the town, dropping six bombs and setting fire to Messrs Latten's timber yard. Although three horses were killed, there were no human casualties.[122] The target had in fact again been the Humber area, and involved three airships, the Navy Zeppelins *L5*, *L6* and *L7*. Peter Strasser, flying in the latter craft, commanded the operation, the net effect of which was £6,500 worth of damage. The combination of navigation difficulties, high winds and British lighting restrictions prevented the raiders from reaching their intended targets. Later, the airship captains confessed they were not sure where they had been.

A sighting of one of the Zeppelins had been made by the sailing trawler *Leslie*. Skipper Borbine reported that just before 1 a.m., when they were anchored two miles SE of Lowestoft, the man on watch on deck shouted down to the cabin that an airship was approaching. The skipper went up on deck and made out a Zeppelin plainly visible against the dark, starry sky. It was flying at a height of 300 or 400 feet and the noise from its propellers was deafening. When the airship was almost above the vessel, something was dropped from it and a blue light shot up to a height of three or four feet. This was followed by a splash as the missile dropped into the water. The skipper could not say whether or not it was a bomb, as there was no explosion. It was conceivably a type of marker.[123] The crew of the *Leslie* immediately extinguished their sailing lights. The Zeppelin hovered over them for a short time then made her way landwards; the fishermen then heard the fire alarm at Lowestoft, immediately after which came two loud reports. Flames could be seen shooting high into the air and this was followed by the cracking of rifles. Skipper Borbine then saw the airship make her way north-eastwards, flying so low that he thought his men could have hit her with rifles had they been armed.

At about 8 p.m. on 11 May 1915, Skipper Frank Bucknole of the Lowestoft sailing trawler *Crimson Rose*[124] saw a Zeppelin in the North Sea some 50 miles NE of Lowestoft. It was growing dusk when he heard the whirring of the airship's engines. He then saw it flying low towards him. It passed over his vessel at a height of about 500 feet and circled. In the distance was a trading steamer, in whose direction the airship then made off. He afterwards heard the sound of an explosion and concluded that the Zeppelin had dropped a bomb. By then it was dark and he could not see what had happened. Fearing the airship would return, he and the crew got into the boat in readiness for an emergency. Eventually, however, the Zeppelin flew away towards the English coast.

Far to the south, on 17 May, a Zeppelin was picked up by the searchlights at Dover (this was the first time an airship had ever been illuminated) and driven inland. The bombs she dropped fell harmlessly near Oxney. On 10 August, Dover was bombed from over the western entrance, and a bomb fell near a trawler. In general, however, the Zeppelins' raids on the Kentish port in 1915 met with very little success, thanks partly to the vigilance of the searchlights and anti-aircraft battery at Langdon.[125]

Reporting from North Shields in May 1915, the RNMDSF Superintendent, Miss Grace, was for her part much relieved at the Institute being spared in:

> ...the late Zeppelin raid ... how much reason we have to thank our God for His protection. The sound of explosion of a bomb near, and the sudden total darkness into which we were plunged, were certainly alarming ...

The following month came the dramatic report that two Lowestoft fishing smacks had fallen victim to a Zeppelin. A Dutch smack, *M.A. 73*, had, according to a telegram sent from Maasluis, landed eight survivors of the *Welfare* and *Laurestina*, allegedly attacked and sunk by an airship while fishing in the North Sea, the crews having been picked up in their own boats by the Dutch vessel. However, this report, as mentioned in Chapter 9, was erroneous, since a U-boat had been the perpetrator.

Writing in December 1915, Skipper Collett, the RNMDSF Port Missionary at Gorleston, reported some narrow escapes:

> Since my last note there has been a great deal of sorrow on the sea, and that has meant great sorrow to those that have been left to mourn. There have been ship-wrecks on our coast through the bad weather, but even those have not been the only dangers of the deep, but there have been the dangers of Zeppelins to our fleet of herring catchers. During the last air raid some of the men told me that the bombs were falling all round the boats as they were adrift at their nets, and they were powerless to get out of their way without cutting their nets adrift. But, thank God, there were no boats damaged, which was just a miracle, as my Scotch friend that was one of them told me.

Incidents involving Zeppelins from 1916 onwards, one of which would become an issue on Germany's part, are described in Volume 2.

Chapter 13

Lifesavers

Weary, helpless, hopeless seamen
Fainting on the deck,
With what joy they hail their Saviour,
As He hails the wreck.
I'll stand by until the morning,
I've come to save you; do not fear!

Quoted in *Toilers of the Deep*, November 1911

Less than a year before the war began, the subject of the safety of life at sea was the focus of international attention. Nearly 130 delegates from most European countries (including Germany) and North America attending the London Conference on the Safety of Life at Sea were entertained at a dinner by the Worshipful Company of Fishmongers on 2 December 1913 at Fishmonger's Hall. The venue was declared by the Prime Warden, Major-General WS Blewitt, to be an appropriate one for what he declared to be 'an international matter ... of the utmost importance'.

Looking back, we can appreciate how fishermen, many of whose vessels have been dubbed the 'lifeboats of the North Sea', have earned universal recognition and the deepest respect for their crews through the hazardous (and occasionally terrifying) rescues of fellow-seamen and survivors from vessels of all kinds.

A number of such exploits before the war involved our future enemy. In March 1911, for example, Skipper Bone of the Grimsby steam trawler *Scarborough* and the members of his crew were publicly presented by the Mayor with rewards for conspicuous bravery in rescuing the crew of a German barque in the North Sea during a gale. The skipper received a certificate from the German Society for Saving Shipwrecked Men and a silver medal of the Laeisz Foundation of the Society, while monetary rewards were handed to the crew. Since the circumstances of the rescue had called for exceptional bravery and risk, the Kaiser notified his consul in Grimsby that further rewards would be given to the fishermen by the German Government. Again, in November 1913, Skipper Oxborough of the Grimsby trawler *Acuba* was the recipient of a handsome pair of binoculars from the Kaiser in recognition of the bravery he and his crew had shown in rescuing the crew of another German barque, *Kathe*, which they had discovered sinking in April of that year. The survivors had narrowly escaped drowning, since the barque had gone down immediately after the rescue.

On 19 January 1914, the masters of two German steam trawlers, the *Caroline Kohne* and *Alice Busse* were landed at Grimsby by the trawler

Semiramis (later hired and armed by the Admiralty for war work). The combined crews, consisting of 27 hands, had first been conveyed to Reykjavik, where most of them received hospital treatment after their terrible experience among the ice floes and icebergs which blocked almost all of Iceland's west coast over the New Year. The *Caroline Kohne* had been struck by heavy ice floes in Isafjord and her rudder and propeller had broken. The *Alice Busse* went to assist the helpless vessel, but she too was caught in the ice, which swept along the fjord in such masses that both vessels were crushed. They sank before the crews could do more than launch their boats on the ice. After covering over 10 miles under appalling conditions, the survivors reached shore and received help at a mission station. When the *Semiramis* entered the fjord for shelter to escape huge icebergs floating down the open coast she took them on board and conveyed them to the capital.

WS Wharton recalled in his reminiscences that two Lowestoft skippers had received monetary gifts from the Kaiser for their lifesaving services. He himself rescued a crew some years before the war and the Germans told his men that they often looked to the fishermen to help them when in distress or danger.

During 1914-18, their gallantry would be called upon more than ever. Trawlers put out their dinghies in the worst weather, as when they rescued airmen from off the dangerous shoal of Longsand when a heavy sea was crashing over it.[126] Their actions contrasted starkly with those of German sailors who, in many instances, deliberately murdered the fishermen crews when they sank their vessels.

Below are some accounts of daring and dangerous rescues from naval vessels by fishermen and officers in fishing vessels on naval service, mainly in home waters. Any not dealt with are covered in those chapters relating to the relevant theatre of war. Also detailed are acts of salvage of various kinds. Rescues from merchant, passenger and fellow fishing vessels necessarily had less of a *direct* impact on the war effort than those from naval vessels and the salvaging of vessels and aircraft yet they were still of importance in many ways. As such they are detailed in tabular form in Appendices 5a to 5c inclusive in this volume and, in the case of post-1915 rescues, in appendices to Volume 2 of this history.

The *Oceanic II* and *Laurentic*

The *Oceanic* was a White Star Line ship in battledress and its loss is thus treated here as a naval casualty. From the outset of the war (and earlier), the Royal Navy had requisitioned such liners for conversion to armed merchant cruisers, mainly to create the 10th Cruiser Squadron. This was employed to maintain the blockade of the North Sea, the patrol area of which extended from the Norwegian coast far into the Atlantic and covered all the approaches to Europe from a northerly direction. They were also intended to relieve the strain on the regular cruisers by undertaking lone patrols and, later, convoy escort work. As a result, 20 or more regular Navy cruisers were freed up for other duties. Forty-one different converted passenger ships, each armed with guns up to 6-inch calibre, served with the Squadron – which was finally paid off on 7 December 1917 – for varying lengths of time.

Regrettably, the *Oceanic*'s naval career was all too brief. She went aground off Foula Island, Shetland, on 8 September 1914. A splendid rescue by a fishing vessel, however, ensured there was no loss of life, as an account in *The Scotsman* on 11 September 1914 illustrated:

> The Glasgow steam trawler *Glenogil*, belonging to Mr John S. Boyle, Aberdeen and Glasgow, arrived at Aberdeen yesterday. Captain Robert Armour reported that he had stood by the White Star liner *Oceanic*, which had been converted into an armed merchant cruiser, for several hours when that vessel went on the rocks, and had been instrumental in getting the whole of the officers and crew safely rescued and transferred to another vessel summoned by wireless. More than one trip by the trawler was necessary before the men were rescued. The trawler, as soon as the signals of distress had been observed, hastened to the rescue. The *Oceanic*, it is stated, could not be towed off, notwithstanding repeated attempts by vessels which went to render assistance, the hawsers parting more than once.

Along with other vessels, including HMS *Forward* which had come out to the scene, the *Glenogil* returned a fourth time to attempt to get the *Oceanic* towed off the reef where she had struck. One after another, however, the strongest hawsers broke, and the attempt was given up. There were 600 men on board, including a German prisoner, who was taken off as carefully as the others. It was a dark and foggy night and, to add to the difficulty of the task, the coast lights had been put out. But the *Glenogil*'s skipper was equal to it – in his own words, 'not a man got his feet wet'. Over £1,000 in money and valuables and the ship's log and papers were salvaged. The *Oceanic* was declared a total loss on 11 September. Following a tremendous storm on the 29th she disappeared, although some remains did lie scattered in relatively shallow water. Breaking-up on the spot would be completed in 1924.

At a court martial at Devonport on 19 November 1914, Lieutenant David Blair, RNR, of the *Oceanic* was found guilty on charges of stranding the vessel or suffering it to be stranded, although at a hearing two days later, also at Devonport, Captain William Slayter, commanding the ex-liner, was acquitted of the charge of negligently, or by default, stranding that vessel.

Like the *Oceanic*, one of her ill-fated sisters, the White Star liner *Laurentic* was requisitioned by the Admiralty as an armed merchant cruiser. When travelling to New York on 25 January 1917 with a complement of 470, she sank after striking a mine off Lough Swilly. Three hundred and fifty lives were lost. Captain RA Norton subsequently told the coroner's inquest that there had been ample time to save all on board who had escaped being killed by the explosion but that the fatalities had been due to severe weather preventing some of them in the boats reaching shore. His own boat was almost full of water when the occupants were picked up by a trawler the next morning, but all the men in the boat survived. Another boat contained five survivors and fifteen frozen bodies. They had been exposed to the bitter cold for over 20 hours. The liner's cargo included a substantial amount of gold bullion, 99 per cent of which was subsequently recovered – at a cost of only 2 per cent of the amount salvaged.

Four Stricken Cruisers and a Mined Submarine

We saw in Chapter 7 how the sister cruisers *Aboukir, Hogue* and *Cressy* were torpedoed in the North Sea on 22 September 1914 with the loss of 1,459 men, although 837 were rescued by nearby Dutch merchant ships and British trawlers. In his statement with reference to this disaster, the Secretary of the Admiralty, on the basis of reports of surviving senior officers, declared:

> The sinking of the *Aboukir* was, of course, an ordinary hazard of patrolling duty. The *Hogue* and *Cressy*, however, were sunk because they proceeded to the assistance of their consort, and remained with engines stopped endeavouring to save life, thus presenting an easy and certain target to further submarine attacks.

Orders were thus subsequently issued that in future no big warship should remain near to render assistance to fellow-vessels in such circumstances.

Despite the appalling death toll, 156 officers and men were picked up by Skipper Thomas N Phillips and his crew in the Lowestoft trawler *Coriander*. The splendid service of these fishermen won warm praise from Commander Bertram WL Nicholson of the *Cressy*. The trawler *J.G.C.* (Skipper George E Jacobs) gave even more valuable help, saving no fewer than 350 men. Both skippers were awarded the Board of Trade Sea Gallantry Medal. Help was also forthcoming, reported Commander Reginald A Norton of the *Hogue*, from the Dutch ships *Flora* and *Titan*. He regretted to add, however, that a Dutch sailing trawler passed close by without rendering any assistance, although signalled to from the *Hogue* to close after she was struck. It was thought by a fair number of the survivors that this 'Dutch' fishing vessel was not Dutch at all, but a German vessel sailing under false colours.

Skipper Wharton, who had been only a few miles away from the scene of the disaster, later wrote:

> Next morning we sailed into all the wreckage and many dead bodies. ... A lot of the wreckage which we found we took into Port and handed over to the Naval Authorities.[127]

Regrettably, the *Coriander* would fall victim to a German submarine within the year.

Scarcely had the shock of the loss of the three cruisers passed when the cruiser HMS *Hawke* was sunk. As mentioned previously, she was torpedoed by *U.9* (Weddigen again) on 15 October 1914, with the loss of 525 men. There were only 70 survivors. Three officers and 49 men were landed at Aberdeen by a trawler, the *Ben Rinnes*. Skipper John Cormack, on landing them at Aberdeen Fish Market, stated that he had taken them off a Norwegian steamer the previous night. The destroyer *Swift* reported having picked up a raft with an officer and 20 men. She was herself subjected to a submarine attack while engaged in her rescue work but managed to convey the men safely to Scapa.

One James Collin was among the 11 recipients, on 7 February 1915, of the BoT's silver medal for gallantry in saving life at sea. This skipper of a Berwick steam drifter (the *Faithful*), in a most unusual rescue, went to the assistance of Submarine *D.5*[128] which had struck a mine in the North Sea and sunk within less than a minute. Despite the danger from mines, Collin and his crew saved four out of five members of the crew. Interestingly, the fifth crew member (Albert Suttill from Leeds) would also owe his life to a fishing vessel, since he was later picked up by a smack, the *Homeland* of Lowestoft. She was skippered and owned by A Jenner, who was also awarded the SGM. As a monetary reward for their gallantry, Collins and his crew shared a prize of £97. The *D.5* was the first of two submarines attached to the 8th Flotilla which were lost in November 1914, the other being the *D.2*, which went missing at the end of the month. It was thought she may have been destroyed by a German torpedo boat.

The *Formidable* Disaster

On New Year's Day 1915, the *Formidable*, a battleship of 15,000 tons, was torpedoed in the Channel by *U.24* with heavy loss of life. No fewer than 547 of the crew from her complement of 780 perished.

The 5th Battle Squadron to which she was attached had been participating in gunnery exercises off Portland, supported by the light cruisers HMS *Topaze* and HMS *Diamond*. At 2. 20 a.m. the next day, the *Formidable*, steaming at 10 knots at the rear of the squadron just 20 miles from Start Point, was struck by a torpedo on the starboard side and then by a second torpedo 45 minutes later. The pinnace and cutter, together with two other boats – one of which capsized soon after – were launched and the cruisers jointly were able to save 114, although 35 officers and 512 men were lost. A passing liner was hailed and asked to assist but refused and continued on her way. HMS *Formidable* remained afloat until 4.45 a.m. and then rapidly sank, with Captain Noel Loxley – and his fox terrier, Bruce – still on the bridge.

A sailor from the *Topaze* gave the following description of the last moments of the *Formidable* to the *Daily Telegraph*:

All the remainder of the Fleet scattered, but we stood by her until she went. We kept sweeping round in circles so as to make ourselves an awkward target for submarines. The first time round we managed to get a line to a cutter and got 35 hands out of her. The coxswain of the boat was a real good Britisher. He remained in his boat calling to his crew to stand by him. He wanted to go back again for another boat-load. He refused to come out until an officer went down and literally hauled him out, and he nearly cried because they wouldn't let him go back.

What struck me most was the coolness of the captain of the *Formidable*. He stood there among the men, cheering them and giving orders quite coolly … . The men had fallen in on the quarter-deck, smoking, and quite orderly. The third and last time we steamed round we went right close to the *Formidable*, and endeavoured to go alongside her, but were unable to do so on account of the sea. We laid off, helpless to save them, and at two minutes past six the poor old *Formidable* went down to Davy. The voice of the skipper could still be heard cheering up the men on deck. Then we saw her settle down by the bows, heard the skipper yell out, 'Good-bye, lads, every man for himself and may God help you all.' His cool and calm voice seemed to reach miles. He was answered with a cheer from the men, and then – I am not ashamed to say that tears were in my eyes and in many others' too – the ship took the final plunge. The lads on her deck went down singing, 'Should auld acquaintance be forgot'. It was so grand, and oh, so pitiful.[129]

In the evidence given at the inquest held at Lyme Regis, AE Cooper, Master-at-Arms of the *Formidable*, who landed at that place in the ship's pinnace with 56 others, stated:

> The boat was absolutely full of water when we started ... we landed on the beach at about 11 o'clock, so that we had been from half-past two in the morning till eleven at night in the water. When we landed six men were dead in the boat and three expired when they got on shore. There was no physical injury to any one.

In a letter from Sidmouth, Stephen Reynolds wrote:

> Horrible job, the *Formidable* – most furious gale I've known here – goodness knows how the boat got to Lyme Regis ... an Exmouth man was among the survivors.[130]

It was the heroism of a Brixham skipper in saving another batch of survivors that would become legendary in connection with the disaster. William Pillar, the owner and skipper of the 50-ton Brixham sailing trawler *Provident*,[131] picked up the men from the cutter of the *Formidable* before she sank, saving 71 members of the crew. There was a strong wind at the time (1 p.m.) and the sea was rising. It was bitterly cold, with squalls of snow alternating with rain. The rescue came not a moment too soon. The cutter had filled with water, having a hole under her hull. This had been stuffed with a pair of pants from one of her seamen. Near Brixham the *Provident* fell in with the tug *Dencade*, which took her in tow, and she was berthed at the pier. By then it was between 7 and 8 p.m. Townsfolk brought blankets, clothing, and boots out to the survivors, who had been in their boat for 12 hours, most of them inadequately dressed. Seventeen were taken to the Fishermen's Institute and it was from these men that some of the earliest information about the disaster to the *Formidable* and the heroism of Pillar and his crew would come. Commending their gallant seamanship, the officer in charge of the cutter, Torpedo-Gunner Daniel Horrigan, characterized it as being beyond all praise.[132] One of the survivors declared, in the course of an interview:

> The way in which we were rescued by the Brixham trawler was a wonderful piece of work. The crew made four attempts to get alongside, and when she succeeded she threw a heaving line. We got hold of the rope and made it fast, and the trawler sailed on, towing us by the rope until she had a favourable opportunity to take the rope on her capstan. She kept on sailing until we were up under her lee quarter, and then every man jumped from the launch into the trawler as best he could. Some were in such an exhausted condition that the others had to help them out, the skipper of the trawler also assisting. Whilst we were on board the trawler the crew gave us some biscuits and coffee, which were very welcome. [At Brixham] the people were wonderfully good to us [and] several of the men were taken to hospital.

Honour and reward would rightly come to the gallant smacksmen. They were received by the King at Buckingham Palace on 7 February and there the Board of Trade Silver Medal was pinned onto the breast of the skipper and his men. Each was handed a voucher for the monetary reward which the Admiralty had bestowed (£250 for Pillar, £100 each for William Carter, mate, and John Clark, second hand, and £50 for Daniel Taylor, the apprentice). Pillar admitted later he had been a 'wee bit' nervous but the King soon put the men at their ease. 'It was a regular beano' was how the skipper described the proceedings. The Shipwrecked Mariners' Society also awarded their gold medal and £5 to the skipper, and their silver medal and £3 to the crew, plus there were presentations from other bodies, such as the Shilling Fund and the London Devonian Association.

The wonderful work of saving life at sea continued during 1915, a year which had begun so disastrously with the *Formidable*'s loss. A letter sent by a fisherlad to the RNMDSF reproduced in the July issue of the *Toilers* shows this:

> I was very pleased to receive your kind and welcome letter, and was also pleased to hear that you and several other ladies take an interest in the welfare of fisherlads who are toiling on the deep and whose lives are in danger at this moment owing to the war. The Mission is doing a great deal of good here. The drifters are saving lots of lives from ships which have been torpedoed. Last week a drifter brought in 18, and today 22 men were rescued by drifters from their ship that had been torpedoed.

Mishap off the Thames Estuary

Quoting an announcement by the Secretary of the Admiralty, the *FN* of 8 May 1915 informed its readers:

> A series of small affairs took place in the neighbourhood of the Galloper and North Hinder Lightships on Saturday [1 May 1915]. During the forenoon, H.M. destroyer *Recruit* was sunk by a submarine, four officers and 21 men being saved by the trawler *Daisy*.[133]
>
> At 3 p.m. the trawler *Columbia* was attacked by two German torpedo-boats, who approached her from the westward and commenced the action without hoisting their colours. The *Columbia* was sunk by a torpedo, only one deckhand being saved by another trawler.

The submarine which dispatched the *Recruit* – actually cutting her in half – was the *UB.6* on her first patrol. Some 35 men were lost. The destroyer's sister-ship, the *Brazen*, attacked the U-boat without success. A more detailed report in the *RUSI Journal*[134] relates that the *Columbia* was one of a division of patrol boats consisting of the *Barbados*, *Miura* and *Chirsit* and that the engagement lasted a quarter of an hour. The deckhand was saved by the 'other trawlers', 16 officers and men being lost. When the boat which sank the *Columbia* was later sunk by British destroyers, strenuous efforts were made to rescue the German sailors, Lieutenant Henry Hartnoll actually going into the water himself to save a German.

Salvage Work

The sea off the Galloper LV where the *Recruit* went down became the location, in November 1915, of good salvage work by the trawler *Resono*. The *Athomas*, a steamer, struck a mine and was badly damaged. Her crew abandoned her and were picked up by the trawler, whose commanding officer felt that, despite her condition, she could be salvaged. With some volunteers from his own crew to man her (in a parallel with the *Carrie* case described below, the original crew refused to re-board her, despite it being explained to them that they would have to go through the minefield in any case and would have been safer in a larger vessel), she was successfully towed away, notwithstanding the heavy weather, and was handed over to the Sheerness Patrol in sheltered waters. Just before this incident, on 17 November, the *Resono* had seen the merchant steamer *Ulrikon* blown up by a mine, also near the Galloper Light Vessel, and had taken all the crew off safely. Regrettably, the *Resono* fell victim to a mine herself the next month, being lost on Boxing Day 1915 near the Sunk LV.

Two curiously similar cases of fishing vessels being salvaged by their sisters took place in April 1915 and January 1917. The *Fishing News* of 1 May 1915 reported:

> The Aberdeen trawler *Envoy* arrived at North Shields on Sunday, to the great surprise of the fishing community. On Thursday the crew were compelled by a German submarine to abandon their vessel, and it was believed she was destroyed. The North Shields trawler *Ethelwulf*, however, picked up the deserted vessel and took her in tow, bringing her to the Tyne. The *Envoy* had a catch of fish, and there was a dog on board. The vessel was undamaged.

Captain Smalley of the *Envoy* said the submarine had been about a mile off when she began shelling his vessel. Nearly 30 shots were fired in rapid succession – even at the men once they were in their small boat. After an hour afloat, they were picked up by the Milford Haven trawler *Fuchsia* and taken into Aberdeen. This trawler was transferred to Grimsby in September that year, becoming GY 669, and within twelve months was herself sunk by a U-boat and her crew were taken prisoner (see Volume 2). For her part, the *Ethelwulf* would meet a sudden and cruel end some years later, as we will see. The *Envoy* survived the war.

In his *Fishermen in Wartime*, Walter Wood points out that it became usual to find HM trawlers included in notices issued by the Department of the Accountant-General of the Navy of intended distribution of salvage awards. Sometimes one vessel would be named, but often several were. Indeed, in connection with the salvage of the steamship *Formosa* on 14 November 1915, no fewer than six were listed – the *Nodzu, Spider, Evangel, King Erik, Thunderstone* and *Esher*. The announcement of the intended distribution was made exactly two years from the date of the salvage operation itself.

In the English Channel, eight vessels out of the 38 in total which were minesweeping patrol casualties through mining, bombing and collisions were subsequently salvaged. Reginald Bacon later wrote:

> The conduct of the officers and ratings of the trawler patrol during the whole of my time in command was very good and compared favourably with the conduct of officers and ratings of the Royal Navy.[135]

The trawler *Etoile Polaire* was employed escorting a vessel engaged in repairing a telephone in the Sunk Light Vessel, when the SS *Volscian* was mined in the vicinity. Her crew abandoned ship and were picked up by the trawler, captained by Lieutenant Allan Lansley DSC RNR. Observing that the steamer, though down by the head, was not sinking rapidly, he decided to try and salvage her. Lines were put on board and although the vessel was in a dangerous area, he succeeded in towing her through the several dangerous areas until he arrived at the Rough Buoy at Harwich, when tugs from that port came to his assistance. He had brought the SS *Volscian* into shoal water, where she was practically salvaged before the arrival of the tugs. The sum of £75 for the officers and crew was awarded for this fine piece of salvage work of a vessel whose value was certainly in excess of £10,000.

Regrettably, the *Etoile Polaire* would herself become the victim of a mine on 3 December 1915 at the South Goodwin LV. She sank almost immediately, although most of her crew were able to get away in her small boat. A strong tide was running to the north-east towards the Goodwins and there was considerable wind and sea from the south-west. Fortunately, it was near the turn of the stream and after the boat had got close to the breakers on the Goodwin Sands the stream did begin to turn and carried her down the Channel again. The officer observed the riding lights of the South Goodwin LV. The men pulled as hard as they could and were much relieved, at length, to reach the Light Vessel. There they were received with great kindness and eventually brought by an armed trawler to Dover.

Rescues of men and vessels from 1916-18 are dealt with in Volume 2.

Chapter 14

Fish on the Table

The husbandman has rent to pay,
Blow, winds, blow!
And seed to purchase every day,
Row, boys, row!
But he who farms the rolling deeps,
Though never sowing, always reaps;
The ocean's fields are fair and free,
There are no rent days on the sea!

Traditional. From *The Fisher's Life*[136]

Presiding at a meeting of the Royal National Mission to Deep Sea Fishermen in 1915, Field-Marshal Lord Grenfell paid a high tribute to the fishermen still pursuing their calling in wartime:

> When we eat our fried sole at breakfast we little think of the trouble and the work that has been carried out in order to provide all of us with fish that is so necessary for us. And now these men are fishing not only with the dangers of the deep before them, but with the dangers created by the most brutal and savage enemy we have ever heard of.[137]

It is doubtful fried sole would have appeared on breakfast tables to any great extent during the war but Grenfell did summarize perfectly the position Britain's fishermen were in and how they were helping the nation against all the odds. Throughout the war they landed some 400,000 tons of fish and lost 672 of their vessels, with a gross tonnage of over 71,000 tons, through enemy action. Among the men, 416 lost their lives through that cause while pursuing their calling and others fell victim to gales and other hazards.

The quantity of fish landed in Britain in the very successful year 1913 totalled 1.2 million tons, with a value of over £14 million. About half of the tonnage had consisted of herring and mackerel (the actual herring catch was 592,279 tons). When war came, great efforts were made by the men still left fishing to continue satisfying home demand and it is remarkable that the industry was able to sustain the production levels it did. The *FN* commented in February 1915 'it seems little short of marvellous that we should be getting any fish at all'. Wet fish landings in England and Wales alone averaged 234,525 tons over the 1915-18 period, even if this was only about a third of the average of 722,560 tons for the years 1909-13. Both branches of the shellfish fisheries (crustaceans and molluscs) also generally held their own well during the war.

Fortunes of War

Remarkable high and low records were set. The market of mighty Grimsby was almost blank on 2 January 1915, with only nine boats landing scanty supplies. Even frying and rough kinds sold at famine prices. A fortnight later the market was absolutely bare, with not a single vessel having berthed in dock overnight. Due mainly to fog, no vessel put into the port between 18 and 19 October 1915 while on the 30th, not a single fish was landed for sale – an unenviable record repeated on 17 March 1916, according to the *FTG* of 25 March, paradoxically below a headline proclaiming 'Excellent supplies: Cod again Plentiful and Cheap'.

Meagre supplies and unheard-of landings and earnings were strange yet frequent bedfellows during the war. The boats the Admiralty didn't want and the men the Navy didn't need were making fortunes. Over on a visit reporting for the *New York World* in March 1917, correspondent Joseph W Grigg remarked:

> Here is an old salt [on a rusty-looking drifter] who, if plying his trade of fisherman, could now be making £100 in a day in these times of high prices.
>
> 'That's what my father made one day last week', said a young fisherman. 'But he can't join up because he's too old.'[138]

At Dundee, phenomenal business was transacted on 7 December 1914 when the 18-strong sprat fishing fleet returned to port. The prices fetched had never been equalled in the industry, in one instance exceeding £2 per cran. In the previous season that measure would often only have fetched 6s or 7s. In Hull, a wonderful catch of plaice from the White Sea fishing grounds was landed on 11 January 1915 by the native trawler *Sir James Reckitt* (Skipper Peter Christiansen). Fabulous prices were paid for the catch over two days. A week earlier the trawler *Stalwart* (owner G Hollingworth), made £1,729 promptly followed by a £1,490 landing by the trawler *Neptune* (Skipper W Johnson) and a catch worth £2,195 – the previous UK record – from the trawler *St Malo* (Skipper W Grantham). Mention is made in Volume 2 of the good fortune of the Banff motor boat *Benison*. Indeed, motor craft using paraffin almost matched the performance of costly steam-powered drifters. One of the latter from Berwick reportedly ran up earnings of £5,000 in the 1915 Yarmouth fishing, while another made £2,400 in 11 days – in fact, none of the Scottish boats did badly there that season. They 'had only to go to sea and put their noses into the fishing grounds', reported the *FN* published on Christmas Day 1915, 'to come back with at least a catch worth £100'. Hull was again in the trade press news in January 1916, when it was reported that record prices had been achieved for haddock at the port on the 7th. Meanwhile, a curer at Grimsby paid over £100 for a few boxes of fish whose weight and quality he had paid less than 30s for at the same market some years previously.

There were odd developments, too, in the species of fish consumed: flake, or dogfish, which a year or two earlier had been regarded as the fishermen's pest, were fetching more than a shilling each at Plymouth's Barbican that January.

Nationally, the cost of food between July 1914 and November 1916 increased by 81 per cent in the large towns and 74 per cent in the small towns and villages, or 78 per cent in the UK as a whole. Yet the respective figures for fish were 157, 108 and 132.[139] The inevitable scarcity of fish on the slab was due in good measure to the depletion of the fleet through requisitioning, leading to high prices. These in turn led to mutterings of profiteering. Such rumours were scotched by the then President of the Board of Trade, Walter Runciman (President of the Board of Agriculture and Fisheries for three years before the war), in the Commons on 17 October 1916:

> Why is fish dearer? Fish is not dearer because there is any undue profiteering out of fish, and not because there is any exploitation of the customer. It is dearer because there are not the same number of fishing boats at sea, because they are engaged in trawling for mines instead of fish. The reason why we have not more fish in England is because there are not the men, the material or the instruments to get them.[140]

The prices bubble ultimately burst when the Fish (Prices) Order of 16 January 1918 laying down maximum prices for fish with effect from 23 January was published. *The Times* of 21 January, however, wryly commented: '...the general experience is that maximum prices become minimum prices.'

The Government had also assisted the industry some years earlier, not through control but by organizational support. The London-based Fisheries Organisation Society Ltd was registered as far back as 28 September 1914 as a result of strong recommendations made by two Government Committees (the 1912-13 Committee of Inquiry into the Fisheries of Devon and Cornwall and the 1913-14 Departmental Committee on Inshore Fisheries) appointed to enquire into the condition of the Inshore Fisheries and advise as to the steps which could advantageously be taken for their preservation and development. Both Committees agreed that the inshore fishermen formed 'a community most valuable to the nation and worth every effort to preserve' and both advocated cooperation as the best means of preserving and reviving the inshore fisheries. They therefore urged the immediate formation of a Fisheries Organisation Society. Among its main objects were fostering cooperation within the inshore fishing industry of England and Wales and forming local fishermen's cooperative societies for the better marketing of fish. It was financed by grants in aid from the Development Fund and by voluntary contributions. It did not trade itself and made no profits.

In its Third Report, for the twelve months ended 31 December 1917, the Society observed:

> Although the fishing industry generally has enjoyed exceptional prosperity during the continuance of the war, it has been found that many fishermen in our small inshore ports have reaped hardly any additional increase in the sale of their catches, owing principally to a surprising lack of knowledge of prevailing conditions and limitation of outlets. Though prices in the open market rose abnormally during the year under review, there was often very little increase, if any, in the prices received by the inshore fishermen, and for lack of other markets, the men were in many cases forced to sell their catches locally.

It further pointed out that the continued withdrawal of the younger men from the inshore fishing communities for service in the Navy, leaving the older men (who were naturally very conservative in their methods) had greatly added to the difficulties in the way of successful cooperative propaganda. By the time the report was prepared (April 1918), however, maximum prices had – as has been noted – been fixed for both wholesale and retail buyers of fish. These maxima became, in nearly all cases, the prices actually paid, so it was easy for any fisherman to discover whether he was receiving the market price for his catch.

Other constructive initiatives to assist small-scale fishermen included the formation of the Motor Loan Committee, appointed on 1 February 1917 and reconstituted a few months later as the Fish Food and Motor Loan Committee.

Rule Breakers, Deserters and Rebels

This volume would fail to be a balanced history of fishermen in the Great War if no reference were made to that body of men hauled before the courts to answer for their misdemeanours. These ranged from fishing – often 'accidentally on purpose' – in prohibited waters to unpatriotic, selfish and uncooperative behaviour which in a couple of instances led to a court martial in the case of enrolled men.

Hardly any mention has been made of such offenders in any of the numerous volumes recounting in varying depth the part played by fishermen during the conflict, although Walter Wood, in his *Fishermen in War Time* (1918), did reluctantly concede that there were 'here and there dubious hearts amongst the fishermen'. Yet he had in mind 'almost exclusively ... men who were in the service from necessity and not from the choice which prompted most of them to go to sea and brave its dangers.'[141] One other reference found was in a war history,[142] where it was, apparently 'somewhat of a relief to see that the old spirit which nerved the British seaman to take risks was as lively as ever'. The sneaking admiration was for one George Lamming, a Grimsby skipper, who was fined £3 on 6 January 1915 for disregarding Admiralty regulations. He was, the writer conceded, in the wrong and ought to have taken a pilot. None had been to hand to show him how to avoid our mine defences so, rather than lose the early market, Lamming came in by himself, trusting to his own skill and to luck. The author felt that the skipper's conduct was reminiscent of 'the adventurous behaviour of traders in the old wars, who gave an immense amount of trouble to naval authorities' yet this element of unruliness had, he claimed, actually contributed to the success of British sea-borne commerce. A scouring of the wartime trade press reveals, however, that Lamming became an arrogant pest. A year after the above offence he was fined 3 guineas for having breached pilotage regulations on Christmas day morning in the *Vernicia* in his anxiety to reach the market (this case is, however, so similar to the one described in the war history that one wonders whether the wrong year was quoted in that volume). Lamming was in court again in May 1916, when he was heavily fined (£50) and ordered to pay 2 guineas costs for being in prohibited waters in the trawler *Andes*, whose pioneering role in this war was detailed in Chapter 2. On that occasion he appeared together with John Oddsson (a naturalized Icelander), master of the *Cayrian*, and William Bore, master of the *Resolute*. Oddson, the only one to plead guilty, was fined £25 plus costs and Bore, whose case was described as 'a very bad one', £50 plus costs. The magistrate remarked that the skipper had only escaped destruction by a mere chance, for the British fleet would have been perfectly within its rights to destroy any vessel in a prohibited area. The action of men like the defendant was a hindrance to the Navy. Lamming, for his part, claimed that by his reckoning he had been nine miles away from the prohibited area.

That same May, three other Grimsby steam trawler skippers – Thomas Wright of the *Lord Shrewsbury*, Albert Young of the *Lord Strathmore* and Charles Mumby of the *Romeo* – were fined £50 and costs. Wright pleaded guilty and the others not. Lieutenant Crossley testified that he was in his patrol ship in the mine area, destroying mines, when he saw the three trawlers. He ordered the skippers to clear out of the area on account of the danger and told them he would be reporting them, which he duly did – this despite happily taking a basket of fish from the *Romeo*. John J Sutton, Secretary to the Grimsby Fishing Vessel Owners Exchange Company Ltd, gave evidence that the owners received Admiralty instructions and that these were given to all skippers.

Lamming's name came up yet again in March 1917, when he had to pay another hefty fine of £50 plus 2 guineas costs for having entered a prohibited area in the North Sea on 6 February. By this time, he was skipper of the *Kalso*.

Infringements of pilotage regulations, like Lamming's, occasionally occurred. One of the stipulations applying in December 1914 as regards the Humber was that vessels had to leave the river in batches of four. The *FTG* reminded its readers of the folly of ignoring the area limits set by the Admiralty: the Wilson liner *Runo* had done so and now lay at the bottom of the sea. Captain Lee had admitted liability. (For details see page 196.)

In the spring of 1915, Fred Firth of the Grimsby trawler *Pelican* used the wrong channel when entering the Humber and was fined £5, including costs. Skipper Walter Haines of the *Horatio* had disobeyed the signals of the Admiralty patrol – instead of stopping, he used strong language, for which he had to pay 3 guineas including costs. The following February, five trawlers – the *Egyptian Prince, Redvers Buller, T. W. Mould, Baden Powell* and *Kielder Castle* – infringed the North Sea regulations under Section 35 of DORA. The skippers, fined £2 each, pleaded that the prohibited area was a very large one and they had been waiting for the weather to turn favourable again. Two months later a substantial fine of £50 including costs was imposed on Skipper Albert Menzies Johnson, master of the Hull steam trawler *Audrey*, for illegally fishing in a 'certain area'. This penalty was also meted out to John Vincent of the *Thistle*, and Cornelius Wynne of the *Falcon* in September at Grimsby for being within the prohibited areas. George Howlett of the *Dee* had to pay £35 and Peter Appleton of the *Titan*, £20. The earnings of the latter vessel were on record as averaging £250 per week – a sum stated to be 'moderate' for ships fishing in the North Sea during the previous 18 months. The month before, a batch of eight Grimsby skippers had got off relatively lightly with fines ranging from £10 to £25, plus expenses, for taking their vessels – the *Viella, Lord Chancellor, Albatross, Douro, Athenian, Larchwold, Weelsby* (a vessel often named in court cases – but see below) and *Recto* into prohibited waters. All of them were big earners.

In a case involving assistance to a stricken vessel, the action of the defendant was given due recognition. At Falcarragh Court, Donegal, in February 1915, Herbert Percy Jones, master of the steam trawler *Niblick*, had the Irish Fisheries Board's charge of being in prohibited waters off Tory Island dropped on account of his gallant conduct in having rescued the crew of the Bangor steamer *Linda Blanche*, blown up a few days earlier. The *Niblick* had picked up a chest containing 40 lifebelts. Jones did, however, have to pay costs.

Many other prohibited area cases from around Britain's coast were heard but space prevents further instances being recorded. It should be mentioned in particular, however, that Start Bay in Devon, closed to trawlers under an 1893 bye-law yet teeming with splendid fish, and, north of the border, Moray Firth and the Firth of Forth – where, at one stage, 80 Pittenweem fishermen were starving on account of the regulations preventing them from pursuing their calling – were especially problematical. The ordinary peacetime fishing restrictions at those locations were compounded by prohibitions from the naval authorities, leading to even further discontent and hardship among the fishing communities concerned.

Breaking Admiralty regulations was one thing, disobedience/desertion quite another. In fishermen cases it denoted 'failing to join a vessel' or jumping ship. Despite the splendid record of most of Britain's sea toilers during the war, there was a constant procession of men to the courts. Nowhere was this stream greater, for some reason, than in Grimsby, unpalatable though that fact may be. It is borne out by the implication in a report heading in the *FN* of 6 March 1915: 'A light list this week'. Only three cases were heard: that of an old offender, Joseph Fern of the *Nubia* (21s or 28 days' imprisonment), that of George Charles of the *Haintow*, (12/6 [62½p]) and that of Robert Scruton of the *Cuirass* (21s or 28 days).

Undoubtedly, the root of the problem in a great many instances at the Humber port and along the entire national coastline was drink. An editorial in the *FN* of 19 June 1915 complained that it was 'deplorable that the nation had not had the courage to grasp this particular evil and deal drastically with it'. The noted novelist Marie Corelli, writing in *The War Illustrated* of 24 April 1915 on the subject of 'Workers and "Shirkers"', referred to the preface of her own book, *Holy Orders* (1908), where she had written:

> As for the drink evil, I wish that everyone into whose hands this book may fall would honestly try to realise the widespread misery, disease, pauperism, crime, and lunacy for which that hideous vice is responsible.

Lloyd George, then President of the Board of Trade, took an interest in her work and earnestly told her that if she could only help in pointing out the mischief of drink, she would perform a national service.

In one extreme case, drinking led to the total loss by stranding of a trawler near Lynton, Devon. The Cardiff steam trawler *Mikasa*, CF 41, built in 1913 and valued at £9,500, had left for the fishing grounds and became a total wreck on 13 January 1915. Skipper James Drennan admitted making a false statement to the Receiver of Wreck when he said he had not given liquor to Joseph Boyce, the bosun. The tot of rum he drank made him go to sleep when in the wheelhouse on watch and the vessel, undermanned with nine men including only four deckhands, ran aground. Judgement was given in May 1915 by the Cardiff Stipendiary in the Board of Trade enquiry. The verdict was that the vessel had not been navigated with proper and seamanlike care. Drennan's certificate was suspended for nine months and Boyce's for three. Blame was also apportioned to the trawler's registered managers and to Charles Russell, the ship's husband, for having permitted the vessel to proceed to sea undermanned, although undermanning had not been the cause of the loss. A replacement namesake was built for the same owners, Neale and West, in that same year and was requisitioned in 1916. She survived to see service as a hired vessel on two occasions in the Second World War.

An attempt to take over a vessel was perpetrated by trawler cook Sydney Skeats in Aberdeen. On 19 and 20 November 1914, he boarded the German prize of war *Else Kunkel* berthed in the port, pretending his name was Captain Thomson and that he had been sent by the Admiralty Marshal, London, to take charge of the prizes of war in Aberdeen Harbour. These included the *Dr Robitzsch, Hemel, Warden* and *Wells*,[143] all berthed in the Upper Dock, Regent Quay. He was discharged after nine days in prison pending further enquiries. No follow-up to the case appeared in the *FN*.

Returning to the drink problem, the names of some vessels just kept coming up. The aged (1900) Grimsby trawler *Serapion* was an example. On 21 January 1915, when a dozen fishermen appeared before the town's magistrates charged with either disobedience or desertion, this vessel was among ten whose crew members had 'let the side down'. They included the *Andromeda* and *Mercury*, which would be lost in the massacre of June 1916. Frederick Greenwood of the *Serapion* pleaded guilty to failing to join his vessel. It was his ninth offence. He admitted he had had 'a lot of booze'. Another fisherman who had had 'a good drink' was George Smith who had indeed joined his ship, the Grimsby trawler *Diamond*, but had 'got ashore at the swing bridge'. It was his first offence.

The *Serapion*'s name came up again in May of that year (once) and in December (twice). In the May case, Sidney Smalley failed to join her and was fined 20s or 10 days. At the same hearing, evidence was given that Robert Mudd had been found hopelessly drunk instead of being aboard the *Halcyon*. 'I was a bit late, that's all', he claimed. His wife, thinking he had joined his ship, drew 10s from the owners, the Cleethorpes SF Co. At another hearing in the same month, Henry Whitburn drew his advance of 10s but when found later in a public house flatly refused to join the *Dominican*. A couple of days earlier, Harry Laing, who ought to have sailed with the *Fleetwood*, explained he had had 'a little too much to drink'. Penalty: 15s or 14 days. The same issue of the *FN*, dated 15 May 1915, reported that a dozen or so Hull fishermen had been charged with neglecting to join their ships and had been fined 15s each. They had refused to go to sea, demanding that the weekly war risk bonus of 5s should be doubled following the destruction of seven Hull trawlers by German submarines. They had been under the impression that engine-room hands had received a double bonus.

In the December case involving the *Serapion*, it was one Henry Tasker who had not joined the ship (two days earlier, on 29 November 1915, the *Diamond* had again featured in proceedings). Appearing in naval uniform, he had joined the minesweepers but had drawn a 30s advance to join the trawler. He had given notice he would not but its acceptance had been conditional on him cancelling the debt. He was fined 30s or 21 days. His record of four previous appearances was dwarfed by that of William Futter, whose tally was no less than 35. Due to a printing error, the trawler he should have joined was not specified in the *FN*. The accused had nothing to say and was sentenced to 28 days' hard labour. That same week, the names came up during proceedings of two ill-fated trawlers, the *Viella* (see above) and the *Fuchsia* (see Volume 2).

Other Grimsby vessels whose names came up more often than others were the *Rodrigo, Lord Shrewsbury, Niblick* and *Lord Selborne*.

Drink was even implicated in a court martial. In June 1915, William Coull RNR, temporary skipper of a patrol trawler, faced four charges. The first was that of wilfully disobeying, on 19 May, the command of Temporary-Sub-Lieutenant Charles William Walters, RNR, of HMS *Vivid* to weigh anchor and proceed to sea on patrol; the second, that of anchoring on 21 May to the prejudice of good order and naval discipline, at about 10 p.m. and remaining at anchor until about daybreak the following day instead of patrolling the sea; the third, that of attempting, on 22 May, to anchor instead of patrolling the sea; and the fourth, that of being drunk on 16 June on duty ashore. Coull did not give evidence. The third charge was not proved but the first, second and fourth were, and he was dismissed the service.

Another naval court martial was held in the same month in Liverpool. Skipper William Hayes of the Grimsby trawler *Alberia* was charged with insubordination to a superior officer. On 2 April, Hayes had been told by his commanding officer, Lieutenant Henry Fisher, that some sealed letters he (Hayes) had taken to his cabin could not be sent off until they had been censored. The skipper retorted that they contained money only and he would take ' ----- good care' to see the lieutenant read none of them. He was suspended from duty that evening, yet six days later allegedly used insulting language to Fisher about being landed in Stornoway. This was the second charge against him. The skipper argued that the officer had been irritating in his remarks about the money, although the Court found that charge partly proved on the grounds of contemptuous conduct and issued a reprimand. The second charge was not proved, since despite orders having been given that Hayes should be sent to the port, he was not. Given his previous good character, he was acquitted of the indictment.

An editorial in the *FN* of 19 June 1915 summed up the disobedience problem:

The question of desertion by trawlmen has long been a cause of difficulty and annoyance at fishing ports. Men who have been engaged for a particular boat neglect to turn up when the vessel sails, with the result that delay and loss are entailed to the owners and to the other members of the crew. The same evil exists in the case of ordinary merchant vessels, and it is still persisting, even where these vessels have been taken over by the Admiralty for transport work. At ordinary times these offences may not matter so much, though they are troublesome and vexatious, but at a time like the present, they are more serious in their conse-quences, and the public will have very little patience with them.

That month, six fishermen deserted from the Grimsby trawler *Shrewsbury*. One of them was George Kelly, making his 24th appearance in court. He was committed for 28 days. The same penalty was meted out a couple of weeks later to Benjamin Lawson (trawler *Egyptian*). In the following February, fisherman Herbert Tidswell, a familiar face in court in Grimsby, failed to join the SS *Lindum* while in April 1917, regular offender Joseph H Middlewood was one of three Grimsby men charged with disobedience in connection with the trawler *King Canute* on 31 March. Penalty: 40s or 21 days.

Among the various cases reported in the trade press during the first year of the war were the following:

ENGLAND
1915

March	Thomas Harris, a cook on the smack *Corona* (sunk in June 1917), summoned at Lowestoft for wilful disobedience. Refused to sail, saying he 'had private affairs to attend to' and was going to have a holiday. Penalty £2 or 14 days. Prisoner: '14 days please'.
April	Grimsby trimmer Harold Walker disappeared from the trawler *Warland* at the lock-pit to 'settle a little dispute'. 21s or 28 days.

SCOTLAND
1915

June	Skippers and mates from the trawler fleet at Granton and Leith went on lightning strike for an increase in weekly earnings. About 30 trawlers belonging to Thomas L Devlin were affected. Some were making as much as £2 a day.
August	Settlement reached in trawl fishermen strike in Dundee due to with-drawal of a war bonus. Affected about 80 men. Small increase awarded – to be handed over to the Royal Infirmary.

The other side of the coin was the enormous help given by fishermen to various causes. In the 1914 season, the Scottish fleet working out of Yarmouth donated one cran of herrings per boat to be sold for the Belgian Relief Fund. They made the same donation the following year, this time to the British Red Cross Society. The figure realized was £372 – nearly two-thirds of the sum raised locally. The *FN* of 13 November 1915 listed the donor vessels by home port and name.

Additions to the Auxiliary Fleet
The Admiralty did not only rely on hirings from the mercantile fleet but ordered vessels to be built to its chosen specifications or acquired a number

before they were launched for subsequent adaptation. As early as 1914, it bought 10 trawlers which were under construction for commercial concerns at the yards of Smith's Dock Company Ltd of Middlesbrough and had nine of them completed as minesweepers. Although generally designated the 'Military Class', the vessels constituted more of a 'Group', so much did they vary in dimensions and even appearance. The largest, *Bombardier* (which, as noted previously, served in north Russia), was just under 100 tons heavier than the smallest. The first, *Lancer*, was launched in December 1914 and the rest followed between January and April 1915. Last in service was *Trooper*, completed in June 1915. The tenth vessel, *Gunner*, was completed as a Q-ship (Q 31) – see Volume 2. She operated as *Planudes* and carried 3 x 12-pounders, 3 x 6-pounders and 2 x torpedo tubes. Three of the class, *Carbineer, Lancer* and *Sapper*, were lost during the war.

Prize vessels, of course, augmented the fleet. In 1914/15, 30 German trawlers fell into British hands and were, quirkily, given names ending in -*sit* initially and -*sin* later. We saw in Chapter 1 how two, finally renamed *Chirsin* and *Clonsin*, were seized at Aberdeen directly war was declared. Many captured at sea and found to have insufficient coal to be steamed back to the UK by prize crews were sunk. Twenty-seven were brought back and converted to Navy minesweepers, save for *Cortasin* which was considered unfit and released to the fishing industry, being renamed *Skerne*. Most saw service on patrol in the Mediterranean, where two of them became war losses.

Particulars of post-1915 augmentations of Admiralty trawler (and drifter) stocks are provided in Volume 2.

Author's note on the next volume

Volume 2, covering the years 1916 to 1918, examines, among other aspects, the continued service abroad by fishermen and fishing vessels; describes in detail the fearful toll of the mine and submarine in home waters and the ways in which it was gradually lessened; looks at more extraordinary feats of life-saving and salvage; reviews the fish supply situation at various key ports in 1916, selected as a specimen year; and devotes further attention to slackers and rebels in the fishing industry. The book ends with a vivid portrayal of the valiant stand made by Skipper Tom Crisp of Lowestoft, the second skipper to be honoured with a VC. Sad to relate, the award in his case was made posthumously.

Notes

1. Published in *The Navy* of December 1915, p. 373.
2. *Submarine Hunting on the North Sea in the Great War 1914-1918*, document held at Lowestoft Public Library. Nd. ca. 1937.
3. A major Prussian city and seaport on the River Oder, in Polish hands since 1945 and named Szczecin. The account of Smith's experiences was recorded in the *FN* of 22.8.14, p. 10.
4. *My Year of the War* (1915), pp. 66-67. Palmer wrote a number of books, including *With Kuroki in Manchuria*, *The Vagabond* and *The Last Shot*; the latter appeared only a few months before the Great War. It was based on his experience in many wars and attempted to describe the character of a conflict between two Great European land powers, such as France and Germany. The prophetic scenario was right in many details.
5. *FTG*, 22.8.14, p. 16.
6. *FN*, 7.11.14, p. 13.
7. *TD*, November 1914, pp. 234-5.
8. Later called the East Anglian Herring Fishing and so named on account of the drifter fleet being away from home most of the year.
9. *Lowestoft Journal*, 3.12.76.
10. Palmer, p. 81
11. In 1908 the cran had been made a legal measure in England and Wales, having previously been legal only in Scotland.
12. *TD* July 1915, p. 124.
13. *FN* 10.10.14, p. 14.
14. Stephen Reynolds (1889-1919) wrote, amongst other works, the classic *A Poor Man's House* (1909), which described the hardship and daily existence of a fishing family in Sidmouth.
15. *TD* June 1916, p. 67.
16. Reported in *TN*, March 1916, p. 86.
17. Falmouth, Glasney Press, 1979, p. 28.
18. *FN* 10.10.14, p. 1.
19. The *Euston, Ashton, Alice Fisher* and *T. B. Miller*.
20. Published in *The Navy*, May 1916. EA Mackintosh (1893-1917) was educated at St Paul's and Christ Church, Oxford. He was sent to France with 5th Seaforth Highlanders and killed at Cambrai in October 1917. He wrote *A Highland Regiment* (John Lane, 1917) and *War, The Liberator* (1918).
21. This Hull vessel had been launched in 1911 and requisitioned in November 1914. It was mined off Dover on 4 March 1916.
22. *FN* 12.6.15, p. 2.
23. Henry Major Tomlinson (1873-1958), journalist and novelist. In 1904, he was engaged as a reporter with the radical *Morning Leader*, a paper to which he had already contributed. His love of the sea was soon turned to good

account by his editor, Ernest Parke, who sent him to live for several weeks, in midwinter, with a fleet of trawlers on the Dogger Bank, followed by an assignment to the naval manoeuvres. His first book, *The Sea and the Jungle*, appeared in 1912 following a voyage, on which he was sent by Parke, to Brazil and 2,000 miles up the Amazon and Madeira rivers in the first English steamer to make that passage. The book was very successful, running into many editions and marking Tomlinson out as a gifted writer. When the *Morning Leader* was amalgamated with the *Daily News* in 1912 Tomlinson stayed on as a leader writer; he became a war correspondent in Belgium and France in August 1914 and was official correspondent at British general headquarters in France in 1914-17. It was in France in 1917 that Tomlinson met HW Massingham, who later offered him the post of assistant editor of *The Nation*, where he remained until 1923. His reputation as a writer grew and in 1927 he was awarded the Femina Vie Heureuse prize for his first novel, *Gallions Reach* (1927). Thirty years later, he told the story of the impact of the blitz on an English family in *The Trumpet Shall Sound*, his last work.

Source: http://www.oxforddnb.com/view/article/36533?docPos=9

24. *FN*, 3.6.16, p. 2.
25. *Highland News*, 14.11.1914.
26. From the Isle of Lewis alone in the First World War there were over 3,500 serving with the RNR, but to get the Western Isles total you would have to add those from Harris, Uist and Barra – probably another 1,000. (Donald MacLeod, Aberdeen, pers. comm., 18.7.07).
27. Letter from Eric Wettern, an engineer, dated 7.10.14 and quoted in Peter Liddle's *Men of Gallipoli* (1988).
28. Published at Cross Deep, Twickenham, nd.
29. The composition of the Volunteer Reserve is complex. It includes all sorts – from mercantile marine sailors and yachtsmen down to bankers and provision merchants. I have met [among them] a captain of a liner, a well-known journalist, a headmaster of a public school, a chartered accountant, an opera singer, a bookseller, an engineer, and an author. (Sydney A Moseley, *SURPRISES OF THE R.N.V.R.*, in *The War Illustrated*, 31.8.18, No 211, Vol. 9, p. 47).
30. The typescript of these memoirs is held by the Imperial War Museum. The text covers the years from 1900 to 1961 and in it he describes his childhood in Tyldsley and his early training in the Manchester School of Art until his call-up. On demobilization, Boydell returned to his studies at the Royal College of Art. The second volume covers his career in advertising and his Second World War work for the Government on propaganda, which included his invention of the `Squander Bug' character.
31. pp. 52-4 of the memoir.
32. Ibid. pp. 76-78.
33. *FN* 10.10.14, p. 7.
34. Campbell's early life was spent in Canada. He worked as Assistant Purser for the Orient Line (his first berth was on the *Orient*, the earliest of the steamships to carry mail to Australia). His next ship was the *Ophir*.

After his involvement with minesweeping, he joined HMS *Otranto* at Liverpool, where her guns were being replaced. This was one of many ships which had to patrol 85,000 miles of trade routes. At sea for months on end, the *Otranto* scoured South American waters for German raiders and was unharmed through three years of duty. Later, however, it was in collision with a Breton fishing vessel and also with the *Kashmir*. Rescue was carried out by the destroyer *Mounsey*, which saved nearly 600 lives. Survivors were landed at Islay. The *Otranto* was swept ashore and only 16 out of 500 who had been left on board got ashore alive.

After being ordered to Sydney then returning to Rio, Campbell travelled to England, escorting 12 decrepit tramps. From England he was sent to New York to escort a convoy of troop ships. He was away from England for four years and was at Chatham barracks when the Armistice was declared. After demobilization in December 1920, he lectured temporarily in maths and geography in a private school. After working as a courier, he turned to writing then set up as a publisher (Campbell & Co), publishing six magazines. He sent the *Otranto* loss story to the BBC and did many broadcasts thereafter.

35. *With the Corners Off – My Adventurous Life on Land and Sea*, nd., p. 198.
36. Ibid., p. 201.
37. Sir Frederick Charles Doveton Sturdee, 1st Bart (1859-1925) entered the Navy in 1871. A Rear Admiral in 1908, he commanded the *Invincible* in the action which wiped out the German squadron under von Spee off the Falkland Islands in 1914. Thereafter he served with the Grand Fleet, including the Battle of Jutland (1916). In 1921 he was promoted to Admiral of the Fleet.
38. Ibid. p. 205
39. Ibid. p. 209
40. Ibid. pp. 209-10.
41. A vessel by this name was hired as an armed merchant cruiser in the next war. She sank on 5 November 1940 in action with *Admiral Scheer* in the Atlantic.
42. See Dittmar, FJ & Colledge, JJ, *British Warships, 1914-19* (1972), pp. 177-213 and 232-62. The figures given in the 1920 BAF Report *Fisheries In The Great War* are 1,502 steam drifters, 51 motor drifters and 1,467 steam trawlers.
43. *FN* 27.9.19, p. 31.
44. *Memoirs of Admiral Lord Charles Beresford, Written by Himself*, Vol. II, (pp. 554 & 555), Methuen & Co. Ltd, 1914.
45. These vessels measured 105 ft in length and had a 21 ft beam, with a draught of 13 ft and about 9 ft forward. Their speed was 8½ knots, their indicated horse power was 240 and they carried 80 tons of coal; their consumption was 5/6 tons per day. Each trawl warp consisted of 250 fathoms of 3-inch wire, and at first the trawlers' own otter-boards were used as kites, though later, after further experiments, the right size and type of kite for mine-sweeping was evolved.
46. *The Naval Review*, Vol. VI., 1919. Paper 2 of 6: *The Work of a Trawler in the Aegean Sea*, pp. 13-68, Ed. WH Henderson. See p. 123 for the surmised identity of the writer.
47. Cf. *The Days That We Have Seen* (1975), pp. 174-80.
48. Tunnel-sweepers were shallow-draught, flat-bottomed vessels designed to sweep for mines at low tide in harbours, river mouths and along the coast. They were acquired by the transfer to the Admiralty in 1917 of the 'Tunnel Tugs' being built for the War Office for river service in Mesopotamia; a

feature of these vessels was the hollow dishing of the plating, or tunnels, under the stern to accommodate the twin propellors – hence their name. The accommodation was anything but comfortable and their usual complement was 24 or 25 officers and men. They nevertheless did good service and all ten of the class were based at Dunkirk during the last few months of the war; during fine weather they were employed clearing up the minefields off the Flanders coast. They bore the names of dances, such as *Hornpipe*, *Mazurka* and *Pirouette*.

49. Admiral Sir Herbert William Richmond (1871-1946) joined the Royal Navy as a cadet in 1885. In 1900-1903, he served in the flagship of the Channel Fleet HMS *Majestic*. Promoted to Commander in 1903, he became first officer in HMS *Crescent*, flagship of the Cape of Good Hope Station. Assigned to the Admiralty in 1906-08, he served briefly as naval assistant to Admiral Jackie Fisher, 1st Baron Fisher. Promoted to Captain, he commanded HMS *Dreadnought* from 1909 to 1911, then, in 1911-12, the Torpedo School training ships HMS *Furious* and HMS *Vindictive*. In 1912, he founded the *Naval Review* magazine to promote innovative thought within the Royal Navy. Richmond became Assistant Director of Operations on the Naval Staff in 1913-15 and Liaison Officer to the Italian Fleet in 1915. He went on to command HMS *Commonwealth* in 1916-18, served as director of staff duties and training in 1918 and commanded HMS *Erin* in 1919. In 1929, he was promoted to Admiral. He held numerous academic posts of distinction and his published writings include *National policy and naval strength and other essays* (1928, 1934, 1993), *Imperial defence and capture at sea in war* (1932) and *Sea power in the modern world* (1934).

50. *The Auxiliary Patrol, 1914-15* (1971), pp. 113-14.

51. Adm 137/1893, p. 464, Pears, Rear-Admiral Invergordon – Beatty, 3 November 1914.

52. JRUSI Feb. 1933, p. 14.

53. Adm 137/1039 pp. 430-1, memorandum by Admiral Sir Henry Jackson, 12 June 1915.

54. Comments made following Lecky's 1933 lecture.

55. Adm 137/173, pp. 176-9, Tupper – Admiralty, July 7, 1915.

56. *The Dover Patrol*, Volume I (ca. 1932), p. 120.

57. *The Grand Fleet 1914-16, Its Creation, Development and Work* (1919), p. 226.

58. From the collection *These Were The Men – Poems of the War, 1914-1918*, (1919), pp. 82-3. Reproduced therein 'By kind permission of the Author and of the *Spectator*'.

59. A picture of Wright appears in Walter Wood's *Fishermen in War-Time* over the caption 'Skipper Wright, who discovered the "Königin Luise", a German mine-layer ...'. Yet the *Lowestoft Journal* for 8 August 1914 reported that a skipper, William Pleasants of the trawler *Loch Nevis,* spotted the German vessel dumping mines overboard whilst fishing. He at once raised his trawl and set sail for Lowestoft. When some 15 miles from Lowestoft, he decided to continue fishing, only to be told by a naval vessel to make for port with all speed as war on Germany had been declared (information courtesy of JE Smith, Hon. Recorder, Lowestoft and East Suffolk Maritime Society, letter dated 23 October 1996). The *Loch Nevis* (LT 696) was owned in 1915 by W Warman (Source: Olsen).

60. Chatterton, E Keble, *The Auxiliary Patrol* (1923), p. 15.

61. A second *Thomas W. Irvin* (SN 265) was built in 1915 and served as a minesweeper from February 1916 until 1919. A second *Crathie* (A 713) was built in 1916 but had a short career. Taken over as a minesweeper in November 1916, she was wrecked on 16 December 1916 on Nizam Point, Barra Head.

62. The name of the auxiliary patrol shore base at Grimsby 1907-19. Trawler No 24 carried this name as tender at the base.

63. In a letter to the author dated 13.6.87, the late Captain ST Smith of Scarborough mentioned that the *Passing,* the largest trawler in the country and only a year old, survived the explosion and was later sold to France by her Grimsby owners.

64. In this trawler, Lt J Pittendrigh RNR, while on patrol in the Kos Channel on 25 October 1917, was fired at from the shore. Seeing a dismasted caique flying the Italian flag drifting towards the enemy coast, he closed on her despite the rough sea and strong southerly gale, took her in tow and brought her to safety while still under hot fire. For this gallant conduct and good seamanship, he was awarded the DSC.

65. Arthur Godfrey, *Yorkshire Fishing Fleets* (1974), p. 42.

66. The *Aquarius* had been taken over in June 1915 yet would be returned to the fishing fleet in August. Requisitioned into the Fishery Reserve in 1917, she was returned to her owners in 1919.

67. Published in *The Navy,* April 1915.

68. Lowell Thomas, *Raiders of the Deep* (1929), pp. 38-9.

69. Ibid. p. 352.

70. More correctly the *Merrie Islington*, although Olsen's gives *'Merry'*. She was built in 1891 and operated by the Humber Steam Trawling Co., Hull (H 183). The incident occurred 6 miles NNE of Whitby Rock Buoy, Yorks. on 6 May 1915. A bomb was placed on board (see Gill, *Lost Trawlers of Hull 1835-1987*, 1989).

71. *FN*, 5.8.16, p. 17.

72. http://www.scottishholidays.net/visit/scotland-tour-shetland-outskerries.html

73. *FN*, 16.10.15, p. 13.

74. *FN*, 18.9.15, p. 9.

75. *FN*, 23.10.15, p. 12.

76. *FN*, 2.10.15, p. 2.

77. *TD*, 7/15, p. 125.

78. Published in the (joint) author's *The History of Ruhleben,* 1919.

79. GERMAN INHUMANITY TO BRITISH PRISONERS in *The Great War – The Standard History of the All-Europe Conflict* (Wilson, HW & Hammerton, JA, Eds.), Vol. 5, 1916, Chapter XCII, 253-4.

80. Dispatch from Sir John French issued on 5 December 1914 as a supplement to the *London Gazette*.

81. Geoffrey Dearmer (1893-1996), poet, novelist and playwright, was born in Lambeth and educated at Westminster and Christ Church, Oxford. He fought at Gallipoli and the Somme. His *Poems* were published by Heinemann in 1918. He was examiner of plays to the Lord Chamberlain, 1936-58, and editor of the BBC's *Children's Hour,* 1939-59.

82. *The Great War,* Volume I (1933), p. 465.

83. See pp. 34-41 of *The Dardanelles – Colour Sketches from Gallipoli,* 1916, for a chapter devoted to the work of the trawlers.

84 *The Naval Review*, Vol. VI. Available online
    www.naval-review.org/pasp/..%5Cissues%5C1918.pdf
85. IWM ID No P217 12146. MS diary of J Clarke RNR in two volumes (48
    pp and 80 pp), which cover his service in HMT *Loch Broom* off the Gallipoli
    peninsula and in the Aegean Sea, 1915-1917, detailing his arrival at Mudros
    in April 1915 and duties including minesweeping in the Gulf of Saros on the
    first day of the Gallipoli landings and describing minesweeping and patrol
    duties in the Aegean. Also recorded are the enforcement of the naval
    blockade of Turkey, a raid on a Turkish-held island and civil disturbances in
    Greece.
86. *The Naval Review*, Vol. IV pp. 184 – 197 (1916 – Part 2).
87. *Fishermen in War Time*, Walter Wood, 1918, pp. 164-5.
88. Reported in the *FN* of 16.12.16, p. 13.
89. *FN*, 17.4.15, p. 13.
90. *Dardanelles Dilemma – The Story of the Naval Operations* (1935), p. 112.
91. Ibid. pp. 160-1.
92. 24.4.15, p. 6. *The Fleets at Sea. Attacks On Fishing Vessels.*, "Wanton
    Murder." In *Swept Channels* (p. 153), Taffrail points out that it was not so
    much the human casualties that prevented the sweeping from being carried
    out but the destruction of the winches, kites and wires without which
    sweeping could not continue.
93. Naval Chief of Staff to Admiral de Robeck. The quotation is from p. 77 of
    his book.
94. Many other awards were made to trawler crew members. For example, the
    Second Supplement to the *London Gazette*, published on 16 August 1915,
    recorded that Skippers William Henry Collins RNR and Albert Edward
    Olley RNR were commended for service in action, while no fewer than four
    Second Hands, one Deckhand and six Enginemen in the Trawler Section of
    the RNR were commended for services during the attack on minefields under
    fire. Mate Joseph Burgon of North Shields was subsequently awarded the
    DCM. In respect of the period from the landings to the evacuation, an
    announcement was made in the Supplement to the *London Gazette* dated 14
    March 1916 of the award of the DSC to four skippers: Frederick W Barnes,
    Robert W Butler, George Mellership and Donald Craig (the latter is referred
    to in the text). All four were among eight skippers commended for service in
    action in dispatches received from the Vice-Admiral Commanding the
    Eastern Mediterranean Squadron.
95. *FN* 12.6.15, p. 1, also *FN* 8.5.15, p. 15.
96. *TD* Oct. 1915, p. 162. The *FN* of 8.5.15, p. 15, refers to five Milford
    skippers being home on leave, including two cousins, H James Snr and H
    James Jnr. An Edwin Banfield James, Second Hand, from Milford perished
    in the Mediterranean on 17 January 1916 when the patrol trawler *Fulmar*
    was blown up in a 'friendly' minefield.
97. *Dardanelles Dilemma*, p. 180.
98. Quoted in Hurd, *The Merchant Navy*, Vol. II, London, John Murray,
    1924, p. 162.
99. Craig, from Torry, Aberdeen, was a fine example of the
    trawlerman/sweeper type in this theatre of war. He was something of a
    minesweeping pioneer, having been a member of the minesweeping section of
    the RNR before the war. When he was called up he joined the Aberdeen
    trawler *Loch Esk*, later designated 340 by the Admiralty. For about a year

prior to serving at the Dardanelles, he was engaged in sweeping off the East Coast.

100. Keyes noted (*The Fight for Gallipoli*, p. 277) that on 4 November 'the Fourth Sea Lord told me that they were sending in addition [to four battle-ships and four destroyers] 24 trawlers armed with 12-pounder guns.'

101. See *The Uncensored Dardanelles* (1928).

102. Viewable online at http://www.archive.org/stream/dardanellescolou00wilk

103. See pp. 34-40 of the e-book for the full account of the trip.

104. Letter to John Collins JP, Secretary of the Grimsby Fishing Vessels' Engineers' Union, reproduced in part in the *FN* of 26.6.15, p. 13.

105. Pages 65 and 66 respectively.

106. Ibid. p. 67.

107. Issue dated 25 November 1916, p. 13.

108. Quoted in *FN*, 5.10.18, p. 11 and *TD* Nov. 1918, pp. 94-5.

109. *TD* May 1920, p. 69.

110. From *The Concise Story of the Dover Patrol* by Admiral Sir Reginald Bacon (1932), p. 300.

111. He devotes a section of his *Keeping the Seas* to Dover's minesweepers.

112. Pages 213-214.

113. Regrettably, the *Abelard* of Milford would be wrecked on Christmas Eve 1916 off Plymouth breakwater, while the *Falmouth* of Blyth, which was renamed *Falmouth III* in April 1915, would be mined off Deal on 19 November 1915.

114. Including *Benin, the City of Blood* (1897), describing the Benin Expedition (he had served as Intelligence Officer in this British naval campaign against the city), biographies of John Jellicoe and Jackie Fisher and, importantly, the 2-volume *The Dover Patrol*.

115. *The Naval Memoirs of Admiral of the Fleet Sir Roger Keyes. Scapa Flow to the Dover Straits 1916-1918*, quoted at http://www.doverwarmemorial-project.org.uk/Casualties/MoreMemorials/Areas/Dover%20Patrol/Dover%20Patrol%20Book%20words.htm

116. Among the dead was Lt-Cdr Henry Thomas Gartside-Tipping of the *Sanda*, who at 68 was the oldest naval officer afloat. He had been a great friend and admirer of the Dover Patrol and his death was a severe blow to Rigg and his sweepers.

117. *The Concise Story of the Dover Patrol*, pp. 66-7.

118. Ibid, p. 68.

119. 'In the measure of SHELLEY's *To a Skylark*'. From *Punch, or the London Charivari*, 15.9.1915)

120. *Eastern Daily Press*, 16.3.81.

121. Cole & Cheesman, *The Air Defence of Britain, 1914-1918* (1984), pp. 24-5. In *Sheringham – A Century of Change* (Poppyland Publishing, 1985), authors Stanley & Roy Craske refer to a bomb dropped that night on a house in the village as reputedly the first to land on British soil. It struck a house in Whitehall Yard, passing through the roof, bedroom ceiling and floor, embedding itself in the kitchen floor. A local girl visiting the house was injured, although the bomb failed to explode and was removed by a fireman. A second bomb fell on open ground near Priory Road and did explode, but did not cause any damage. (p. 25).

122. *Eastern Evening News*, 16.4.15.

123. Muhlhauser came across a floating lighted marker, flashing at irregular

intervals, which he reported to the shore authorities, who decided it was a calcium flare dropped by raiding Zeppelins to discover whether they were over water or land. If the calcium lit up, they were over water.

124. On 16 November 1914, this vessel had landed at Lowestoft the crew of the Dutch herring catcher *Poolester* of Maasluis, which had been sunk with 230 barrels of salted herrings on board as a result of a mine explosion some 30 miles ENE of Lowestoft.

125. Firth, *Dover and the Great War*, nd, p. 84.

126. Knight, *The Harwich Naval Forces – Their Part in the Great War*, (1919), pp. 215-16.

127. Page 3 of *Submarine Hunting on the North Sea in the Great War 1914-1918*.

128. The submarine's captain, Lt Cdr Godfrey Herbert, was no stranger to mishap, having been the first lieutenant of *A.4* when she had been nearly sunk during underwater signalling experiments. After a spell of duty on surface vessels, he had returned to submarines in 1910 on appointment as captain of the *C.36*, which he took on a record-breaking voyage to the China Station.

129. Quoted in Cdr E Currey's *How We Kept the Sea* (1917), pp. 56-7.

130. Letter to Vaughan Nash, 11.1.15.

131. Persistently described as the *Providence*, an error perpetuated by news-papers and historical works.

132. Both E Currey and Walter Wood, the latter copying from the former, spelled the name 'Hurrigan', which caused this author problems of verifica-tion.

133. One internet source states 'a Dutch steamship saved four officers and 22 ratings'.
http://www.naval-history.net/WW1NavyBritishDestroyers.htm

134. Of August 1915, pp. 215-6.

135. *The Dover Patrol*, p. 135.

136. *Sea Songs and Ballads* (1906).

137. Reported in *FN*, 19.6.15, p. 10.

138. From *The War Budget*, 29.3.17, p. 216.

139. Board of Trade statistics reproduced in the *FTG* of 18.11.16, p. 16.

140. Quoted in the *FTG* of 21.10.16, p. 14.

141. Page 44.

142. Vol. II, p. 132, of *The Great World War – A History*, Gen. Ed. Frank A Mumby.

143. The latter two vessels' names are as printed in the *FN* of 5.12.14. They are not listed as prizes in Dittmar & Colledge, although 'Hemel' could be 'Elma', 'Warden' could be 'Varel' and 'Wells' could be 'West'.

Appendix 1

(The appendices have their own notes on p. 204)

Vessels purchased by the Admiralty, 1909-1915

HMT	Tons	Built	Builder	Notes
Alnmouth	236	1912	Cochrane	Purchased 7/14. Sold 1919, retaining the same name. Acquired by the Vulcan STC of Fleetwood.
Daisy	510	1911	Duthie	Survey vessel fitted for minesweeping. Sold 1919, same name. Owned later by the Government of Newfoundland.
Daniel Stroud	209	1912	Hall	Purchased 7/14. Sold 1919. Renamed *Loch Esk* (served under this name in the Second World War).
Driver	107	1910	Duthie	Purchased 1910. From 1914 based at Devonport as mine sweeping training ship for Trawler Reserve Crews. Renamed *Nairn* in June 1919. Returned to the mercantile. Went ashore off Collieston, 2.12.1931.
Esther	510	1911	Duthie	Survey vessel fitted for minesweeping. Transferred to Board of Customs & Excise, 25.9.19
Jackdaw	250	1903	Goole SB	Purchased 10/14, sold 1919. Named *Excellent* from 2/17, then *Jackdaw* again from 2/19.

Janus	243	1911	Goole SB	Purchased 5/14. Renamed *Kilda* 1919. Sold 1920 and renamed *Tubal Cain*.

HMT	Tons	Built	Builder	Notes
Jasper	221	1912	Hall	Ex-*Rayvernol*, Smiths Dock. Purchased 1914. Mined 26.8.15 in Moray Firth.
Javelin	205	1913	Hall	Ex-*Braconlea*. Renamed *Javelin* (1914). Sold to Admiralty in September 1914 by the Don Fishing Co. Mined 17.10.15 off Longsand.
Osborne Stroud	209	1912	Hall	Purchased in July 1914. Sold to mercantile in 1920, when renamed *Beathwood*. Requisitioned in December 1939 and designated an APV. Returned to owners in 1940. Bombed and sunk, 11.9.40.
Rose	243	1907	Smiths Dock	Purchased 1910 for M/S trials & experiments at Portland. 1914: Based at Devonport as an M/S training ship for Trawler Reserve crews. Sold 1921 to the mercantile and renamed *Aby*.
Seaflower	275	1908	Goole SB	Ex-*Osprey II*. Purchased by Admiralty 4/09 & converted into a Trials M/S. 1914: Based at Chatham/Sheerness ICW *Seaflower* as M/S Training Ship for Trawler Reserve crews. 1920: Renamed *Sea Rover* in January. Sold to mercantile and renamed *Heinrich Beerman*.
Seamew	248	1909	Smiths Dock	Ex-*Nunthorpe Hall*. Purchased by Admiralty 4/09. Based at Portland on M/S trials. 1914: Based at Chatham/Sheerness ICW *Seamew* as M/S Training Ship for Trawler Reserve crews.

Re-assigned her old name, 1/1920. Sold to mercantile in May, retaining that name.

HMT	Tons	Built	Builder	Notes
Sparrow	266	1908	Goole SB	Ex-*Josephine I*. Purchased by Admiralty 4/09. Based at Portland on M/S trials. 1914: Based at Portsmouth as M/S training ship for Trawler Reserve crews. Re-assigned her old name, 1/1920. Sold to mercantile and renamed *Orion*.
Spider	256	1908	Cochrane	Ex-*Assyrian*. Purchased 4/09 & employed on M/S experiments at Portland. In 1914, based at Portsmouth as M/S training ship. Wrecked off Lowestoft 24/11.
Xylopia	262	1911	Cochrane	Purchased 7/14. Sold to mercantile in 1919, retaining same name. Owned in Grimsby in 1938.

Appendix 2

2a: Mine victims (total losses) - Auxiliary Patrol vessels, minesweepers, etc., 1914

Name	Duty	Date of loss	Position
Thomas W. Irvin	Sweeper	27 Aug	Off River Tyne
Crathie	Sweeper	27 Aug	Off River Tyne
Eyrie (D)	Sweeper	2 Sept	Off Outer Dowsing
Lindsell (D)	Patrol	3 Sept	Off Outer Dowsing
Princess Beatrice	Sweeper	5 Oct	Off Belgian Coast
Drumoak	Sweeper	5 Oct	Off Belgian Coast
Mary	Sweeper	5 Nov	Off Yarmouth
Orianda	Sweeper	19 Dec	Off Scarborough
Garmo	Patrol	20 Dec	Off Scarborough
Night Hawk	Sweeper	25 Dec	Off Scarborough

Total vessels 10

(D) = Drifter

(Source: List of Auxiliary Patrol Vessels, Mine Sweepers, &c., which have become total losses since the declaration of war, Auxiliary Patrol Office, 17.11.18)[1]

In addition, six auxiliary vessels (four patrol) were wrecked during November and December 1914.

2b: Mine victims (total losses) - Fishing vessels, 1914

Name	Date of loss	Position
Barley Rig	27 Aug	Off Tyne
Ajax	2 Sept	Off the mouth of the Humber
Fittonia	2 Sept	27 miles E by S from Spurn
Imperialist	6 Sept	40 miles ENE from Tyne
Revigo	7 Sept	25 miles E ½ N from Spurn
Kilmarnock	22 Sept	31 miles E from Spurn
Rebono	23 Sept	25 miles E by N from Spurn LV
Rosella	29 Oct	25 miles SE from Tyne
Our Tom	29 Oct	45 miles SE from Southwold
Fraternal	3 Nov	16 miles NE by N from Lowestoft
Will and Maggie	3 Nov	17 miles E by N from Lowestoft
Copious	3 Nov	15 miles E by S from Yarmouth
Speculator	10 Nov	Near Smith's Knoll
Seymolicus	18 Nov	12 miles E by N ½ N from Smith's Knoll
Lord Carnarvon	20 Nov	Off Yarmouth
Earl Howard	11 Dec	90 miles NE by N from Spurn LV (believed mined)
Ocana	23 Dec	75 miles NE by E from Flamborough Head

Total vessels 17

(Source: *British Vessels Lost at Sea 1914-1918*, HMSO, 1919)

2c: Mine victims (total losses) - Auxiliary Patrol vessels, minesweepers, etc., 1915

Name	Duty	Date of loss	Position
Banyers	Sweeper	6 Jan	Off Scarborough
Bedouin	Patrol	13 Feb	Off Tory Island
Okino	Sweeper	8 Mar	Dardanelles. Struck mine
Manx Hero	Sweeper	10 Mar	Mediterranean
Schiehallion	Sweeper	9 June	Mediterranean
Agamemnon II	Sweeper	15 July	Off Shipwash
Briton	Patrol	21 July	Off Longsand
Leandros	Sweeper	6 Aug	Off North Knock
Ben Ardna	Sweeper	8 Aug	Near Elbow Buoy
Worsley	Patrol	14 Aug	Off Aldeburgh
Japan	Patrol	16 Aug	Off Shipwash
Miura	Patrol	23 Aug	Off Yarmouth
Jasper	Sweeper	26 Aug	Moray Firth
Dane	Patrol	28 Aug	Off Aldeburgh
Nadine	Patrol	1 Sept	Off N. Shipwash Buoy
Malta	Patrol	1 Sept	Off N. Shipwash Buoy
Lydian	Patrol	18 Sept	Off South Foreland.
Greatheart	Net drifter	24 Sept	Off Dover. Cause unknown. Probably by explosion of own mine
Frons Olivae	Armed Drifter	12 Oct	Off Elbow Buoy
Javelin	Patrol Sweeper	17 Oct	Off Longsand
Erin II	Patrol	19 Oct	Off Nab
Star of Buchan	Drifter	20 Oct	Off Nab
Scott	Patrol Sweeper	22 Oct	Off Tongue
Othello II	Patrol	31 Oct	Off Leathercoat
Falmouth III	Patrol Sweeper	19 Nov	Off Dover
William Morrison	Patrol Sweeper	28 Nov	Near Sunk Head Buoy
Etoile Polaire	Patrol	3 Dec	Off S. Goodwin
Carilon	Patrol Sweeper	24 Dec	Off Margate
Resono	Patrol	26 Dec	Near Sunk Light
Speeton	Patrol	31 Dec	Off Lowestoft

Total vessels 30

(Source: AP List, 1918)

In addition, seven patrol vessels, two net drifters and one sweeper (total 10) were wrecked during the year. The patrol trawler *Ruby* was wrecked in Grandes Bay, Crete.

Fourteen vessels sank after a collision, eight of them patrol vessels and three of them net drifters. *Lord Denman* was lost in this manner in the White Sea, while the *Strathgarry* went down when on boom defence duties.

2d: Mine victims (total losses) - Fishing vessels, 1915

Name	Date of loss	Position
Windsor	22 Jan	55 miles E from Spurn Point
Golden Oriole	22 Jan	37 miles E by N from Lowestoft
Sapphire	1 Mar	Off Filey
Recolo	26 Apr	60 miles E by N from Spurn Point
Uxbridge	3 May	North Sea
Don	6 May	100 miles E by S from Spurn
Hellenic	8 May	98 miles E by S from Spurn
Angelo	21 May	Dogger Bank
Sabrina	21 May	160 miles ENE from Spurn LV
Condor	29 May	30 miles NE from Scarborough
Dovey	11 Jun	50 miles E by S from Spurn
Queen Alexandra	13 Jun	8 miles E by S ½ S from Tod Head
Cheshire	7 Jul	50 miles E by S from Spurn
Tors	30 Jul	43 miles E from Spurn
Grimbarian	4 Aug	56 miles E by N from Spurn
Devonian	9 Sept	30 miles NE ½ N from Spurn LV (believed mined)
Albion (smack)	30 Sept	8 miles S by W from Berry Head
King William	5 Nov	125 miles E by N from Spurn LV

Total vessels 18

(Source: *British Vessels Lost at Sea 1914-1918*, HMSO, 1919)

Appendix 3

3a: Trawlers at the Dardanelles named in
The Work of a Trawler in the Aegean Sea (to 10.1.16)

Admiralty No. & Port Reg	Name	Entry date/Notes
350 A 113	Balmedie ('Balmeade')	24.4.15 'under protection of *Doris* at midnight swept Xeros Bay, close to peninsula'. 29.4.15 Sunk [on 27th] 'hit, getting towed in to beach; the crew, will have to abandon her; sinking fast; been struck by transport propeller whilst dodging shell; run aground, water over her engine-room, total loss; crew went to H.M.S. *Queen*.'
279 A 500	Ben Loyal	24.8.15 'Heard from *Ben Loyal* that the Suvla troops have been put on half rations. Cannot land the stores; shelling the beaches heavily.'
344 H 973	Coltman	25.5.15 'hit off Gaba Tepe; not exploded'
706 GY 1235	Elk	24.4.15 6 a.m. 'proceeded to sea [from Lemnos] under sealed orders' [with *Lord Wimborne*, and *Balmedie* and three more sweepers] 'under protection of *Doris* at midnight swept Xeros Bay, close to peninsula'.
448 GY 804	Fentonian	29.5. 15 'has to run ammunition and stores to the peninsula with the fleet sweepers *Newmarket, Hythe, Clacton*'

		1.6.15 'on transport duty with fleet sweepers' 31.8.15 '[703] proceeded to Osiris, Port Kondi, for boiler cleaning with 448. Ordered, on arrival, to Mudros again, to *Aquarius*, to be fitted with gun-mounting and gun.'
332 H 496	*Lizzie*	21.4.15 'Captain Hope, of the *Lizzie*, and many more officers and all the old shipmates of former days' 24.4.15 'under protection of *Doris* at midnight swept Xeros Bay, close to peninsula'. 13.6.15 'loads wounded for hospital ships' 7.8.15 'aground off B Beach, loaded; [703] went to her assistance, got her in tow for two hours; could not move her, had to slip tow.'
26 A 141	*Loch Broom*[2]	24.4.15 'under protection of *Doris* at midnight swept Xeros Bay, close to peninsula'.
703 GY 916	*Lord Wimborne*[3]	Lt. Gowthorpe in command.
294 SN 277	*Soldier Prince*	8.11.15 'bears a charmed life, sweeping in the Dardanelles in the early days'
719 A 165	*William Allen*	24.4.15 'under protection of *Doris* at midnight swept Xeros Bay, close to peninsula'. 25.5.15 Assisted in rescue from the *Triumph* 29.5.15 Running troops to the peninsula 1.6.15 'on transport duty with fleet sweepers'

3b: Trawlers at the Dardanelles named in the *Log on Active Service*[4] (to 10.1.16)

Admiralty No. & Port Reg.	Name	Entry date/Notes
288 A 505	*Dinorah*	Ex-*Picton Castle*
696 GY 696	*Helgian*	Lost. Mined in the Gulf of Ruphani (or Orphano) on 6.9.17 with the loss of 10 men. Two survived.
327 A 414	*Northman*	
281 BL 9	*Yarmouth*	Renamed *Yarmouth II* in 2/15

On the British Memorial at Cape Helles are inscribed the names of 25 trawlers, including 341 *Prince Palatine*; 1043 *Renarro* and 258 *Richmond Castle* not referred to in the Dardanelles chapter. The names inscribed are as follows, with the Admiralty numbers supplied where absent:

293 *Achilles*	308 *G.M.*	48 *Restrivo*
705 *Avon*	354 *Gwenllian*	258 *Richmond Castle*
362 *Beatrice II*	324 *Koorah*	284 *Soldier Prince*
[323] *Coronatia*	340 *Loch Esk*	318 *Star of the Empire*
706 *Elk*	[339] *Manx Hero*	92 *Strathlossie*
43 *Escallonia*	[285] *Okino*	102 *Strathord*
448 *Fentonian*	341 *Prince Palatine*	269 *Syringa*
49 *Frascati*	1043 *Renarro*	10 *Vidonia*
		719 *William Allen*

(Listing courtesy of Oliver Lörscher, Germany)

Appendix 4

Drifters in the Adriatic - The first 60 units

1)	*Admirable*	31)	*Ivy*
2)	*Aivern*	32)	*John Mitchell*
3)	*All's well*	33)	*Lily Reaich*
4)	*Ben-Bui*	34)	*Lord Stradbroke*
5)	*Beneficent*	35)	*Lottie Leask*
6)	*Bon Espoir*	36)	*Manzanita*
7)	*Bono*	37)	*Mary Adeline*
8)	*British Crown*	38)	*Maud Evelyn*
9)	*Burd*	39)	*Mill o' Buckie*
10)	*Capetown*	40)	*Morning Star I*
11)	*Clach-Na-Cudin*[5]	41)	*Morning Star II*
12)	*Clara & Alice*	42)	*Norlan*[7]
13)	*Clavis*	43)	*Ocean Spray*
14)	*Colonial*	44)	*Our Allies*
15)	*Craigneen*[6]	45)	*Plantin*
16)	*Craignoon*	46)	*Prime*
17)	*Evening Star*	47)	*Remembrance*
18)	*Felicitas*	48)	*Restore*
19)	*Floandi*	49)	*Sedulous*
20)	*Foresight II*	50)	*Select*
21)	*Frigate Bird*	51)	*Selina*
22)	*Golden Gift*	52)	*Serene*
23)	*Gowan Lea* [sic]	53)	*Speranza*
24)	*Guerdon*	54)	*Sunnyside*
25)	*Guide* [Me] *IV*	55)	*The Prince*
26)	*Hastings Castle*	56)	*Three Boys*
27)	*Helenora*	57)	*Unicorn*
28)	*Helpmate*	58)	*Union*
29)	*Herring Queen*	59)	*Young Fisherman*
30)	*Holly Bank*	60)	*Young Kenneth*

Source: Manfroni, Camillo, *I Nostri Alleati Navali - Ricordi della Guerra Adriatica* [Our Naval Allies - Memories of the Adriatic War] 1915-1918, Milan, A Mondadori, 1927. Manfroni writes on page 55 'I found a list of the first sixty units among some old notes ... By June 1916, I find fully eighty units registered ... in July the number of units rose to one hundred, and this figure remained unchanged for quite a long time'. [author's translation].

Appendix 5

5a: Some rescues by fishermen from passenger vessels, 1914-18 (in chronological order)

Date	Rescuing vessel(s)	Vessel assisted & notes	Lives saved (where known/as stated)
5.9.14	Steam trawlers (a) *Cameo* (b) *Euripides* (c) *Silanion* (d) *Straton* and (e) *Prince Victor*	*Runo* This Hull steamship of the Wilson Line was bound from Hull to Archangel. Her passengers (nearly 300) were mostly Russian reservists from America, returning to Russia with their women and children and she carried a cargo of rubber. She was mined in a known field 20m off the east coast when deviating from Admiralty directions. Ten lives were lost. The BoT Silver Medal for Gallantry at Sea was awarded to all five skippers.	(a) ca. 100 (b) 31 incl. capt (c) 128 (d) + (e) ca. 40 jointly
15.3.15	North Shields fishing boat *Ayacanora*	*Fingal* Leith passenger steamer en route from London to its home port. Torpedoed without warning and sunk by submarine 6 miles E by S from Coquet Island, 1.2 km off Amble on the Northumbria coast. Six lives were lost. Survivors landed at North Shields quay.	21, including Capt. Dawson
28.3.15	(a) Lowestoft steam drifter *Eileen Emma* (b) Lowestoft steam drifter *Wenlock*	*Falaba* The s.s. *Falaba* (Liverpool) was one of the Elder Dempster line's fleet of West African service vessels. With 100 crew, 140 passengers and a cargo valued at £50,000, she was en route from Liverpool to Sierra Leone when, some 36m SW by W of the Small Lighthouse, she sighted *U.28* and unsuccessfully tried to outrun her. Only five boats had been swung out when the submarine torpedoed the *Falaba* amidships from only 150 yards. She sank within 10 minutes. She was the first unarmed passenger	(a) 100 - 116 and 6 recovered dead (b) 14

liner to be sunk during the First World War.

The death toll was 111. The *Eileen Emma* was luckily within 200 yards of the ship when she foundered and performed valuable rescue work. Her skipper, George Wright, had seen the submarine and chased it for half an hour.

The drifter *Wenlock* took in tow the lifeboat with 14 on board. The survivors were landed at Milford Haven.

£225 was later presented in Lowestoft to the *Eileen Emma*'s skipper and crew, £125 of it being donated by the shipping company.

7.5.15

(a) Peel (IOM) *Wanderer*
(b) Fleetwood AP Trawler *Brock*
(c) Hull AP Trawler *Indian Empire*
(d) Grimsby AP Trawler *Bradford*
(e) Fleetwood AP Trawler *Sarba*
(f) AP Drifter *Golden Effort*
(g) and (h) Arklow fishing boats *Daniel O'Connell* and *Elizabeth*
(i) local fishing boat *Lady Elsie*

Lusitania

This famous Cunard liner, carrying 1,959 persons, was torpedoed by *U.21* off the south coast of Ireland en route from New York to Liverpool and sank in about 20 minutes. The death toll was 1,198, many of the victims being American citizens.

(a) 160
(b) ca. 100
(c) ca. 180[12]
(g) 65[13]

Following a wireless message from the vessel received at Queenstown asking for assistance, all available vessels made for the scene, including the Cruiser HMS *Juno* (the flagship of the Irish Coast Patrol), the tugs *Warrior, Stormcock* and *Julia*, the *Katerina*, a Greek steamer, the *Flying Fish* (one of the last side-wheelers and normally used as a tender in Queenstown) together with four trawlers (as detailed left) and the local lifeboat in the tow of a tug.

The only vessel in sight at the time of the sinking was the *Wanderer*[8] (PL 11), close inshore, with a crew of 7. Making all possible sail, she slowly came up to the scene of the disaster and was able to pick up 160[9] of the survivors, taking 110 on board, and towing the remainder in a lifeboat and a raft until she was able to transfer them to other vessels.

Company officials in London announced some hours after the sinking that they had received information that 16 of the ship's boats were engaged in the work of rescue and that 20 boats from the adjacent coast were also on the scene.

Elias Hall, a fisherman from
Fleetwood serving on that port's
patrol boat *Brock,* wrote to his
parents: 'We had a very busy and
exciting time picking up the
survivors. We got 65 aboard our
ship, besides putting some on other
ships. I daresay we saved about 100
altogether.[10]

Skipper Simpson of the patrol boat
Indian Empire wrote from
Queenstown to his father in Leeds:
'We were the first trawler to arrive on
the scene - late, it is true, for she had
sunk when we got there, though we
went for all we were worth. ... we
succeeded in saving about 180 passengers, and you can guess there were
some awful scenes. Several of those
whom we rescued died on board. I
shall never forget the sight as long as
I live. The ship was torpedoed twice
at about 2 o'clock, and we arrived on
the scene about 3 o'clock.'[11]

1.6.15	(a) HM Trawlers *Eske* and	*Saidieh*	(a) 46[14]
	(b) *Strathalladale*		(b) 2

Bound from Alexandria to Hull
when, at 2 pm, she was torpedoed
about 6m to the NE of the Elbow
Buoy, just beyond Broadstairs. In 6
minutes she had foundered.

HM Trawler *Eske* (Lt. Green RNR)
was on patrol and steering for the
Buoy when the steamer passed ¼-
mile distant on his port beam. Feeling
the explosion and seeing the crew
taking to the boats, Green made
towards her, lowered a boat and
signalled another trawler,
Strathalladale (patrolling not far off),
to do the same. The U-boat was still
in the vicinity and the *Eske* went
after her but her gun was mounted
on the starboard side and the
submarine was on the port side. The
marauder then made off for
Zeebrugge.

In answer to a wireless summons,
destroyers quickly arrived on the
scene. Seven on board had no time to
get away and were drowned in the
stokehold. The first boat launched
from the steamer capsized before

reaching the water and all its occupants were thrown out.

17.11.15	Trawlers on patrol	*Anglia* (hospital ship) At 1230 hit a mine while off Folkestone. She sank bow first and 129 people lost their lives. Over 170 were rescued by other vessels but those confined to cots below decks with serious injuries could not be reached. The trawler *Falmouth III*, when sweeping in the vicinity of the wreck of the *Anglia*, struck a mine and actually sank on top of it, as did the rescuing collier *Lusitania*.	A large number
12.11.16	Trawler(s)	*Britannic* White Star liner launched in February 1914 and converted into a hospital ship with over 3,300 beds on the outbreak of the war. On 17 November 1916 she ran into a minefield in the Zea Channel, 4 miles west of Port St. Nikolo, Kea. The mines had been laid by German submarine *U.73* and some had remained, despite the Channel having been swept the day before. The survivors were picked up by the escorting destroyers *Foxhound* and *Scourge* and the armed merchant cruiser *Heroic*. The light cruiser HMS *Foresight* berthed at Port St. Nikolo and the French tug *Goliath* also assisted in the rescue. Captain Bartlett was the last to leave the ship and only 30 people died from the large number on board.[15]	A very large number About 166[16]

5b: Some rescues by fishermen from merchant vessels, 1914-18 (in chronological order)

Date	Rescuing vessel(s)	Vessel assisted & notes	Lives saved (where known/as stated)
1.9.14	Grimsby trawler *Pearl*	***Kamma*** Danish steamer bound from Odense for the Tyne (light) for coal. Struck a mine 45m off Tyne. All survived except the dog.	19
27.10.14	A trawler	***Manchester Commerce*** Struck a mine 20 miles off Tory Island. See also Chapter 6.	30
301.15	(a) Fishing smack *Margaret* (re: *Ben Cruachan*), Capt. Leadbetter. (b) Fleetwood steam trawler *Niblick* (re: *Linda Blanche*)	***Ben Cruachan*** British, laden with coals from Orkney to Liverpool. Crew of 23. Scuttled by *U.21* 15m NW from Morecambe LV. All crew picked up and landed in Fleetwood. ***Linda Blanche*** British, general cargo from Manchester to Belfast. Crew of 10. Scuttled by *U.21* 18m NW ½ N from Liverpool Bar LV ***Kilcoan*** British, Garston to Belfast. Scuttled by *U.21* 18m NW from Liverpool Bar LV. The steam collier *Gladys* of the Liverpool Monks Line was made by *U.21* to convey the crew to Douglas, IOM, where 11 persons were landed.	(a) 23 (b) 10
8.2.15	Steam trawler *Relevo*	***Frigga*** Norwegian steamer bound from Goole to Rotterdam sank following a collision with a submerged object. The crew got off in two boats, the *Relevo* taking one boatload of them to Grimsby.	7

14.2.15	Smack *General Leman*, Skipper Johnson	*Industry* Schooner of Bridgewater bound for Dublin with bricks, tiles and pipes. Sprang a leak. Vessel salved by trawler *Ebor* and taken into Milford.	4

Florazan

11.3.15 Steam drifter *Wenlock*

Torpedoed without warning and sunk by submarine, 53m NE ½ E from Longships when en route from Le Havre to Liverpool. One life lost (a fireman). *Wenlock* rescued all the other officers and men from the boats,
On the following day she was still afloat and taken in tow by 8 drifters but finally sank.

Amstel

25.3.15 Steam trawler *Pinewold*

The crew of this Dutch steamship 16
drifted in an open boat in the North Sea for five hours after their vessel had struck a mine. They were landed in Grimsby.

Aguila

27.3.15 Steam trawler *Ottilie* with SS *St. Stephen*

Steamship bound for Lisbon and the Some of
Canary Islands with 46 persons, of the 38
whom 3 were passengers. Sighted survivors
and overhauled by *U.28* some miles off Pembroke. The first boat lowered capsized on launching and drowned a woman passenger and a stewardess. Only 4 minutes elapsed between the launching of the boats and the submarine's shelling of the vessel. The chief engineer and two men were killed by the firing and 20 shells struck the ship before she was sent to the bottom 47m SW of the Smalls Light by a torpedo which split her in two. Eight lives were lost. The survivors, including Capt. Bannerman, were picked up shortly afterwards by the SS *St. Stephen* and the *Ottilie*.

Fulgent

30.4.15 Steam trawler *Angle* with SS *Tosto* of Newcastle

Sailing from Cardiff on the evening 9
of 28 April under Admiralty orders for Scapa Flow. She had passed the Blaskets Lighthouse, off the coast of Kerry, on the morning of the 30th when it was found she was being shadowed by a U-boat. She tried without success to zigzag away and was sunk. The crew got off in two boats and on 2 May the SS *Tosto* of

Newcastle picked up the first mate and eight hands, while the trawler Angle landed 9 other men at Cappa (Kilrush), where the body of Captain CW Brown was borne ashore.

| 1.5.15 | Patrol vessels Smack *Our Friend* |
| | |

Gulflight

Despite American neutrality at the time, this American oiler was torpedoed by *U.30.* She beached on the Isles of Scilly and was later repaired and refloated. Three of the 38 crew died. She was the first American ship to be torpedoed during the First World War (the German government apologised for the error yet continued to wage unrestricted submarine warfare).

The skipper of the smack *Our Friend,* fishing out of Lowestoft, witnessed the attack from his fishing-boat and remarked later how prominently the American flag had been flying. He hauled in his nets and went to try and save the lives of the crew.[17] Ten minutes later, patrol vessels raced up and one took them off; the wireless operator and a seaman drowned. Captain Alfred Gunter of the *Gulflight* died of shock Soon 4 patrol vessels were on the spot and 3 put men aboard with wires. The fourth, the 'Trawler Leader', steamed round and round in the vicinity, keeping a careful watch. The oiler was towed to Crow Sound with the trawlers in attendance, while the crew were landed at Penzance.

Salvador

2.6.15   Grimsby trawler *Fermo*[18]

A 3-masted Danish schooner bound from Gothenburg to Bideford with timber and carrying a crew of 6. She was stopped by a German submarine, set on fire and shot at. The crew were picked up by the trawler and landed at Lerwick after drifting in their boats for 12 hours in heavy rain.

6

5c: Some rescues by fishermen and naval trawler/drifter officers from fishing vessels, requisitioned or otherwise, 1914-18 (in chronological order)

Date	Rescuer(s)/rescuing vessel(s)	Vessel assisted & notes	Lives saved (where known/as stated)
6.3.15[19]	Percy Brookes, steam trawler *Eric Stroud*	***Eric Stroud*** Brookes saved the life of William McKenzie, a fireman on the *Eric Stroud* under particularly difficult circumstances. Awarded the Royal Humane Society's Medal and Parchment in Aberdeen.	1
27.5.15	Brixham smack *Sunstar* owned and skippered by John Friend	***St. Georges***[20] French trawler of Boulogne torpedoed without warning ca. 3-4m SE of Brixham. Sole survivor, Capt. Condert, saved by Friend. Thirteen lives lost.	1
11.6.15	Trawler *King James*	***Plymouth*** Grimsby trawler captured by UB and sunk by gunfire 67m miles NE ½ N from Spurn. Crew adrift for one day & night before being picked up.	9
11.7.15	GY trawler *Helvetia*	***Syrian*** Grimsby trawler sunk by *U.25*, which destroyed the trawler *Hainton* and damaged the trawler *Fleetwood* on the same day.	9
24.7.15	Grimsby trawlers *Buckingham* & *Ostrich*	***Diligent*** One of numerous small petrol inshore fishing boats based at Grimsby. Caught in severe storm and abandoned by crew. *Ostrich* salved boat.	Not stated

Notes to Appendices

1. Henceforth 'AP List, 1918'.
2. The vessel of James Clarke, writer of *Log on Active Service*.
3. References to activities throughout the text, since this was the diarist's own vessel.
4. Other than any mentioned elsewhere.
5. Spelled *Clachnacuddin* in the original text.
6. The original reads *Craigneen II* but no vessel of that name has been traced.
7. Spelled *Morland* in the original text.
8. Renamed *Erin's Hope* and fitted with a motor, *Wanderer* was still fishing in Irish waters in 1930 (source for this and for *Wanderer* information in the table is Edgar J March, *Sailing Drifters*, 1952). An *Erin's Hope* is shown in Olsen's *The Fisherman's Nautical Almanack* for 1920 as S (Skibbereen) *504*.
9. From a letter from Skipper William Ball to Charles Morrison (owner of the *Wanderer*): 'We couldn't take any more, as we had 160 - men, women, and children. In addition, we had two boats in tow, full of passengers, We were the only boat there for two hours.' All seven of the crew were awarded medals. A plaque for the *Wanderer* was unveiled at Weatherglass Corner, Peel, in 2004.
10. Published in the *FN* of 22.5.15, p. 10. The letter had previously been published in the *Fleetwood Express*.
11. Published in the *FN* of 22.5.15, p. 10.
12. Another source (http://navalhistory31.googlepages.com/history-326.html) states 170 but in any case adds that this was 'the largest number of survivors brought in by any one vessel'.
13. From two of the ship's boats, mostly women and children. When taking these survivors to Kinsale, this steam trawler was intercepted by a Government tug, which took them to Queenstown (*Cork Examiner*, 8.5.1915, p. 8).
14. Including a woman who died from shock.
15. Source : http://www.ocean-liners.com/ships/britannic.asp
16. More than half of whom were women and children, according to a Mr Prentice of the Indian Civil Service, relayed to the Marseilles correspondent of *The Times*. He added: 'We set off in a calm sea for Malta, 270 miles away … . They were 37 hours of utter misery.' (Source: *TD* December 1916, page 138).
17. This informant narrated these events to Alfred Noyes when serving on HM Drifter *Contrive*; his brother had been a naval skipper who had lost his life in November 1914 in charge of the *Will and Maggie* of Lowestoft.
18. See also Chapter 7 concerning this vessel.
19. Date of report in the *FN/FTG*.
20. Also referred to in the *FN* report of 29.5.15 as the *St. Just* of Arcachon.

Bibliography

A. BOOKS

Aflalo, FG, *The Sea-Fishing Industry of England and Wales – A Popular Account of the Sea Fisheries and Fishing Ports of those Countries*. London, Edward Stanford, 1904

Alward, GL, *The Sea Fisheries of Great Britain and Ireland – Notes from the Author's Diary, 1854-1928*, with Charts, Photographs and Illustrations, Grimsby, Albert Gait, 1932

Anson, Peter, *Fishing Boats and Fishing Folk on the East Coast of Scotland*, London, JM Dent & Sons Ltd., 1930

Ashmead-Bartlett, CBE, *The Uncensored Dardanelles*, London, Hutchinson & Co. Ltd., 3rd Impression, 1928

Ashmead-Bartlett, CBE, *Some of my Experiences in the Great War*, London, Geo. Newnes Ltd, 1918

Atkinson W et al., *The Log of HMS Gunner, 1914-1919*, nd. [c.1920]

Auten, Lt-Cdr Harold, VC, *"Q" Boat Adventures: The Exploits of the Famous Mystery Ships by a "Q" Boat Commander*, London, Herbert Jenkins Ltd, 1919

Bacon, Admiral Sir Reginald, KCB, KCVO, DSO, *The Dover Patrol* (2 Vols.), London, Hutchinson & Co., nd. [c. 1932]

Bacon, Admiral Sir Reginald, KCB, KCVO, DSO, *The Concise Story of the Dover Patrol*, London, Hutchinson & Co., 1932

Bagshawe, Gerard W, *The Wooden Ships of Whitby (being some account of the Fishermen and Fishing Craft, past and present, of the North Sea)*, Whitby, Horne & Son Ltd, 1933

Ballard, Robert D., with Dunmore, Spencer, *Exploring the Lusitania*, London, Weidenfeld and Nicolson, 1995

Balneaves, Elizabeth, *The Windswept Isles – Shetland and its People*, London, John Gifford, 1977

Bartimeus [Paymaster L Da Costa Ricci], *The Navy Eternal*, London, Hodder & Stoughton, nd

Berry, Claude, *Portrait of Cornwall*, 3rd Edn., London, Robert Hale, 1984

Beveridge, Sir William H, *British Food Control*, Carnegie Endowment for International Peace, London, H Milford, Oxford University Press, 1928

Bone, David W, *Merchantmen-at-Arms – The British Merchants' Service in the War*, London, Chatto & Windus, 1919

Boswell, David, *Loss List of Grimsby Vessels, 1800-1960*, Grimsby Public Libraries & Museums, 1969

Buchan, Jim, *Bygone Buchan*, Buchan, The Field Club, 1987 (Centennial Year)

Burrows, C, *Scapa and a Camera – Pictorial Impressions of Five Years spent at the Grand Fleet Base*, London, Country Life Ltd, 1921

Bush, Eric W, *Gallipoli*, London, Allen & Unwin, 1975

Butcher, David, *The Driftermen*, Tops'l Books, Reading, 1979
—*The Trawlermen*, Tops'l Books, Reading, 1980
— *Living from the Sea*, Tops'l Books, Sulhamstead, Berks., 1982
— *Following the Fishing*, Tops'l Books, Newton Abbot, London, 1987
Campbell, Commander AB, *With The Corners Off (My Adventurous Life on Land and Sea)*, London, GG Harrap & Co. Ltd, 1937
Carolan, Victoria, *WW1 At Sea*, Harpenden, Pocket Essentials, 2007
Carpenter, Captain Alfred FB, *The Blocking of Zeebrugge*, Uckfield, The Naval & Military Press Ltd, repr. 2003
Carr, William G, *Out of the Mists*, London, Hutchinson & Co. (Publishers) Ltd, 1942
Chack, Paul, *Sea Fights [On Se Bat Sur La Mer] – The Entente upon the Seas, 1914-18,* Tr. Cdr L B Denman RN, Liège, Imprimerie Vaillant-Carmanne, 1928
Chalmers, WS, Rear-Admiral, CBE, DSC, *The Life and Letters of David Beatty, Admiral of the Fleet*, London, Hodder & Stoughton, 1951
Chatterton, E Keble, *Q-Ships And Their Story*, London, Sidgwick and Jackson, 1922 Republished 1972, New York, Naval Institute Press, 1972
— *The Auxiliary Patrol*, London, Sidgwick & Jackson, 1923
— *On the High Seas*, London, Philip Allan & Co. Ltd, 1929
— *The Sea-Raiders*, London, Hutchinson & Co., nd [c.1931]
— *The Big Blockade*, London, Hurst & Blackett Ltd, 1932
— *Danger Zone – The Story of the Queenstown Command*, London, Rich & Cowan Ltd, 1934
— *Dardanelles Dilemma – The Story of the Naval Operations*, London, Rich & Cowan Ltd., 1935
— *Seas of Adventure – The Story of the Naval Operations in the Mediterranean, Adriatic and Ægean*, London, Hurst & Blackett Ltd., 1936
— *Fighting the U-Boats*, London, Hurst & Blackett Ltd, 1942
Churchill, The Rt. Hon. Winston S, *The Great War*, 2 vols, London, Geo. Newnes & Co., 1933
— *The World Crisis, 1911-18*, 2 vols, New Edition, London, Odhams Press Ltd, 1938
Clark, F Le Gros & Titmuss, Richard M, *Our Food Problem – A Study of National Security*, Harmondsworth, Middx, Penguin Books Ltd (Pelican Books), 1939
Clark, Roy, *The Longshoremen*, Newton Abbot, David & Charles, 1974
Clark, Victoria E, *The Port of Aberdeen*, Aberdeen, D Wyllie & Son, 1921
Cocker, MP, *Mine Warfare Vessels of the Royal Navy – 1908 to date*, Shrewsbury, Airlife Publishing Ltd, 1993
Cole, C & Cheesman, EF, *The Air Defence of Britain, 1914-1918*, London, Putnam, 1984
Colledge, JJ, *Ships of the Royal Navy, Vol. 2 (Navy-Built Trawlers, Drifters, Tugs and Requisitioned Ships, From the Fifteenth Century to the Present)*, London, Greenhill Books, 1989 (revised edition)
Coppack, Tom, FICS, *A Lifetime with Ships – The Autobiography of a Coasting Skipper*, Prescot, Lancs., T Stephenson & Sons Ltd., 1973
Copplestone, Bennet (Frederick H Kitchin), *The Secret of the Navy – What it is and what we owe to it*, London, John Murray, 1918
Corbett, Sir Julian S, *Official History of the War, Naval Operations*, Official

History Of The Great War Series, based on official documents, [5 vols.], London, Longmans, Green & Co., 1920-1935.

Corbett Smith, A, *The Seafarers*, London, Cassell & Co. Ltd, 1919

Corin, John, *Provident and the Story of the Brixham Smacks*, Reading, Tops'l Books, 1980

Cornford, L. Cope, *The Merchant Seaman in War*, London, Hodder & Stoughton, 1918

Cox, Charles B, *The Steam Trawlers and Liners of Grimsby*, published by the author, 1990

Coxon, Stanley W, *Dover during the Dark Days – by a "Dug-Out", with contributions by other officers of the Dover Patrol*, London, John Lane, The Bodley Head, 1919

Crane, Jonathan, *Submarine*, London, BBC, 1984

Craske, Stanley and Roy, *Sheringham – A Century of Change*, North Walsham, Norfolk, Poppyland Publishing, 1985

Currey, Cdr EH, *How We Kept the Sea*, London, Thos. Nelson & Sons Ltd., 1917

Davis, Lt Noel (US Navy, Editor-in-chief), *Sweeping the North Sea Mine Barrage*, New York, Press of J.D. McGuire, 1919

Denham, Henry M, *Dardanelles, A Midshipman's Diary, 1915-16*, John Murray Ltd, 1981

Dittmar, FJ & Colledge, JJ, *British Warships, 1914-19*, London, Ian Allan, 1972

Dixon, W Macneile, *The Fleets behind the Fleet – The Work of the Merchant Seamen and Fishermen in the War*, London, Hodder & Stoughton, 1917

Drummond, JC & Wilbraham, A, *The Englishman's Food – A History of Five Centuries of English Diet*, London, Jonathan Cape, 1939 (rev. 1957)

Dudley, Ernest, *Monsters of the Purple Twilight*, London, G. G. Harrap & Co. Ltd., 1960

Dudszus, Alfred & Henriot, Ernest, Tr. Thomas, Keith, *Dictionary of Ship Types – Ships, Boats and Rafts under oar and sail* (Eng. lang. version), London, Conway Maritime Press, 1986

Dunlop, Jean, *The British Fisheries Society*, Edinburgh, John Donald Publishers Ltd, 1978

Dyson, John, *Business in Great Waters – The Story of British Fishermen*, London, Angus & Robertson, 1977

Eames, Aled, *Ships and Seamen of Anglesey, 1558-1918*, Anglesey, The Antiquarian Society, 1973

Edwards, Brian, *Scottish Seaside Towns*, London, BBC, 1986

Elliott, Colin, *Sailing Fishermen in Old Photographs*, Reading, Tops'l Books, 1978

— *Steam Fishermen in Old Photographs* (from the Ford Jenkins Collection), Reading, Tops'l Books, 1979

Evans, AS, *Beneath the Waves – A History of HM Submarine Losses*, London, William Kimber, 1986

Evans, Capt ERGR, DSO CB RN, *Keeping The Seas*, London, Sampson Low, Marston & Co. Ltd., nd [c.1920]

Evans, George Ewart, *The Days That We Have Seen*, London, Faber, 1975

Fairbairn, Douglas, *The Narrative of a Naval Nobody, 1907-1924*, London, John Murray, 1929

Fayle, C Ernest (Ed.), *Harold Wright – A Memoir*, London, Geo. Allen & Unwin Ltd., 1934

Festing, Sally, *Fishermen*, Newton Abbot, David & Charles, 1977

Fewster, Kevin, *Gallipoli Correspondent – Frontline Diary of C. E. W. Bean*, Sydney, Geo. Allen & Unwin Pty. Ltd., 1983

Firth, JB, *Dover and the Great War*, Dover, Alfred Leney & Co. Ltd, nd

Fokeev, KF, *Activities of the Russian Arctic Ocean Flotilla – 1914-1917, Vol. I Operations of the Russian Fleet* (translation) Ministry of Defence, USSR, Moscow, 1964

Foreman, Susan, *Loaves and Fishes – An illustrated history of the Ministry of Agriculture, Fisheries and Food, 1889-1989*, London, HMSO, 1989

Forshaw, Alec & Bergstroem, Theo, *Markets of London*, Penguin Books, 1983

Freeman, Lewis R, *Sea Hounds*, London, Cassell & Co. Ltd., 1919

Frost, Ted, *From Tree to Sea*, Lavenham, Terence Dalton, 1985

Gardner, Brian (Ed.), *Up the Line to Death – The War Poets 1914-18*, London, Methuen, 1976

Gerard, James W, *My Four Years in Germany*, London, Hodder & Stoughton, 1917

Gibson, RH, *Three Years of Naval Warfare*, London, Wm Heinemann, 1918

Gibson, RH and Prendergast, M, *The German Submarine War, 1914-1918*, London, Constable and Co. Ltd, 1931

Gibson, WM, *The Herring Fishing – Stronsay, Vol. 1*, Edinburgh, BPP, 1984

Gilbert, Martin, *First World War Atlas*, London, Weidenfeld & Nicolson, 1970

Gill, Alec, *Lost Trawlers of Hull 1835-1987*, Beverley, The Hutton Press Ltd., 1989

Godfrey, Arthur, *Yorkshire Fishing Fleets*, Clapham (via Lancaster), North Yorkshire, Dalesman Books, 1974

Goldrick, James, *The Kings Ships Were at Sea*, Maryland, Naval Institute Press, 1984

Goodey, Charles, *The First Hundred Years – The Story of Richards Shipbuilders*, Ipswich, The Boydell Press, 1976

Goodlad, CA, *Shetland Fishing Saga*, Shetland Times Ltd, 1971

Graham, Cuthbert, *Portrait of Aberdeen and Deeside*, London, Robert Hale, 1974

Grant, Robert M, *U-Boats Destroyed – The Effect of Anti-Submarine Warfare, 1914-1918*, London, Putnam & Co. Ltd, 1964

Gray, Malcolm, *The Fishing Industries of Scotland, 1790-1914 – A Study in Regional Adaptation*, Oxford, OUP, for the University of Aberdeen, 1978

Green, Neal, *Fisheries of the North Sea*, London, Methuen & Co. Ltd, 1918

Greenhill, Basil, *A Quayside Camera, 1845-1917*, Newton Abbot/London, David & Charles, 1975

Greenhill, Basil & Giffard, Ann, *Victorian and Edwardian Ships and Harbours from Old Photographs*, London, BT Batsford, 1978

Griff (ASG), *SURRENDERED – Some Naval War Secrets*, published by the author, Cross Deep, Twickenham, nd

Gwatkin-Williams, Captain Rupert S, CMG Royal Navy, *Under the Black Ensign*, London, Hutchinson & Co., 1922

Halpern, Paul G, *The Naval War in the Mediterranean, 1914-1918*, London, Allen & Unwin, 1987

Halpern, Paul G, *A Naval History of World War I*, London, UCL Press, 1994

Halpern, Paul G, *The Battle of the Otranto Straits – Controlling the Gateway to the Adriatic in World War I*, Bloomington and Indianapolis, Indiana University Press, 2004

Halpern, Paul G. (Ed.), *The Royal Navy in the Mediterranean, 1915-1918*, Publications of the Navy Records Society, Vol. 126, Aldershot, Temple Smith for the Navy Records Society, 1987

Harvey, FW, *Gloucestershire Friends: Poems from a German Prison Camp*, London, Sidgwick & Jackson, 1917

Hasenson, Alex, *The History of Dover Harbour*, London, Aurum Special Editions, 1980

Hashagen, Ernst, *The Log of a U-Boat Commander, or U-Boats Westward, 1914-1918*, London, Putnam, 1931

Hawkins, LW, *The Numerical Fleet of Yarmouth*, Sprowston, Norwich, (self-published), 1982

Hepper, David, *British Warship Losses in the Ironclad Era, 1860-1919*, London, Chatham Publishing, 2006

Herubal, Marcel, *Sea Fisheries – Their Treasures and Toilers*, London, T Fisher Unwin, 1912

Hewison, WS, *This Great Harbour – Scapa Flow*, Aspects of Orkney series, Orkney, The Orkney Press, 1985

Holme, C (Ed.), *The War depicted by distinguished British Artists*, London, The Studio Ltd, 1918

Hopwood, Capt. Ronald A, RN, *The Old Way and Other Poems*, London, John Murray, 1917

Horton, Edward, *The Illustrated History of the Submarine*, London, Sidgwick & Jackson, 1974

Hough, Richard, *The Great War at Sea 1914-18*, Oxford, Oxford University Press, 1983

Hoy, Hugh Cleland, *40 O.B., or How The War Was Won*, London, Hutchinson & Co., 1932

Humphreys, Roy, *The Dover Patrol 1914-1918*, Stroud, Alan Sutton Publishing, Ltd, 1998

Hurd, Archibald, *The Command of the Sea*, London, Chapman & Hall Ltd, 1912

— *Ordeal By Sea*, London, Jarrolds, nd. [ca. 1918]

— *Italian Sea Power and the Great War*, London, Constable & Co. Ltd., 1918

— *The Merchant Navy, Vol. I*, London, John Murray, 1921

— *The Merchant Navy, Vol. II*, London, John Murray, 1924

— *The Merchant Navy, Vol. III*, London, John Murray, 1929

Jackson, Robert, *The Prisoners, 1914-18*, London, Routledge, 1989

Jackstaff (JJ Bennett), *The Dover Patrol – The Straits: Zeebrugge: Ostend*, London, Grant Richards Ltd, 1919

Jellicoe, Admiral Viscount of Scapa GCB, OM, GCVO, *The Grand Fleet 1914-16, Its Creation, Development and Work*, London, Cassell & Co. Ltd, 1919

— *The Crisis of the Naval War*, London, Cassell & Co. Ltd, 1920

— *The Submarine Peril – The Admiralty Policy in 1917*, London, Cassell & Co. Ltd, 1934

Jenkins, JT, *The Sea Fisheries*, London, Constable, 1920

— *The Herring and the Herring Fisheries*, London, PS King & Sons Ltd, 1927

Jones, Cecil Barclay, *Memorandum upon the Inception and Progress of the Auxiliary Patrol Service, 1914-18*, London, Admiralty Patrol Office, 1918

Jones, David T, CBE, FRSE; Duncan, Joseph F; Conacher, HM; Scott, WR, Appendix by Day, JP, *Rural Scotland During the War (Ch. II, Scottish Fisheries during the War), Publication of the Carnegie Endowment for International Peace, Division of Economics and History*, London, Humphrey Milford, Oxford University Press, 1926

Jones, JH (Ed.), *The German Attack on Scarborough*, December 16 1914, Huddersfield, Quoin Publishing 1989

Kaye, David, *The Book of Grimsby*, Buckingham, Barracuda, 1981

Keith A, *A thousand years of Aberdeen*, Aberdeen UP, 1972

Kerr, J Lennox & Granville, Wilfred, *The RNVR – A Record of Achievement*, London, Harrap 1957

Keyes, Sir Roger, *The Fight for Gallipoli: from the naval memoirs of Admiral of the Fleet, Sir Roger Keyes*, London, Eyre & Spottiswoode, 1941

Knight, EF, *The Harwich Naval Forces – Their Part in the Great War*, London, Hodder & Stoughton, 1919

Knight, W Stanley MacBean, *The History of the Great European War – Its Causes and Effects, Vol. II*, London, Caxton Publishing Co. Ltd, nd

Lake, Deborah, *Smoke and Mirrors: Q-ships Against the U-boats in the First World War*, Stroud, Sutton Publishing Ltd, 2006

Lakeman, Mary, *Early Tide – A Mevagissey Childhood*, London, Wm. Kimber, 1978

Layman, RD, *The Cuxhaven Raid – The World's First Carrier Air Strike*, London, Conway Maritime Press Ltd, 1985

Leyland, John, *The Achievement of the British Navy in the World-War*, London, Hodder & Stoughton, 1917

Liddle, Peter H, *Men of Gallipoli*, Newton Abbot, David & Charles, 1988

— *The Sailor's War 1914-18*, Dorset, Blandford, 1985

— (Ed.), *Home Fires and Foreign Fields – British Social and Military Experience in the First World War*, London, Brasseys Defence Publishers, 1985

Lummis, Trevor, *Occupation and Society – The East Anglian Coast Fishermen 1880-1914*, Cambridge, Cambridge UP, 1985

Maclean, Charles, *The Fringe of Gold – The Fishing Villages of Scotland's East Coast, Orkney and Shetland*, Edinburgh, Canongate Publishing Ltd., 1985

Malster, Robert, *Lowestoft – East Coast Port*, Lavenham, Suffolk, Terence Dalton Ltd, 1982

Manfroni, Camillo, *I Nostri Alleati Navali – Ricordi della Guerra Adriatica [Our Naval Allies – Memories of the Adriatic War] 1915-1918*, Milan, A Mondadori, 1927

March, Edgar J, *Sailing Drifters – The Story of the Herring Luggers of England, Scotland and the Isle of Man*, London, Percival Marshall & Co. Ltd., 1952

— *Sailing Trawlers – The Story of Deep-Sea Fishing with Long Line and Trawl*, London, Percival Marshall & Co. Ltd., 1953

— *Inshore Craft of Great Britain (in the Days of Sail and Oar)*, Vols. 1 & 2, Newton Abbot, David & Charles, 1970

Marcus, Geoffrey, *Before the Lamps Went Out*, London, Geo. Allen & Unwin, 1965

Marder, Arthur J, *From Dreadnought to Scapa Flow – The Royal Navy in the Fisher Era, 1904-1919,* [5 vols.], London, Oxford University Press, 1961-70

Masters, David, *"I.D."* – *New Tales of the Submarine War*, London, Eyre & Spottiswoode, 1935

Maurice, Henry G (contributor), *The Fisheries Department* (Chapter XVII of *The Ministry of Agriculture and Fisheries* by Froud, Sir Francis LC., KCB), London, Putnams Sons Ltd., 1927

Maxwell, Gordon S, Lieut. RNVR, *The Naval Front*, illustrated by Maxwell, Donald, Lieut. RNVR, London, A & C Black Ltd, 1920

Maynard, Major-General Sir C, *The Murmansk Adventure*, London, Hodder & Stoughton, nd (ca. 1928)

McCarthy, Dan J, AB, MD, *The Prisoner of War in Germany*, London, Skeffington & Son Ltd, 1918

McGreal, Stephen, *Zeebrugge and Ostend Raids*, Barnsley, Leo Cooper/Pen and Sword Books Ltd, 2007

Messimer, Dwight R, *VERSCHOLLEN* – *World War I U-Boat Losses*, Naval Institute Press, Annapolis, Maryland, 2002

Millholland, Ray, *The Splinter Fleet of the Otranto Barrage*, Brooklyn, New York, Bobbs-Merrill Company, 1936.

Molony, Senan, *Lusitania, An Irish Tragedy*, Cork, Mercier Press, 2004

Moynihan, Michael (Ed.), *People at War, 1914-18*, Newton Abbot, David & Charles, 1973

Muhlhauser, GHP Lt. RNR, *Small Craft*, London, John Lane The Bodley Head Ltd, 1920

National Association of Head Teachers, *Grimsby*, Grant Educational Co. (London) EC4, 1948

Neurether, Karl & Bergen, Claus (Eds.), *U-Boat Stories* – *Narratives of German U-Boat Sailors*, Trans. Eric Sutton (pictures by C Bergen), London, Constable & Co. Ltd., 1931

Nevinson, Henry W, *The Dardanelles Campaign*, London, Nisbet & Co. Ltd, 1918

Newbolt, Henry, *Submarine and Anti-Submarine*, London, Longmans, Green & Co., 1918

Nicholls, Mark, *Norfolk Maritime Heroes and Legends*, Cromer, Poppyland Publishing, 2008

Nicolson, James R, *Food from the Sea*, London, Cassell Ltd., 1979
— *Shetland's Fishing Vessels*, The Shetland Times Ltd, 1981
— *Shetland*, Newton Abbot, David & Charles, 1989

Noall, Cyril, *Tales of the Cornish Fishermen*, Truro, Tor Mark Press, 1970

Noble, Edward, *The Naval Side*, London, Cecil Palmer Hayward, 1918

Noyes, Alfred, *Mystery Ships (Trapping the "U" Boat)*, London, Hodder and Stoughton, 1916

Paine, Ralph D, *The Fighting Fleets (Five Months of Active Service with the American Destroyers and their Allies in the War Zone)*, London, Constable & Co. Ltd, 1918

Palmer, Frederick, *My Year of the War*, London, John Murray, 1915

Parmelee, Maurice, Ph.D., *Blockade and Sea Power* – *The Blockade 1914-19 and its significance for a world state*, London, Hutchison & Co., 1924

Peak, Steve, *Fishermen of Hastings* – *200 Years of the Hastings Fishing Community*, St Leonards-on-Sea, News Books, 1985

Pengelly, Alfred John, *Oh, For a Fishermans Life* – *An Autobiography*, Falmouth, Glasney Press, 1979

Powell, Joseph & Gribble, Francis, *The History of Ruhleben: a Record of*

British Organisation in A Prison Camp in Germany, London, W Collins & Co. Ltd, 1919

Punch, *Mr Punch's History of the Great War*, London, Cassell & Co. Ltd, 1919

Purves, Alec A, *The Medals, Decorations and Orders of the Great War, 1914-18*, London, J B Hayward & Son, 1975

Reeves, Nicholas, *Official British Film Propaganda during the First World War*, Croom Helm (in assoc. with IWM), nd

Reid, J, *Steam Drifters Recalled – Whitehills to St. Combs*, self-published, Enzie, Moray, 2001

Reynolds, Stephen, *A Poor Man's House*, London, John Lane, 1908
— *Letters* (Ed. Wright, Harold), Richmond, Leonard & Woolf, 1923

Rimell, Raymond L, *Zeppelin! A Battle for Air Supremacy in World War*, London, Conway Maritime Press, 1984

Ritchie, Carson, *Q-Ships*, Lavenham, Terence Dalton Ltd, 1985

RNV, *Pushing Water*, London, John Lane The Bodley Head, 1919

Robinson, Joe, *The Life and Times of Francie Nichol of South Shields*, London, Geo. Allen & Unwin, 1975

Robinson, Robb, *A History of the Yorkshire Coast Fishing Industry 1780-1914*, Hull, Hull University Press, 1987

Royal Italian Navy, *The Italian Navy in the World War 1915-1918 – Facts & Figures*, (Office of the Chief of Staff of the Historical Section), Rome, Provveditorato Generale dello Stato, Libreria, 1927

Samuel, Arthur Michael, *The Herring and its Effect on the History of Britain*, London, John Murray, 1918

Sargeaunt, BE, MVO, OBE, *The Isle of Man and the Great War*, IOM, Brown & Sons Ltd, Douglas, 1921

Scheer, Admiral Reinhard, *Germany's High Sea Fleet in the World War*, London, Cassell and Company Ltd, 1920

Scottish Tourist Board, *Scottish Tourist Board/Fishing Heritage Trail 1985-6*

Sea Fish Industry Authority Publicity Booklet, *Herring*, Edinburgh, nd

Shaw, Capt. Frank H, *Seas of Memory*, London, Oldbourne Book Co., 1958

Simper, Robert, *Scottish Sail – A Forgotten Era*, Newton Abbott, David & Charles, 1974

Smith, Peter, *The Lammas Drave and the Winter Herring – A history of the Herring Fishing from East Fife*, Edinburgh, John Donald 1985

Smiths Dock Co. Ltd., *The Origin and Growth of British Fisheries and Deep Sea Fishing*, North & South Shields & Middlesbrough-on-Tees, nd [c.1908]

Stanley, C & Banks, L, *Britain's Coastline – History from the Air*, London, Batsford, 1986

Starkey, David J; Ramster, John (Eds.), *England's Sea Fisheries – The Commercial Sea Fisheries of England and Wales since 1300*, London, Chatham Publishing, 2000

Steel, Nigel & Hart, Peter, *Defeat at Gallipoli*, London, Macmillan, 1994

Stewart, A T & the Revd C J E Peshall, BA, *The Immortal Gamble – and the part played in it by HMS Cornwallis*, London, A & C Black, 1917

Sutherland, Iain, *From Herring to Seine Net Fishing on the East Coast of Scotland*, Wick, Camps Bookshop, nd

Taffrail (Dorling, Capt. Taprell, DSO, FRHistS), *The Watch Below – Naval Sketches and Stories*, London, C Arthur Pearson Ltd., 1918

— *Endless Story*, London, Hodder and Stoughton, 6th Edn., 1938

— *Swept Channels – Being an Account of the Mine-Sweepers in the Great War*, London, Hodder & Stoughton, 1935

Taylor, James, *Fishing the North-East, from Whinnyfold to Whitehills*, Northern Books, nd

Terraine, John, *Business in Great Waters – The U-Boat Wars, 1916-1945*, London, Leo Cooper, 1989

Thomas, Lowell, *Raiders of the Deep*, London, William Heinemann Ltd, 1929

Thompson, Francis, *The Uists and Barra*, Newton Abbot, David and Charles, 1974

Thompson, Julian, *Imperial War Museum Book of the War at Sea 1914-18*, London, Pan Books, 2006

Thompson, Michael, *Fish Dock, The Story of St Andrew's Dock*, Hull, Beverley, The Hutton Press Ltd, 1989

Thompson, M; Newton, Dave; Robinson, Richard & Lofthouse, Tony, *Cook, Welton & Gemmell – Shipbuilders of Hull and Beverley, 1883-1963*, Beverley, The Hutton Press Ltd, 1999

Thompson, Paul, with Wailey, Tony and Lummis, Trevor, *Living the Fishing, History Workshop Series*, London, Routledge & Kegan Paul, 1983

Tindale, John, *Fishing out of Whitby*, Dalesman Books Ltd, Clapham, Lancaster, The Dalesman Publishing Company, 1987

Toghill, Gerald, *Royal Navy Trawlers, Part 1: Admiralty Trawlers*, Maritime Books, Liskeard, Cornwall, 2003

Toghill, Gerald, *Royal Navy Trawlers, Part 2: Requisitioned Trawlers*, Maritime Books, Liskeard, Cornwall, 2004

Tregenza, Leo, *Harbour Village – Yesterday in Cornwall*, London, Wm. Kimber, 1977

Tunstall, Jeremy, *The Fishermen*, London, MacGibbon & Kee, 1962

Turner, John R, *Scotland's North Sea Gateway – Aberdeen Harbour AD 1136-1986*, Aberdeen, Aberdeen University Press, 1986

Usborne, Vice-Admiral C V, CB, CMG, *Smoke on the Horizon – Mediterranean Fighting 1914-18*, London, Hodder & Stoughton, 1933

Warner, Philip, *The Zeebrugge Raid*, London, William Kimber & Co. Ltd, 1978

Waterman, JJ, *Freezing Fish at Sea – A History*, Edinburgh, HMSO, 1987

Watts, Anthony J, *The Royal Navy – An Illustrated History*, London, Arms and Armour Press, 1995

Weldon, Capt. L B, MC, *Hard Lying – Eastern Mediterranean, 1914 1919*, London, Herbert Jenkins Ltd, 1925

Wester-Wemyss, G CB, Admiral of the Fleet, *The Navy in the Dardanelles Campaign*, London, Hodder & Stoughton, 1924

Wheeler, Harold FB, *Daring Deeds of Merchant Seamen in the Great War*, London, Geo. G Harrap & Co. Ltd, 1918

Wilkinson, Norman, *The Dardanelles – Colour Sketches from Gallipoli*, London, Longmans, Green & Co., 1916

Willis, Jerome, *The Last Adventurers (The Story of the Lives of Trawlermen from Hull and Grimsby)*, London, Hurst & Blackett Ltd, 1937

— *Trawlerman's Town*, London, Hurst & Blackett Ltd, 1947

Wilson, Gloria, *Scottish Fishing Craft*, London, Fishing News (Books) Ltd., 1965

— *More Scottish Fishing Craft*, London, Fishing News (Books) Ltd., 1968

Wilson, HW, *Hush, or the Hydrophone Service*, London, Mills & Boon Ltd, 1920

Wilson, Trevor, *The Myriad Faces of War – Britain and the Great War*, 1914-18, Cambridge, Polity Press, 1986

Winter, JM, *The Great War and the British People*, Basingstoke & London, Macmillan Education Ltd, 1986

Winton, John, *Below the Belt – Novelty, Subterfuge and Surprise in Naval Warfare*, London, Conway Maritime Press, 1981

Wood, Walter, *The Enemy in Our Midst*, London, John Long Ltd., nd [c.1908]

— *North Sea Fishers and Fighters*, London, Kegan Paul, Trench Truebner & Co. Ltd., 1911

— *Fishermen in War Time*, London & Edinburgh, Sampson Low, Marston & Co. Ltd., [1918]

— *Fishing Boats and Barges from the Thames to Land's End*, London, John Lane, The Bodley Head Ltd, 1922

Woollard, Cdr. Claude LA, FRGS, *With the Harwich Naval Forces 1914-18, or under Commodore Tyrwhitt in the North Sea*, Antwerp, 1934

Wren, Wilfred J, *Ports of the Eastern Counties*, Lavenham, Terence Dalton Ltd., 1976

Wyllie, RA & Wren, MF, *Sea Fights of the Great War*, London, Cassell & Co. Ltd, 1918

Wyness, Fenton, *City by the Grey North Sea*, Aberdeen, Impulse Books, 1965

B. NEWSPAPERS, PERIODICALS, BOOKLETS AND PARTWORKS

MacDonald, Henry, *Chamber's Journal*, 22 May 1915 (contains *The Mine-Sweepers* 3 pp.)

Commemorative brochure for the opening by HM The Queen of Aberdeen Harbour Fish Market, 5.8.1982

Cornhill Magazine, December 1918 (contains *Patrol*, by Lewis R Freeman, 15 pp.)

Fish Trades Gazette & Poultry, Game & Rabbit Trades Chronicle – The Official Organ of the North Sea Fisheries, London, Monument St, EC4

Fishing News, Prop.: Aberdeen Free Press, Aberdeen, first published 1914

Grimsby Roll of Honour, 1914 – 1919. An account of the Borough's Effort during the Great War, 1914-1919, together with the ROLL OF HONOUR, County Borough of Grimsby, Printed and Published by W. H. JACKSON & Co., 318 Victoria Street, Grimsby

Caborne, WF, *Journal of the Royal United Service Institution*, Vol. 59, No. 438, pp. 495-506, November 1914 ('The Royal Naval Reserve'), London.

Lecky, Capt HS, CB AM RN *Journal of the Royal United Service Institution*, Vol. 78, No. 509, February 1933 ('The Auxiliary Patrol in War'), London. Published in 'The Dolphin', July 1933

Robinson, Cdr CN, RN, *London Magazine*, January 1917 (contains *Emergency Craft – About the Queer Fighting Units rushed out by the Forcing-House of War*, The Times Naval Correspondent)

Godfrey, A, *Scarborough Evening News*, 29.8.85, pp. 14-15, 'Scarborough Fishermen and the U-Boats'

Divry Oakeshott, W, *Sussex County Magazine*, 'Decline of the Sussex Fishing Industry', in Vol. XXIV, No. 7, July 1950, pp. 282-4

The Church and the Sailor, Monthly publication of the former Missions to Seamen, since 2000 the Mission to Seafarers. The journal, previously *The Word on The Waters*, was so named from 1911 to 1957

Olsen, OT, *The Fisherman's Nautical Almanack, Tide Tables, and Directory of British and Foreign Fishing Vessels, Sail and Steamers*, Grimsby [various years]

Wilson, HW (ed), *The Great War – A Weekly History*, London, Amalgamated Press Ltd

Wilson, HW & Hammerton, JA (Eds.), *The Great War – The Standard History of the All-Europe Conflict*, London, Amalgamated Press Ltd, published from 1914 to [?]1918

Mumby, FA, (Gen. Ed.), *The Great World War – A History*, London, The Gresham Publishing Co. Ltd., From 1915-1920 (9 vols.)

Henderson, WH, (Ed), *The Naval Review, Vol. VI.*, Produced by The Naval Society for private circulation among its members. Paper 2 of 6: 'The Work of a Trawler in the Aegean Sea', pp. 13-68, 1919 (22 November)

The Navy was the organ of the Navy League. The title *The Navy* was adopted in 1909. The journal survives today within *Jane's Navy International* .

The Quarterly Review, 'The Territorial Waters and the Sea Fisheries', No. 435, April 1913, pp.433-456

The Royal Navy List, or *Who's Who in the Navy*, London, Witherby & Co., Jan 1915

The Times History of the War (22 volumes), [especially Chapter 121 (Vol. VII), pp. 449-464, 'Fishermen and the War', pub. 1916; Chapter 172 (Vol. XI), pp 177-196, pub. 1917; Chapters 303 & 304 (Vol. XXI), pp 25-36, (pp 31-36, 'Auxiliary Patrols'), pub. 1920], London, 1914-1921

Hammerton, JA (Ed.), *The War Budget Illustrated – A Pictorial Record of the Great War*, London, The *Daily Chronicle* [various war years]

Hammerton, JA (Ed.), *The War Illustrated – A Pictorial Record of the Conflict of the Nations*, London, The Amalgamated Press Ltd, various dates.

The Yachting Monthly and Marine Motor Magazine (Illustrated)/*The Yachting Monthly and Magazine of the R.N.V.R.*, London, 1914-18, Herbert Reiach Ltd, various issues

Toilers of the Deep, A Monthly Record of Mission Work Amongst Them, London, RNMDSF, various issues

Wing, Tom, *Windsor Magazine*, March 1916 (contains *North Sea Fishermen and the War*), London, Ward Lock and Company

C. PRIVATE PAPERS, DIARIES, DISSERTATIONS, LECTURES, ETC

Alward, GL, 'The Development of the British Fisheries during the 19th Century, with special reference to the North Sea'; Lecture delivered before the Grimsby Institute of Engineers and Shipbuilders, 1 February 1911. Grimsby.

Clarke, James, *First World War Diaries of James Clarke*, (17/3/1915 – 12/4/1917), London, Imperial War Museum Collection

Reynolds, Stephen, BAF – The Inshore Fisheries together with a Memorandum of a Scheme for their Assistance and Development and a Note on Decentralization, 23.2.1913

Suddaby, Roderick W.A., MA, *The Auxiliary Patrol, 1914-15*, Thesis submitted to the Department of History, Queens University, Kingston, Ontario, Canada, April 1971

Thompson, Prof. D'Arcy W, CB, MA, *The North Sea and its Fisheries*, Discourse delivered at the evening meeting of the Royal Institution of Great Britain on 22 March 1912. Reported in Notices of the Proceedings at the Meetings of the Members of the RIGB, Vol. XX, 1911-13, pp. 414-426; London, Wm Clowes & Sons Ltd, 1914

Wharton, Skipper W S, RNR, DSC, *Submarine Hunting on the North Sea in the Great War, 1914-18*, Unpublished memoirs deposited with Lowestoft Public Library, 1937

D. OFFICIAL REPORTS AND PUBLICATIONS

— *Instructions for Vessels of the Auxiliary Patrol based on the Firth of Clyde* – issued to HMS *Pactolus*, 1916

— *Patrol Standing Orders, Area XII*, Portsmouth 1918

Board of Agriculture & Fisheries, London, *Report of Proceedings at the 23rd Annual Meeting of Representatives of Authorities under the Sea Fisheries Regulation Act, 1888*, 24.6.1913, Cd. 7014

— *Annual Report on Sea Fisheries for the Year 1912, Part I – Report*, Cd. 6994.

— *Annual Report on Sea Fisheries for the Year 1912, Part II – Tables & Charts*, Cd. 6998

— *BAF Departmental Committee on Inshore Fisheries*, Reports of the Tours made by the Three Sub-Committees of the Departmental Committee on Inshore Fisheries in the Summer of 1913, *Volume I – Report and Appendices*, London, HMSO, 1914 – Cd. 7373; *Volume II – Minutes of Evidence and Index*, London, – 1914 – Cd. 7374.

— *Report of Proceedings at the 25th Annual Meeting of Representatives of Authorities under the Sea Fisheries Regulation Act, 1888*, 22.6.1915. HMSO, Cd. 8018, 1915

— *Fisheries In The Great War*, being the Report on Sea Fisheries for the Years 1915, 1916, 1917 and 1918, Parts I and II, London, HMSO, Cd. 585, 1920

Fisheries Organisation Society, London, Reports for the years 1917, 1919, 1920 (Jan-Dec)

Fishery Board for Scotland, Edinburgh, *33rd Annual Report – Being for the Year 1914*, HMSO, Edinburgh, [Cd. 7976] 1915

— *34th Annual Report – Being for the Year 1915*, HMSO, Edinburgh, [Cd. 8281] 1916

HMSO, *Annual Statement of the Navigation and Shipping of the United Kingdom for the year 1917*. Cd. 327, London, HMSO, 1919

— *Annual Statement of the Navigation and Shipping of the United Kingdom for the year 1919*. Cd. 1419, London, HMSO, 1921

Lancashire and Western Sea Fisheries District, *Superintendent's Report for the Quarter ending 30th September 1914*, Preston, 23.10.14.

Ministry of Agriculture and Fisheries, *Report on Sea Fisheries for the Years 1919, 1920, 1921, 1922 and 1923*, London, HMSO, 1925

Ministry of Agriculture and Fisheries – Fisheries Department, *Sea Fisheries – Statistical Tables, 1922* (in lieu of Part II of the Sea Fisheries Report for the same period), London, HMSO, 1923

Ministry of Reconstruction, *British Fishermen and the Nation, I – Sea Fisheries*, London, HMSO, 1919

Scottish Departmental Committee on the North Sea Fishing Industry, *Report* of the SDCNSFI appointed by the Secretary for Scotland to Inquire into and Report upon certain matters connected with the Development of the Scottish Sea Fishing Industry, after visiting the various Countries engaged in fishing in the North Sea, 1914, HMSO, London. Report – Part I with Appendices, Cd. 7221

Stephens, Patrick (Pub.), *British Vessels Lost at Sea, 1914-18* (a reprint of the original official publications *Navy Losses and Merchant Shipping (Losses)* , first published in August 1919 by HMSO, London).

E. CD-ROMs/DVDs

World War One – Royal Navy Lists, 1914-1918 DVD Collection, Your Old Books and Maps, Dewsbury, W Yorks, 2008.

3 CDs entitled *In Ruhleben Camp*, subtitled *Issues 1-3, Issues 4-6 and Issues 7 to 9* respectively. For details visit http://ruhleben.tripod.com

F. USEFUL WEBSITES

http://www.naval-history.net/index.htm
(Casualty Lists of the Royal Navy and Dominion Navies, World War 1. Researched & compiled by Don Kindell)

http://www.uboat.net/history/wwi/index.html
(Excellent site for anything pertaining to German submarines and their crews in both wars)

http://www.cwgc.org/
Commonwealth War Graves Commission website

http://1914-1918.invisionzone.com/forums/
The Great War Forum

The Times archive
http://archive.timesonline.co.uk/tol/archive/
(generally available free via the public libraries network)

The Hansard archive
http://hansard.millbanksystems.com/

The *London Gazette* archive
http://www.gazettes-online.co.uk/

General Index

Index of Vessels

(Admiralty numbers, where quoted in the text, are shown after the name of the vessel concerned. A number of smaller foreign vessels are excluded from the listing. Only wartime name changes are shown. The queried entries refer to captured German trawlers named differently in the *FN* and Dittmar & Colledge, 1972)